CW00666118

PIONEERING SOCIAL RESEARCH
Life Stories of a Generation

Paul Thompson, Ken Plummer and Neli Demireva

First published in Great Britain in 2021 by

Policy Press, an imprint of
Bristol University Press
University of Bristol
1-9 Old Park Hill
Bristol
BS2 8BB
UK
t: +44 (0)117 954 5940
e: bup-info@bristol.ac.uk

Details of international sales and distribution partners are available at policy.
bristoluniversitypress.co.uk

© Bristol University Press 2021

British Library Cataloguing in Publication Data
A catalogue record for this book is available from the British Library

ISBN 978-1-4473-3352-4 hardcover
ISBN 978-1-4473-3354-8 ePub
ISBN 978-1-4473-3353-1 ePdf

The right of Paul Thompson, Ken Plummer and Neli Demireva to be identified as authors of
this work has been asserted by them in accordance with the Copyright, Designs and Patents
Act 1988.

All rights reserved: no part of this publication may be reproduced, stored in a retrieval system,
or transmitted in any form or by any means, electronic, mechanical, photocopying, recording,
or otherwise without the prior permission of Bristol University Press.

Every reasonable effort has been made to obtain permission to reproduce copyrighted
material. If, however, anyone knows of an oversight, please contact the publisher.

The statements and opinions contained within this publication are solely those of the authors
and not of the University of Bristol or Bristol University Press. The University of Bristol and
Bristol University Press disclaim responsibility for any injury to persons or property resulting
from any material published in this publication.

Bristol University Press and Policy Press work to counter discrimination on grounds of
gender, race, disability, age and sexuality.

Front cover image: Ray Finch © Jacqueline Sarsby; Havana
© Olga Lidia Saavedra Montes de Oca; © Hilary Rose.

Bristol University Press and Policy Press use environmentally
responsible print partners.

Printed in Great Britain by CPI Group (UK) Ltd, Croydon,
CR0 4YY

Contents

List of abbreviations

ASA	Association of Anthropologists in the UK
BL	British Library
BSA	British Sociological Association
CATs	colleges of advanced technology
CSO	Central Statistical Office
ESN	educationally sub-normal
ESRC	Economic and Social Research Council
ILP	Independent Labour Party
ISA	International Sociological Association
LSE	London School of Economics
NGO	non-governmental organisation
ONS	Office of National Statistics
OPCS	Office of Population and Census Studies
PEP	Political and Economic Planning
PPE	Philosophy, Politics and Economics (BA degree at Oxford)
PRO	Public Record Office
RAF	Royal Air Force
SCELI	Social Change and Economic Life Initiative
SOAS	School of Oriental and African Studies
SPSS	Statistical Package for the Social Sciences
SSRC	Social Science Research Council (from 1983 Economic and Social Research Council: ESRC)
WRNS	Women's Royal Naval Service

Authorship

Paul Thompson is Emeritus Professor in Sociology at the University of Essex. He is Founder-Editor of *Oral History* and founder of National Life Stories at the British Library. He is a pioneer of oral history in Europe and author of the international classic *The Voice of the Past* (4th edn, 2017). His other books include *The Edwardians*, *Living the Fishing* and *The Work of William Morris*. He is co-author of *Growing Up in Stepfamilies* (with Gill Gorell Barnes, Gwyn Daniel and Natasha Burchardt), of *The Myths We Live By* (with Raphael Samuel) and (with Daniel Bertaux) *Pathways to Social Class*.

Ken Plummer is Emeritus Professor in Sociology at the University of Essex. His research has highlighted narrative, life story and humanistic research. He is author of *Documents of Life* (2nd edn, 2001), *Telling Sexual Stories* (1995) and *Narrative Power* (2019). His other books include *Intimate Citizenship* (2003) and *Cosmopolitan Sexualities* (2015). He is the founder editor of the journal *Sexualities*; and has authored several text books including *Sociology: The Basics* (3rd edn, 2021).

Neli Demireva is Senior Lecturer in Sociology at the University of Essex. Her research interests include migration, interethnic ties, social cohesion, ethnic penalties and multiculturalism. Neli uses a variety of methods in her research: quantitative and qualitative.

As authors, we have worked together. Paul Thompson organised and first drafted Chapters 1, 2, 9 and the Voices; Ken Plummer Chapters 3, 4, 6 and 7; and Neli Demireva Chapter 5. We discussed and wrote the final copy together with Paul as lead. Our aim has been not to produce a definitive history but to give a taste of the rich evidence of the collection and the multiple viewpoints it offers. In the same spirit, as joint authors we gave ourselves room to disagree.

Acknowledgements

Pioneering Social Research is the culmination of 21 years of fieldwork. This began in 1997 as a side-activity of Qualidata, which had been set up by the Economic and Social Research Council to locate, rescue and archive significant fieldwork data from earlier social research projects. From 1997 Qualidata became absorbed into the UK Data Archive. Subsequent funding support came from the Fuller Bequest, the British Academy (2009–11), and most recently the Leverhulme Trust (2016–18). We are very grateful to all these funders, without whose help our continuation of the work would not have been possible.

The project was led by Paul Thompson, who at the start was a part-time professor at the University of Essex as well as Director of Qualidata in 1994–2001. He continued working on the project as a volunteer and is currently an Emeritus Professor of Sociology at Essex.

Our most fundamental debt is to all the interviewees who gave us their time and patience. In some instances they also provided much unexpected source material: most strikingly *Peter Townsend*, whose interview lasted 17 hours over five sessions, for each of which he produced a thick pile of newly unearthed documentation, now archived in the library of the University of Essex.

The project is also crucially indebted to the interviewers. Paul Thompson interviewed 46 of our Pioneers, wholly or in part, while other interviews were carried out by Blanche Girouard, Elaine Bauer, Julie Boekhoff, Karen Worcman, Anne Murcott, Liz Spencer, Michele Abendstern and Ray Pahl.

Lastly for their continuing support over more than 20 years we are especially indebted to Marion Haberhauer for her transcribing, and for their lead in archiving and making available these interviews Louise Corti at the UK Data Service (Associate Director of the UK Data Archive) and Rob Perks at the British Library. Most recently we also warmly thank Hilary Rose, Jacqueline Sarsby and Olgar Saavedra for the cover photos and Camille Corti-Georgiou for creating the audio clips now on YouTube.

Finding and using the pioneers' interviews

UK Data Service

The Pioneers collection has been successively initiated, processed and archived by the UK Data Service (of which the UK Data Archive is the lead partner). Today, the UK Data Service holds the recordings and transcriptions from interviews with 58 Pioneers. The transcribed interviews, interview summaries and selected thematic text extracts for most of the Pioneers can be downloaded in rich text format (RTF) together as a 'bundle' from the UK Data Service data catalogue: https://beta.ukdataservice.ac.uk/datacatalogue/studies/study?id=6226. Simply click on the purple box 'Access Data'. The data are openly available under a Creative Commons Attribution 4.0 International Licence.

Selected interview transcripts and summaries are also openly available to read online through Qualibank:
https://discover.ukdataservice.ac.uk/QualiBank/?f=Collection Title_Pioneers

Audio clips from the Pioneers can be found from the project's playlist on the UK Data Service's YouTube Channel:
https://www.youtube.com/channel/UCmK1mj5dCq0Xu CWI7DVKx2w/playlists

Finally, summary information on the Pioneers can also be browsed at https://ukdataservice.ac.uk/teaching-resources/pioneers.aspx, where open resources are available for teaching with this interview collection.

British Library

At the present stage the copyrights of both the interviewee and the interviewer have all been transferred to the British Library (BL). The transcripts and audio files in the collection are available via each person's Sound and Moving Image (SAMI) catalogue entry (http://sami.bl.uk). The summaries are used for content discovery when searching the catalogue. The collection title for the Pioneers project is *Pioneers of Social Research* and the collection reference is C 1416.

The data from the SAMI catalogue entries also appear on the main BL 'Explore' umbrella catalogue (http://explore.bl.uk/). When searching by author name, the summary of the interview will appear under 'details'. The 'Explore' catalogue entries also display a full list of each author's publications held by the Library. The text extracts from the interviews have been archived with the British Library Sound Archive but are not listed in the catalogue.

The BL's oral history collection is one of the most extensive in the world and includes interviews on a vast range of subjects. There are over 6,500 life story interviews in the Millennium Memory Bank recorded jointly with the BBC in 1998–99. A series of projects have been recorded in parallel with the Pioneers for National Life Stories, based at the British Library and founded by Paul Thompson in 1987. For more information on life story recording and oral history at the British Library, see: http://www.bl.uk/oralhistory and www.bl.uk/nls.

University of Essex Library

The University of Essex Library holds in its archives Paul Thompson's lifetime research materials, including a full digital set of the Pioneers' interviews, hard copies of documents including correspondence before 2011, and also a full set of the text extracts chosen by Paul Thompson from each interview.

Related interviews

Mark Abrams: in 2019 after we wrote this book the UK Data Service was given a valuable life story interview of the survey pioneer, recorded in 1984 by his grandson Dominic Abrams.

Heather Joshi: we recorded the first stage of her interview but it was not finished, so could not be used for this book. The 2017 recording is held by the BL.

Carl Moser's Pioneer interview is a supplement to the full life story recorded by Jennifer Wingate in 2008 for National Life Stories and held by the BL.

Marilyn Strathern's Pioneer interview is a supplement to her interview recorded for Leading Thinkers by Alan Macfarlane.

Michael Young's Pioneer interview was recorded in 2001 as a supplement to his full life story of 1990 recorded by Paul Thompson for National Life Stories and held by the BL as C 408/012.

Asa Briggs, Lord Briggs, social historian: a full life story interview also recorded by Paul Thompson and held by the BL as C 408/022.

Names

Partly because interviewing brings empathy on first name terms, and also because we mostly quote the Pioneers recalling earlier phases in their lives before they may have achieved baronies, damehoods or knighthoods, we drop titles when referring to them, and call them by first names, except in the Biographical summaries. The one exception is *Raymond Firth* who retained the manners of an earlier generation, which we have respected.

Transcripts

The quotations from interviews are cited in this book simply by page references to the transcripts (which are available online) in 10 pt type. Transcripts are an intermediate form between the audio, which is the ultimate source, and the printed word. They are an interpretation of the audio. Whatever the purpose, in the printed word punctuation is likely to be in different places from the speech pauses. If our purpose was to study speech patterns, we would also need to annotate them to indicate volume, feeling, extreme hesitation and so on. For this book we focus on their meaning. Hence – sometimes with advice from an interviewee – we have edited them more tightly, cutting out distracting circular repetitions and 'fillers' like 'you know' which nearly everybody uses in talk. The interviewees were then sent the draft for corrections and comments. Following this, we sometimes added an explanatory phrase, and put this in square brackets. Otherwise the sequence and the words are those of the transcript from the audio, with hesitations marked '–' and cuts marked '…'.

CHAPTER 1

Introduction: the pioneers of social research study

This book is doubly unusual. First, it does not argue a single hard-shaped account of British social research, but a way into exploring its diversity. Second, it does not stand alone as a book, but is the frontispiece, the doorway, for a remarkable set of life story interviews. These 58 interviews are all available in full as both audio and transcript online, through both the UK Data Service and the British Library. You can find basic information on each interviewee in our Biographical summaries (see pp 219–231). For each interview there is also a summary, a brief bio, lists of publications and sets of text and audio highlight extracts. The audio clips can be heard through YouTube. So this book is the front door for a multimedia resource for all interested in learning and teaching about the development of British social research.

Essentially, it highlights the experiences and practices of the generations who were active from the 1950s to the 1980s, the crucial founding generations for today's social research scene. These were the decades which saw the final phase of colonial anthropology, the explosive growth of sociology in universities, and then the founding of theme-based women's, ethnic and cultural studies and the development of ethical practices and systematic methodologies.

The archive started from the work of Qualidata, now absorbed into the UK Data Service, which was set up by the Economic and Social Research Council (ESRC) in 1994 to search out and rescue un-archived data from major post-1945 research projects. An earlier survey had shown how very few projects had safely archived their data, and many had been already lost or deliberately destroyed: among them *Michael Young* and Peter Willmott's famous studies of family and kinship in East London, John and Elizabeth Newson's 30 years of research on childrearing, all the fieldwork data from the two Banbury community studies, and astonishingly, almost all the data of all the early British black community studies. But Qualidata were able to rescue the fieldwork data of many other sociologists, including *The Affluent Worker* study of Luton car workers, *Stan Cohen*'s work on youth and moral panics, *George Brown*'s on women and mental illness, and *Peter Townsend*'s national projects on poverty and ageing.[1]

1

Inspired by this rediscovered richness, Qualidata began life story interviews with researchers whose work was being deposited, in order to provide crucial information about the purpose and practice of the projects. The interview guide which has been used explores family backgrounds, parents, education, other work, and leisure, but the main focus is on the interviewee's research ideas and practice. The early interviews proved so rewarding that recording was soon broadened to include other distinguished British social researchers whose data was unavailable or already archived elsewhere. This in turn led to recording leading quantitative as well as primarily qualitative pioneers. With support first from the ESRC (1994–99) and then from the UK Data Archive and the Fuller Bequest, the British Academy (2009–11), and most recently the Leverhulme Trust (2016–18), the recording of researchers has continued for just over 20 years, concluding in the summer of 2018.

Who was interviewed?

There is no satisfactory way in which a conventional sample of 'pioneer' social researchers could be created. Inevitably, some key researchers had already died before we could record them. We miss especially the stories which we might have had from Richard Titmuss (d. 1975), Max Gluckman (d. 1975), John Rex (d. 2011), Edward Shils (d. 1995) and Cathie Marsh (d. 1993). A few interviews were started but discontinued due to ill health or – most rarely – through dissatisfactions with the process. The many missing fieldworker voices include Paul Atkinson, Michael Banton (d. 2018), Julia Brannen, Bob Burgess, Tony Coxon (d. 2012), Angela McRobbie, Liz Stanley and Paul Willis.[2] We could have also interviewed methodologists such as Alan Bryman (d. 2017), Martin Bulmer and David Silverman. We could have reached out further to where social research crossed social boundaries, as with social geography, or in the earlier work based on literary approaches by Raymond Williams (d. 1988) and Richard Hoggart (d. 2014), or in Sir Michael Rutter's powerful combination of psychiatry and social science. The choices we were able to make were decided through many discussions, and there were always far more suggestions than we had the resources to record. There are many more original researchers that we wish we could have included.

The whole collection now consists of 58 interviews. The oldest, *Raymond Firth*, was born in 1901 and is exceptional in already being an active researcher in the interwar years. He is followed by *Jack Goody*, born in 1919, who like others of his age was not able to begin until after the end of the Second World War in 1945. Like others of the older interviewees, his wartime was an important experience. The youngest interviewee was born in 1948, and all had begun their research careers by the 1970s. They had mainly made their key contributions by the 1980s, but several continued publishing into the 2000s. Altogether, 33 are with sociologists – most of whom first trained in other disciplines, especially anthropology – and 14 with lifelong anthropologists. There are also three from politics, two each from geography and economics, another two from statistics, and one from cultural studies.

These are essentially British pioneers, although they worked worldwide. We have included two other researchers with British links: *Daniel Bertaux*, who co-researched social mobility with Paul Thompson, and *Glen Elder*, who more briefly connected with *John Bynner*. Through their interviews we glimpse innovation in contrasting neighbouring research cultures: with *Daniel Bertaux* the constraints of a hierarchical patronage system in France, and with *Glen Elder* the can-go scene in the United States (US) – where new approaches did encourage mixed methods. But in terms of birthplace most of our interviewees were born in England, with just one from Wales, one from Northern Ireland, and none from Scotland. Only three were born elsewhere in Europe. However, an important minority of ten came from Jewish families who typically had migrated in the previous generation to escape persecution and extermination. This group includes *Leonore Davidoff*, who was born in the US. Many other interviewees spent important times in America, often taking up the new quantitative developments from visits to Madison, or being inspired by the new American research approaches to sexuality. *Raymond T. Smith* spent most of his working life based in Chicago.

Many of our Pioneers' lives were shaped by the declining decades of the British Empire. Ten were born in the Empire, *Firth* in New Zealand, another in Australia, two in India, one in Malta, two in South and East Africa, and four in the Caribbean. Half of these were white, half non-white, but they all operated in an Anglophone intellectual space, based on the Empire, and in practice also including the US. In the 1940s and 1950s British research within the Empire was financed and – as *Jack Goody*'s story vividly illustrates – to some extent controlled by the Colonial Social Science Research Council and British representatives and local governors out in the colonies.

Geographically, again their work took many of them into new terrains. *Frank Bechhofer* moved to Scotland. *Ronald Frankenberg* set out for the Caribbean, but was refused entry by the British authorities because he was a Communist. So he switched his attention to North

Wales, a part of Britain where the vernacular language was not English. Learning a language was then regarded as an essential step to becoming an anthropologist.

Few of these social researchers showed much interest in continental Europe – apart from *Daniel Bertaux*, who is himself a French sociologist, and *John Goldthorpe* and *Duncan Gallie*, who were both influenced by French theoretical ideas and married French wives. The other exceptions were all anthropologists. Their work focussed on the Mediterranean, which was seen as more primitive – and there had been notable earlier research studies in Spain and Greece. *John Davis* researched in southern Italy and *Peter Loizos* in Cyprus. However, later on *Judith Okely* worked in northern France.

A larger group worked in more distant settings. *Maxine Molyneux* carried out remarkably challenging research in Yemen, Ethiopia and Afghanistan, as did *Stan Cohen* in Israel. *Pat Caplan* worked in Nepal and in Southern India, as well as primarily in Tanzania. Four others worked in Africa: *Jack Goody* in Ghana, *Mary Douglas* in Congo, and *Ruth Finnegan* in Sierra Leone. *Bruce Kapferer* went to Zambia (then Southern Rhodesia), to the innovative Manchester-run Rhodes Livingstone Institute, studying African factory workers, a notable turn in colonial anthropology. Bruce had earlier worked in Fiji, and his later research was in Sri Lanka. *Raymond Smith* researched in the Caribbean, initially in Trinidad. *Harry Goulbourne* came from Jamaica, migrated as a child to England and studied there, worked in newly independent Tanzania, returned to Jamaica, and then back to England, where his final project was on transnational Caribbean migration.

Interpreting the interviews

What can we learn from these interviews? It is important to remember that in reading or hearing them we are listening to people's voices, to their own accounts of their life experiences.[3] The interviews are an interaction between interviewee and interviewer, and what is in them was partly determined by what was asked of them, but equally by their own vision of what mattered most in their lives and what they would like to be remembered. Typically, they held back to some extent – but not usually entirely – in telling about difficulties, whether in the family or their own marriages, or painful conflicts at work and with colleagues. But the interviews give us unique information, especially in two respects. The first is about their early years, their families and childhoods, and their influences through schooling and university, which led them to become social researchers and influenced the themes they chose and where they went to research.

The second is about the research itself. Why and how was it done? What were the difficulties, the shortcuts they took? The published outcomes from research projects usually give smoothed-out accounts of the research, with its problems and difficulties at best hinted, rarely explored. There are innumerable published books about how to do research. But how many are there of how it actually happens?

Precedents and parallels

There are some important parallels and precedents for our work. Thus, since the 1970s Jennifer Platt has made a valuable early contribution to the history of research methods in both Britain and the US. And more recently, Mike Savage draws on the material we have collected in his major overview, *Identities and Social Change in Britain since 1940: the Politics of Method* (2010).[4]

However, in terms of presenting researchers' own accounts the precedents almost all take the form of written autobiography, which is typically more formal and cautious and less expressive of feeling than oral recording. They have come most often from anthropologists, perhaps because life story work with their subjects has been a common practice. Some of the early social researchers in Britain, like Henry Mayhew and Charles Booth, did include some details about their research approaches in their publications. Nevertheless, *Colin Bell*'s championing of 'owning up' was a major innovation for sociologists. Frustrated by what he saw as undiscussed failures in his own team's work in the second Banbury community study, he edited three collections of confessional essays by other sociologists. These began with *Doing Sociological Research* (with Howard Newby, 1977), followed by an Australian collection with Sol Incel, *Inside the Whale* (1978), and a third set, *Social Researching: Politics, Process, Practice* (1984), with Helen Roberts, who had herself meanwhile edited *Doing Feminist Research* (1981).

Unfortunately, there has been much less subsequent 'owning up' by British sociologists. There is one inspiring exception: Ann Oakley's exceptionally candid and perceptive double biography, professional and personal, of herself and her father, Richard Titmuss, in *Father and Daughter: Patriarchy, Gender and Social Science* (2014). She has unusually diverse talents: not only the observational eye of a sociologist, but also a sense of time and history, and the imaginative insights for fiction in novels and on screen. Earlier, she had written a semi-autobiographical novel, *Taking It Like a Woman* (1984). Most recently, in *Women, Peace and Welfare: a Suppressed History of Social Reform, 1880–1920* (2019), she has reflected on how and why the contributions to social research of women who were activists in First Wave Feminism have become forgotten – and sought to reassert their importance.

In the US, by contrast, major sociology departments such as Berkeley and Chicago have developed collections of recorded life stories from their own staff. There have also been significant publications of written autobiography, such as Bennett Berger's *Authors of their Own Lives* (1990) and Mathieu Deflem's *Sociologists in a Global Age: Biographical Perspectives* (2007).

There has been a more sustained recent interest in 'owning up' among anthropologists. Most famously, Malinowski in 1914–18 kept candid diaries while researching in the Trobiand Islands and wrote a long introduction to *Argonauts of the Western Pacific* (1922) describing his fieldwork. However, after his death his fieldwork diaries were translated from Polish and published in 1967, and proved a sharp challenge to his reputation. In the same year, Hortense Powdermaker, an American anthropologist who was a pupil and great admirer of Malinowski, and researched first in Australian-controlled New Ireland in Melanesia and later among the black communities of the southern US, published *Stranger and Friend: The Way of an Anthropologist* (1967), which tells in exceptionally full and fascinating detail about how she worked to become accepted and carry out her fieldwork.[5]

There has also been a fruitful influence from the anthropological tradition of recording and publishing life stories from men and women of other cultures. Beginning in 1982 as the filming of Cambridge anthropology seminars – at the suggestion of *Jack Goody* – Alan Macfarlane has developed an important series of films of anthropological 'ancestors'. Often, the early films were very short, but many of the later ones are full life stories – to the extent that for *Marilyn Strathern* we only carried out a supplementary interview for our own archive. Macfarlane has subsequently broadened out his series to include a wide range of 'Leading Thinkers' – now an online collection of over 200 writers and scientists connected with Cambridge.[6]

This raises the question as to whether or not it is an advantage to film such life stories, rather than simply record in audio. A film of a single talking head from the same angle quickly becomes boring and hence distracting. Few British academics have interesting or revealing gestures – the most striking exception among Macfarlane's interviewees is *Jack Goody*, whose presentation is odd, although the meaning of his gestures is not easy to understand. Filming to a better level requires more than one camera, each with an operator to control angles and close-ups. It is therefore somewhat less relaxed, as well as much more expensive. It also locates the account in the present, mediated through an ageing person. But the voice changes much less with age than the face, so listening to the voice alone, especially if supplemented by photos from the time of the story, can become more powerful in re-evoking time past. So – listen to the voices of our Pioneers on YouTube!

VOICES 1

Moments of discovery

So what can the voices of our researchers tell us? Let us begin with some of their thoughts about the nature of creativity. Social researchers typically reach their most important discoveries through slow processes, beginning with observation, and building up interpretations through their own experience and also through borrowing from others. Transposing an accepted idea into a new concept can be a crucial step. But – especially it seems among men – there may also be vividly remembered moments in a life when a new key idea comes home to stay.

Why is there this difference between men and women Pioneers? It does seem that the men are more likely to tell a story in which they are surprised by their own success, but know that they performed well themselves: for example, *John Bynner* on the impact of his student survey, or *David Butler* on his first television performance. By contrast almost all our women Pioneers present themselves as working as part of a big social movement with shared new perspectives. Thus, when *Sara Arber* takes up gender and ageing, she knows that she will find inequalities in resources between men and women; and when she moves into the sociology of sleep, she is not surprised that women more often suffer from sleep disturbance, or that men snore more.

Meghnad Lord Desai: economists don't do fieldwork

Not all social scientists believe in fieldwork or observation. Meghnad Desai, whose many writings include a book on the power of landowners in India, describes his early experiences of rural fieldwork as fruitless. For him, listening to villagers is a waste of time.

> I remember when we had one of those conferences, and I said, 'I took a bus from Delhi to Jaipur, and I looked out of the window, and that was my fieldwork', and the anthropologists were very upset! They said, 'You're too arrogant, you shouldn't do things like this.' That's how I do my fieldwork! What can I say? Yes, it is, I'm in economics, economists don't do fieldwork. It is a specialist thing. One should not go and do things that are not your specialisation. Economists basically sit at a desk, and think a problem through, because there are data. They do

some statistical calculation. They don't do fieldwork. We are a very *a prioristic* science – if you are a science. Very *a priori* discipline. (p 24)

Stan Cohen: social marginality in racist South Africa

Most of our social researchers, however, have learnt from observing and listening. Thus, Stan Cohen first understood the concept of marginality, which became a lifetime theme in his work, through childhood observation.

> I remember from childhood, looking out of the window at night, and seeing a black 'night watchman' – as they used to be called – from a private security firm, who was guarding the house because my father was away. It was a cold Johannesburg night, and I suddenly saw the man huddled over this coal stove, and I was inside, and I suddenly had this epiphany of... 'Why is he there, and why am I in here?' There seemed something inexplicable about this poor old man having to stand outside, and here I was, inside, in this warm bed. What had made the world like that? And I think once you start thinking like that, you always think like that...
>
> And I could never, I couldn't understand – well, I suppose what we now call 'the order of things'. It didn't make sense to me that, as somebody, and I was 13 or 14, but I had this black servant who would call me 'Master', and he was 20, 30 years older than me, and an adult, but we would call him a 'boy'. And the house servant, the woman, we would call a 'girl'. And things like that which are so obvious to an outsider, but to an insider, are part of reality... I think, from a very early age, I was aware of the strangeness of the social order there, and things which were taken for granted. (pp 1–3)

Claus Lord Moser: learning statistics as an alien internee

Claus Moser discovered the potential of statistics when he was sent to an internment camp at the beginning of the Second World War.

> I was interned with my brother and father, and I was interned at Huyton, Liverpool, with 5,000 other Jewish refugees, and if you get 5,000 Jewish refugees, we all find something to do, we all find a role, some important role. Well, I was only 13, but

I didn't want an important role, but one day I was sitting next to a mathematician, at lunch – he was called Landau, there is a famous Landau, but that wasn't him. Anyway, this guy was called Landau, and he had something to do. He was a mathematician, and he'd set up a statistics office. In the camp. To keep account of the numbers and categories and so on. Would I like to help him? 'Yes'. And that's how I became a statistician…

So it was a very simple causation – imprisonment. I was purely his helpmate, keeping records of the numbers who came, who were admitted, who were released, what we knew about them. Keeping records. I was like a minor statistical assistant, and I loved it. (pp 1–2)

George Brown: suicide in the family

For two others, the spur came from within their own families. With George Brown, the future well known medical researcher on depression in women (not to be confused with the Labour politican), the suicide of his cousin's wife pushed him towards his own lifelong research on the causes of depression among women.

She was very nice to me, and would come to see me. I wasn't intimate or confiding in her, but felt close. One of the crises in my life was when she committed suicide… It must have been just about the time I started research, when I was about 26, and it was post-partum depression, and everybody was ashamed. Her mother, particularly, was ashamed that her daughter should be [mentally ill]. I was very moved and felt that I could have done more, if I'd known what was going on… I don't think she'd even gone to see a doctor about it, and she went into – jumped in the canal, the Grand Union canal, and the baby was only a few months old.

This was important to me, intellectually, because I partly gained my reputation from arguing the social causes of depression. I had no reason to doubt that it was a happy marriage. I'd be very surprised if it wasn't, because they were such extraordinarily nice people. And again, jumping ahead a long way, I've always been aware that you can't reduce psychiatric disorder to only social factors or psycho-social factors, that one has to struggle with the fact that this was almost certainly essentially a biological response to the birth, although subsequently, in my research, I've shown that most post-partum depression is psycho-social. (pp 8–9)

Peter Loizos: first visit to Cyprus to meet his father's family

Peter Loizos told a happier story. His father was a Greek Cypriot communist refugee in London, but separated from his mother, so that as a child he only saw him twice. He spoke no Greek. Peter was in his late twenties when he started to study anthropology. After his mother died he got into active contact with his father, who in turn wrote to his family in Cyprus, and helped him to organise his first visit to the island at the age of 29. The welcome he got was an overpowering experience which set him on his lifetime research theme: community in Cyprus, and the impact of its loss when Cyprus was divided.

So the boat gets to Limassol, and while we're waiting to disembark, and people are waiting – you have to go on small boats, because the boat can't come into the quayside, it anchors half a mile out, so there's a queue, and it's hot, and people are jostling and things, suddenly a young policeman appears in front of me, and asks my name. And at this point, I think, 'This is it! The Cypriots are going to take their revenge on me, as a sort of hybrid British renegade. I'm going to be in some kind of trouble in this place before I've even stepped off the boat!' But not at all! He's come to find me because he's my first cousin, and my father's written, and they've responded, and he's come to take me – in a privileged way – ashore. So I jump the queue, and he takes me in, walk through Customs, they all say, 'Hello', and he says, 'He's my cousin, and there's his passport', and I'm through, you know! Wow!

Then when we come out on to the dockside, there's three carloads of guys, who all introduce themselves, very solemnly, and with great dignity. Some can't speak any English and are being translated for by the one or two who can, and they are my cousins, and they've come all this way, a three-hour drive, in the heat, to collect me off a boat! Which for a man who'd had no brothers and sisters, and hardly any cousins – three cousins by one aunt – this was pretty amazing. Emotionally overwhelming. Remind ourselves, I had just lost my mother... We're in the dog days of the marriage, it's in trouble. Here I am being taken into something. And they take me off to the village and I have a marvellous time.

They feast me. The food is amazing, delicious, generous, unfamiliar. Lots of strong drink served with it. Lots of toasting. It's very decorous. You don't drink at will in Cyprus, you drink in rounds and toasts. So if I raise my glass, everybody raises their glass... There's speeches of welcome – and I have to respond, so I make a speech about having had to carry my father's name as a child, and it not making any sense to me, and having suffered in some small way for it, it now all suddenly seems worthwhile and makes sense. And I look around the room and even the men are wiping their eyes because of this story about kinship, and separation. (pp 28–30)

Ken Plummer: coming out and coming out stories

In the same year, 1966, Ken Plummer also found a lifetime theme through coming out, recognising, observing his own sexuality.

There's a genealogy now of the notion of coming out, and I experienced it personally, and I read it in books in the sixties and I watched it kind of unfold in different ways. There's a big chunk of it in my book on *Sexual Stigma*, and I was applying it to these other groups about when they come out – when can a paedophile come out, for example? Or, indeed, a sadomasochist. So you can apply it all the way through. And then by the late eighties and nineties, there were archives of it, and there were coming out stories all round the world. So you had coming out in India, coming out in Africa, everybody was doing coming out stories. Then there came the deconstruction of coming out. So nobody's coming out any more because everybody's come out already, or it's not straightforward. So there's a whole big story to be told about coming out!

I'm part of that story, like anybody who's gay is, and has a different set of responses. My own coming out was, first of all, to myself, then I told my parents, and I told my parents, well, in this critical year, 1966, and they sent me to see a therapist and all the rest of it. And then coming out to my friends, and the first friend I told it to, I said, 'You know, well, I've got something to tell you. I'm gay'. He said, 'So am I'. And so it went on. So 1966 was my critical coming out year. But there was another coming out, which was in the Gay Movement in 1970, which is when I first marched in the streets, and then that became the real meaning of coming out, publicly, in the streets, for everybody to know. So there are lots of different meanings of it. (pp 51–52)

So my coming out experience, my first gay bar experience, was about 1966, and that was right in the heart of Soho, in a top bar; and then the following night I was taken right down into a basement... That was really my immersive fieldwork moment! (p 21)

Mary Douglas on dirt

Among our women pioneers, many recalled their transition to marriages and motherhood as a difficult turning point. Among them, two especially emphasised how this led them to crucial new research perspectives: with *Mary Douglas* to examine cleaning household dirt as ritual, with *Ann Oakley* to look at child-rearing as an unpaid form of work.

> *You get married, and then you have the children, and then you write about dirt. Do you think this is partly because of being involved in keeping a house?*
>
> Well, in a sense, I look back on *Purity and Danger* and think I wrote it because I didn't believe in dirt. That there was too much pressure to keep things clean! And that this was ritual, not meaningless ritual, but ritual that meant something different from looking after bacteria, or preventing them from entering your food, but ritual about occasions and about continual celebrations of different relationships. That was a hierarchical thing. (p 63)

Ann Oakley: 'What I am doing is work'

For Ann Oakley, then a young mother, feeling perplexed, isolated and depressed, the new perspective on her situation came as a crucial 'conversion moment':

> Of course, a lot of my work, subsequently, has interrogated this whole notion of post-natal depression, which most of the time is actually a label for women who are chronically exhausted and sleep-deprived, and just have too much to do, and I think that was probably my situation. But I remember there being a

sort of conversion moment when I was dusting bookshelves in [husband] Robin's study and found these books on the sociology of work, and I thought, 'What I'm doing is work'. And I looked in these books, and I looked in the index of various books, and there was nothing about housework. There were quite a few references to the fact that employed women's orientation to their employment work was always different because their primary commitments were to the home. And I thought, 'Well, what I am doing here, which is looking after children and cleaning houses, would be paid work. So why is it that this whole area of women's labour is completely missing?' So I decided I wanted to do a study of housework, and I registered at Bedford College and spent quite a long time trying to find a supervisor who understood what I was trying to do. (Part 1, pp 9–11)

John Bynner: the Bristol Student Union – research making an impact

With others, the crucial moment was to see how research could bring results. With John Bynner, future champion of British longitudinal studies, this recognition came as a student activist.

I became quite active in that. I was the Chairman of the Grants and Welfare Committee. From the moment I arrived, the Union appealed to me. It was that political side of my personality… The Grants and Welfare Committee actually handed out money to students who were in difficulty.

But the main thing, in terms of research careers, was actually inheriting this survey of student opinion about the University refectory, and suddenly getting interested in what this data from students could tell us about what was right and what was wrong with the facilities, and the whole approach, the whole policy towards student eating. And the University responded very well to this report, and immediately set in an action plan for doing what I recommended! So I was absolutely amazed! And so doing work, using things like statistics, collecting data, and then seeing action arising from it, became a very important theme of my career. And one of the things that satisfies me most is the thought you've actually made a contribution, as well as just improving understanding, you improve action. That's stayed with me ever since. (p 11)

Sir David Butler: on to electoral television

David Butler remains surprised by how his unexpected invitation to join the BBC's *Election Night* programme in 1950 launched him on a lifelong career as an election pundit and analyst.

> The BBC was going to put on an Election Night programme that had never been done before on television, and radio had always been extremely dull, just reading out the results in a totally formal way. The wonderful lady, Grace Goldie, who was then Deputy Head of Current Affairs at the BBC, had the idea of having a good Election Night programme. She asked Ronald MacCallum, because MacCallum had written a book on the '45 Election, to come on the programme. MacCallum, knowing that he didn't know anything about figures, said he wouldn't come on it unless I could be there, sitting beside him.
>
> So I got involved in Election Night preparations, and then suddenly I was on the screen – I'd hardly seen any television at the time – I was on screen on the 23rd February, 1950, available when results came in. And I found that I could talk, spontaneously, about them. I was doing, in front of a camera, what I would have been doing if I'd just been alone at home, or with friends at home – interpreting the election results. And it was thought to be a success. So I stayed doing Election Night television at the BBC, beside the anchor man, for the next ten Elections, and my last performance – one on telly – was 1979. But from 1950 to '79 I was a sort of fixture there… It really, it was just a very exciting thing to do… One didn't need to sleep, one could go through for 36 hours without stopping, and would be – totally excited, totally immersed in all that was happening…
>
> It was a great help to me. I wasn't a great person at television… But it meant that I was known to the political class. When, later on I was spending a lot of time writing books on General Elections and thinking about British politics, I had an entrée simply because I was known as a television person, as a pundit on elections, and thought to be learned in a way I certainly wasn't. So that well, in a sense, changed my life. It opened doors for me. (pp 8–9)[1]

Ruth Finnegan: listening and watching for hidden meanings

Ruth Finnegan began recording storytelling in Sierra Leone, as she had been advised, and documenting their variations, as if they were stories only destined for print, products for the Western world. The key to understanding some of their hidden meanings came when she not only listened, but also watched, taking in their African context:

> So I began to realise how important creativity was, and individual tellers. I was very moved by some of them because, really, the kind of view of a tragedy, of certain relationships, or the humour of others, or the funny little twists of character that were put in just by a kind of wink of the eye, they were so moving and so deep in the storytelling. I did all the proper things that I thought a scholar should do then. I transcribed them from the tape at the time, because if you leave it till you get home... you'll forget. So there they were, translated, and all written down, and then in my thesis I put them all down in the text with the Limba on one side and the English on the other side, and some word for word and some freer. That's the proper way, as a classical scholar, you know! Learnt how to deal with text! The real thing were texts! That's what reality is, you captured it!
>
> But when I got back and showed some people my texts, they didn't think that they were deep or profound or moving at all, and I was really upset and puzzled by this, until I realised that, of course, the text didn't capture the reality, the stories – the reality lay in the performance, the audience interaction... Also there were often – not always – songs in the stories, and the storyteller would sing the first line – typical call and response situation – and the audience would all sing the chorus. It was part of taking the action of the story on. So all this, and all the kinaesthetic and the gestures and the movements, and the atmosphere, and the amazing thing you can do with your voice – lengthening, and loud and soft, and dynamic, and stopping, and silences, and exaggerations, and the wonderful idiophones that you have in African languages – a sort of symbolic sound – all that is missing from the text. (pp 43–44)

Sir Jack Goody: the culture of flowers

Jack Goody is unusual in the extent to which he took up new themes right through his long research life. These new themes were very often based on comparisons between cultures. Here he describes the origin of his work on the culture of flowers in different societies, which he started after his retirement. It began with a comparison between what he had noticed in Africa, and what he saw in Asia.

> Flowers was rather similar to cooking, in the sense that, just as I find no haute cuisine in Africa, ... you never had domestication of flowers. You had some flowers in Africa, growing wild in the forest, but you didn't have the sort of thing that you have in Asia or in Europe, but mostly in Asia, as chrysanthemums being planted for sacred and to offer either to a god or to a human being, or to decorate the house, or decorate the garden, but that sort of aesthetic activity – if you want to take aesthetic cultivation – was not really practised...
>
> I remember one Japanese anthropologist, who I knew well, Junzo Kawada... I remember Junzo saying that when he first went to Upper Volta, being Japanese he looked around, and he asked the chief, 'Where are you growing flowers?' And the chief looked at him as though he was mad! 'Why should we grow flowers? You can't eat them'. And the idea that you should be planting and growing things which you couldn't eat in that way was incomprehensible to him...
>
> You didn't even get any fruit trees in Africa. You never got the domestication of fruit trees, except one in South Africa, I think, and the idea of growing a peach tree, simply so you could cut it down and display it at the beginning of the New Year, as many families did – most of the families did in Hong Kong – you cut down a peach tree, which is a growing tree, which could have fruit on. That would have horrified my Presbyterian mother, let alone an African, since I was never allowed to break down a branch off an apple tree, let alone a cherry tree. But they are in China and Japan, and now here, you're... growing fruit trees for flowering – not for their fruit, but for the flowers on them – and you're growing chrysanthemums and so on, which were very important. So I was interested in that...
>
> The West rejected the growing of flowers at one time... Do you remember a graveyard in the Protestant United States, in the eastern United States? There's not a flower to be seen.

There's not even a cut flower to be seen, except possibly around a patriot's grave. Scotland is the same, you do not see many flowers in the graveyards up there. And the Protestants kept out flowers out of the graveyards, because, ... if you're growing these things, or presenting these things, you're presenting them to the dead – you're worshipping the dead instead of worshipping God... There's another reason for the Protestant one, and that was to do with the Protestant Ethic that Weber talks about. That as my mother would say, in Scotland, if they go with flowers, you say, 'I'd rather hae eggs'. (pp 96–97)

Peter Townsend: a bath attendant in an old people's home

One last example, this time of Peter Townsend's crucial deepening of understanding of the impact of old-age institutions which took place when he was already researching *The Last Refuge*. It seems fair to ask, what already well-recognised leading social researcher today would take so much trouble as to work as a bath attendant for elderly men? Have we still got that degree of social and scientific commitment?

I was in Newholme, in Manchester... And my job, after doing all these various interviews around the Home, I then became an attendant, looking after the bathing of the old men. And I think what forced itself upon my consciousness was a number of things.

One was the extraordinarily kind of – abject passivity of some of these elderly men. It was almost as if the process of institutionalisation had forced upon them how to behave, and how to be, as it were, preserve their integrity only within – it's almost like the ways in which we have fantasies, we have an inside life and we have an external life, and some of them communicated this by talking a bit about their past and about what their feelings were for their loved ones. And mostly it was feelings of being bereft and being abandoned. But it was also feelings of being neglected by staff, who didn't want to know, and didn't have any forms of communication. It was almost as if they were – I know it's not, it wasn't a situation where they were like in a solitary confinement or in a prison where the doors were locked at such and such hours, and you were only let out at such and such hours, but they led a routine which was amazingly limited.

That aspect of their demeanour and their behaviour, I think, was terribly important, and although this was only the one experience, it obviously then got related by me to all kinds of other interviews I'd had across the country, and helped to inform those interviews and the experiences other people touched upon.

But it was also physically the problem of seeing these very thin, many thin characters, how gentle one had to be to get them into the bath, how careful one had to be in using one's elbow to make sure the water wasn't too hot, how little they had in the way of personal belongings, how the underpants they had, the kind of combinations they were wearing, sometimes had six, seven, eight, ten laundry marks, or tabs attached, which almost underlined their loss of identity. They were just numbers in an institution where they didn't even possess underpants of their own. And although it isn't like some of the terrible experiences people recount about refugee camps and somebody who suddenly comes in and smashes somebody to death – yes, it's not as extreme as all that, but it's equally disconcerting and devastating to absorb what the process of institutionalisation had done to people, without them having any means of fighting back. Yes, of course there were those characters, some of them had enormous resources in terms of personality, but they'd turned it inwards, in order to – oh, I don't know, make sure that they got another slice of toast at breakfast. It was conforming. They knew that conformity was the order of the day. (pp 87–88)

CHAPTER 2

Life stories: biography and creativity

To be recorded among our pioneers implies in itself some kind of success story in research: primarily in terms of intellectual discovery and influence, sometimes later linked to taking a key position in the academic world and achieving, in *Colin Bell's* words, 'a degree of celebrity' (p 15). (If you want to know more about who they all were, see the Biographical summaries on pp 219–231.) The engine of their success had to be the research work, but many of our Pioneers spoke perceptively of their lives much beyond this, especially their earlier lives, hinting or reflecting on how these experiences may have shaped their research. Thus, the sociologist *Peter Townsend*, whose single mother was a struggling singer, frequently away from home, described his grandmother as the emotional and practical 'rock' of his childhood: 'Nowadays, I reflect a lot on the question of being an only child and what that means. It led, in part, to my enormous interest in family relations and extended family life, and the structure of families' (pp 5–6). So, among our Pioneers, how did life experience feed creative research?

The influence of childhood communities

First, how were they influenced by the communities where they grew up? Almost half of our Pioneers were Londoners, but it is striking that only two, *Peter Townsend* and the social geographer *Peter Hall*, focussed on London in their early work. Of the others, some did local fieldwork on non-local issues, but half researched elsewhere in Britain or abroad.

There was a second important group, probably particular to the early decades in which sociology became established in British universities, who came from working-class families in the north of England. Throughout their research lives they shared a key concern with the significance and subtleties of social class: *John Goldthorpe* and *David Lockwood* on class and social mobility in *The Affluent Worker* (1963–69), *David Hargreaves* on school cultures, and *Dennis Marsden* with Brian Jackson on schooling and leisure in *Education and the Working Class* (1962) and *Working Class Community* (1972). Marsden and Goldthorpe especially spoke of the complexities of class differences in their own families and communities. But not all the northerners were so keen on this local culture. Thus, *Raymond Smith* grew up as a policeman's son in Oldham. He describes it as 'a miserable place', 'a dirty northern town', 'No. No, as I say, my – my ambition was to escape!' (pp 1–4). He became an anthropologist of the Caribbean.

Lastly, there was a third important group whose families were from overseas. Ten were the second generation from families who had fled persecution in the East European *pogroms* or from Nazi Germany, including two central figures in post-war mainstream British sociology, *Ronald Frankenberg* and *Frank Bechhofer*, and three leaders in the development of statistically based quantitative sociology, *Claus Moser, Harvey Goldstein* and *Jonathan Gershuny*.

The others were scattered through the colonial British Empire. The most positive influence of birthplace here was with the anthropologist *Raymond Firth*, who as a teenager in New Zealand found books on the Maori and went on to learn their language, seek out their culture, and make Maori friends. This set him on the path which led him to a lifelong concern with Polynesian culture, and to his classic *We, the Tikopia* (1936).

Firth was unusual: the others all moved away by early adulthood, some to research elsewhere in the Empire, but most to England. It is striking how few of them later researched their original homeland. Indeed, the economist *Meghnad Desai* was emphatic that listening to village voices in India would be a waste of time. Two Jamaican researchers, *Harry Goulbourne* and *Elizabeth Thomas-Hope*, did return to work in the Caribbean. There were others, too, both white and of colour, who remained haunted by childhood memories of the fading days of Empire: for *Maxine Molyneux* the 'colonial bubble' in India and Latin America, for *Avtar Brah* the 'colonial sandwich' in East Africa, which remained crucial to their concerns. Both became feminists. The human rights sociologist *Stan Cohen* never forgot the night watchman in his hut in apartheid Johannesburg; nor did the cultural studies pioneer *Stuart Hall* forget his own family's attitudes to race.

Stuart was a dark-skinned son in a light-skinned Jamaican middle-class family who were anticipating an independence in which they would replace the British as the new elite. They identified with the colonial power – 'my mother really thought she was English'. Stuart, by contrast, who never accepted their aspirations, was always disapproved by the family as 'the bad one, the naughty one'. 'I never felt at home in that place.' He carried uncomfortable memories of his grandmother's pinpointing of people's racial backgrounds, and family friends chatting about colour-based class distinctions. But the crucial moment when he knew that he had to leave Jamaica was when his sister fell in love with a black student and the love relationship was smashed by Stuart's family. 'She was sacrificed to the social system' (pp 4–13). Racial prejudice was to become a key theme of his work in cultural studies.

Social mobility

Looking at the Pioneers' families as a whole, even though this generation for which unprecedented university expansion brought rare opportunities for upward mobility, only nine came from – mostly skilled – working-class families. On the other hand, only two, the political scientist *David Butler* and the sociologist *Duncan Gallie*, could claim descent from the old Oxbridge intellectual aristocracy. David Butler's pedigree was spectacular. But the others ranged right across the middle classes, from teachers and accountants, colonial civil servants and clerks, doctors and journalists. There was also a group of small businessmen – including one with a barber's shop, an optician and a razor blade factory owner – of whom two went bankrupt. Another was *Frank Bechhofer*'s father, who ran his own small factory producing tinsel ribbon. Can it be wholly a coincidence that Frank was to research *The Petite Bourgoisie* (1981)?

Family relationships

Two researchers from colonial cultures, one Jamaican and the other Indian, grew up in extended family households. Otherwise almost all of these families were small, as was typical for those born in Britain in the 1930s and 1940s: only five families had more than three children, while a quarter were only children. In the pre-internet era this could push them towards self-reliance and developing interests through reading. Some Pioneers do recall feeling loneliness as children. *Mildred Blaxter* – despite having a brother – described hers as 'an extremely happy and intensely solitary childhood. Solitary in terms of being devoted to books, being totally absorbed by the world of books, from a very early age. And devoted to place, to the countryside, to the fields, the rivers, the old castles I used to go and play in. The rooftops I used to climb on, in [Richmond, Yorkshire] – my own private place was the roofscape around the Market Place, and I used to sit up there reading my books. And nobody ever knew this' (p 3).

These parents stuck together much more than they would today. Only five couples divorced, but another seven lost a parent through death. No parents were remembered as violent or abusive, and almost all were supportive of their child's education. Surprisingly, the very few parents who were unsupportive included the sociologist *Mildred Blaxter*'s father, who was a bank manager. 'My father was anti-intellectual, actively anti-intellectual! Didn't even approve of my going to Oxford!' (p 2). But Mildred grew up with a house full of books, and – like many other Pioneers – she was close to her mother. There are also instances of male bonding. Thus *Robert Moore*, who grew up in a skilled house-owning family in South London, described a four-generational transmission of household maintenance skills centred on their workshops. They also made toys. 'It never occurred to me that other people's fathers might not help them with their algebra homework, or that they were not good at woodwork, electrical work, bricklaying and so on' (p 1).

John Bynner was powerfully influenced by his father, who was an active socialist and spiritualist, but in a more contradictory way. Unsettled by his feeling that his father was not practising the doctrines he propagated, and doubting the authenticity of his spiritualism, John chose to become a scientist – which in turn led him to social science. The anthropologist *Pat Caplan* describes a more coherent extended family culture. This was partly through travelling – 'I was a child of Empire' – but also through writing and journalism, and through public speaking in the Methodist chapel.

By contrast some working-class households could offer much less backing. The sociologist *David Lockwood* had to leave school early because his father had died. The extreme case was that of the medical sociologist *George Brown*, who eventually found his way into research, starting from a household with no books, and uncomprehending unsupportive parents. He passed the 11 plus without having any preparation or even warning, and when he nevertheless passed his form teacher ridiculed him. 'I was the only boy from my whole area to go to grammar school. It was, essentially, a working-class area. I mean that literally, there was no one – so I would walk to Kilburn, from Kensal Green, to get to school, but hiding my cap on the way home' (p 4). Interestingly, both Lockwood and Brown first found inspiration in another resource, then much more common – lingering and working in bookshops.

Secondary schooling

Nevertheless, it is clear that it was with entry to secondary school that the pathway to social research drastically narrowed. With one exception – to which we must return – all the Pioneers who were in Britain as teenagers went either to state-supported grammar schools or fee-paying public schools, split almost equally between them. Only six Pioneers were critical of their schools' teachers. *Duncan Gallie* was especially upset by a preparatory school which he describes as 'brutal' for its harsh discipline and continual shouting, 'hell on earth'. The future quantitative sociologist *Jonathan Gershuny* 'hated' his time at Hasberdashers' Aske's. He was a keen reader, and regularly skipped school to read in the Wembley public library, where he educated himself, reading everything from historical fiction to Freud.

On the contrary, most felt they had been well taught, and some described their teachers as 'inspiring'. At best this influence was on ways of thinking, rather than tied to a particular subject. Thus, the educationist *David Hargreaves* recalled how his Bolton French teacher Kenneth Haig 'always challenged me', forcing Hargreaves to think for himself. 'He would say, "Just read some Rousseau and then tell me what you think". And this was really very difficult, you know, for a 16-year old! But in many ways he was the most important teacher because he constantly forced me back on my own resources' (p 5). *Frank Bechhofer* remembers how his Nottingham physics teacher got his pupils to conduct live experiments in the school labs. The oral historian *Paul Thompson* recalls a biology teacher who took boys out into the countryside in new research plotting bird migrations, while he owes more to his French teacher Walter Strachan for kindling a passion for art than for teaching the French language. These schools set out to convey culture as much as prepare for exams.

At the extremes, two Pioneers, each of whom had lost a parent through death or divorce, had exceptional educational experiences. The anthropologist *Mary Douglas* found comforting certainties in a Jesuit-style education by nuns, focussing on structure, hierarchy, and philosophical discussion of doctrinal problems. The polymath *Michael Young*, by contrast, found a lifetime inspiration in Dartington and its encouragement of individual creativity and enterprise, learning small-business enterprise alongside painting and pottery.

In between, the focus was on inculcating a broad middle-class culture. This could result in trampling on the feelings of pupils from working-class homes. Thus, the sociologist *Janet Finch* resents how at Merchant Taylors' School she was forced to drop her Liverpool accent. 'The one thing which they did do, which I've always deeply resented, was take my Liverpool accent away. It was, it was the school's policy. The small number of us who had got into the school, with a Liverpool accent, had to stay back for elocution lessons after school' (p 14). On the other hand, some head teachers were liberals or socialists with a strong commitment to the education of bright working-class children. *Peter Townsend* describes how at University College School in London Cecil Walton organised discussion days with senior boys about how the school could be changed, and introduced an eccentric form of 'commando exam', combining running and swimming with writing papers, which was intended to balance out skills.

Just one Pioneer went to a comprehensive. *Harry Goulbourne* had migrated from Jamaica, where he was top of his school class, to rejoin his parents in London. He chose Peckham Manor School, where he was one of ten black children in a school of 1,600. Soon he was languishing way down in the 'technical' stream. But he was spotted by a history teacher, idealistic ex-Etonian Fred Murphy, who got him moved up into a top stream, putting him on the path to university, and so to researches on migration and transnationalism. And Murphy also introduced Harry to high culture, taking him to plays and concerts.

Gender in education

Both race and gender were to become key educational issues in future decades, but at this point were just beginning to rumble. *Pat Caplan* and *Margaret Stacey* both have affectionate memories for the skills of their older never-married women teachers, and Stacey sees her school's ethos as proto-feminist. 'The School song began, "Women of England, the heart of the nation, here the full share of our birthright we claim." It was the entire ethos of the School. Women were as good as men, you could do what men did, which people didn't then any more than they do now – but they do now in a way that's completely revolutionary to me. So, yes, it was a strong feminist ethos' (p 11).

This was far from good enough for younger women. The anthropologist *Judith Okely* was sent to a boarding school on the Isle of Wight after her father's death. She was nine, and felt suffocated in this disciplinarian school in which she was discouraged from applying to university, and even from reading her own books. 'You couldn't talk in the passage, you couldn't talk after lights out. When could you talk?' Their posture was under constant control. Time was constantly measured. 'The electric bell would go every 20 minutes.' For Judith, 'it was a place of prison' (pp 23, 27–28). She managed to leave at the age of 15.

The sociologist *Ann Oakley* was similarly very unhappy at Haberdashers' Aske's, with its conflicting ideals for women's lives.

'I absolutely hated the School. It was a girls' school, it was very conventional, you weren't allowed to have opinions of your own, it was terribly regulated.' She saw her educators as 'very unclear about what it was that women were supposed to do. On the one hand, obviously women were supposed to be educated, but on the other hand, they were supposed to be wives and mothers. What was never explained, was how you were supposed to do both!' (p 4). An issue to be crucial in her own research.

Before university, and the wartime gap

After schooling and usually before university there was briefly more variety of pathways before our Pioneers went forward into focussed academic and research lives. This was because of the Second World War and the National Service two-year conscription which followed it. The seven involved in the war itself included *Margaret Stacey*, who worked in a Clyde armaments factory, and *Mildred Blaxter*, who volunteered for the Women's Royal Naval Service (WRNS) and briefly 'fell totally in love with the Navy'. This also gave them a phase of adult independence before marriage, which in their generation was normal for men, but not for women. Among the men *Raymond Smith* flew for the Royal Air Force (RAF) and *David Cox* researched bomber aircraft design, while *David Lockwood* joined the Intelligence Corps, assisting de-Nazification in Austria. The two others had both sharply different and parallel memories.

W. M. Williams, community researcher, was called up for the Welsh Guards. 'I absolutely hated it. Because, for example, you weren't allowed to have any books or a newspaper, you weren't allowed any reading material... If they found a book in your belongings, you were put on a charge.' The Guards were disciplined 'to ensure that you did exactly as you were told, and you did nothing for yourself' (pp 11–12). He was fortunate later in becoming an officer in an Indian regiment, a stimulating exposure to other cultures. The anthropologist *Jack Goody* also served as an infantry officer, and was proud to have volunteered, but his crucial experiences were as a prisoner-of-war and escaped prisoner in Italy. When he escaped he lived for six months with two Nottinghamshire miners, at first in a cave and then hiding in the houses of local peasants 'to get food and to get a night's rest'. Again, this was a crucial and inspiring exposure to 'people who were in a completely different way of life'. Up until then he had been 'simply somebody concerned with books and books and books, you weren't concerned with doing things like cutting up meat' (p 23).

Seven others, all men, spent time in the armed forces after 1945. The sociologist *Robert Moore* was a Navy volunteer from a working-class family, for whom becoming an officer in charge of a ship at sea proved a crucial boost to his social confidence. The rest were National Servicemen. Some were simply bored, but the sociologist *Ray Pahl* had 'an amazing time' in the RAF, including a trip with ballerinas to Canada. *George Brown* first met psychologists at an army training camp, pointing towards his future interest in mental health. *Peter Townsend* recalled how meeting fellow conscripts could be revealing, such as two Geordies sleeping next to him, 'who were illiterate, and where, regularly, I wrote their love letters home to Newcastle' (p 9). But otherwise his two army years simply provided a model of how society should *not* be run. For him the Army was 'an important negative experience. I learned a lot of the things about the class system, as operating through the Army. And I learned about all those skills which I didn't really, personally, want to possess... Square-bashing. Shouting, shouting, becoming a sergeant-major, and shouting at troops, and getting them up at 5.30 in the morning. All of those sort of things' (pp 9, 19).

Marriage and divorce

For both men and women the other crucial non-academic influence by this point was whether or not they were to marry and have children.[1] Not all of these pioneer researchers gave much information on marital relationships, partly because the interviews were intended to be openly accessible, and especially the divorced – roughly half of both men and women – did not want to reveal old wounds in public. The anthropologist *Marilyn Strathern* says no more about her difficulties with Andrew while in New Guinea than that 'managing relationships was fraught' and gave her indigestion (Macfarlane interview summary, p 5). Several men were equally terse and three did not even give a wife's name.

More specifically with women, not speaking openly on record could be a way of dealing with humiliation by men. Thus, with one couple, both equally distinguished sociologists, the wife seriously studied the husband's publications but the husband refused even to read any of her work. With *Margaret Stacey* the trouble came not from her supportive husband Frank, but from the young *Colin Bell*, whom she had promoted as her lead fieldworker for the second Banbury study. She chose never to reply openly to Colin's subsequent public denunciations of the project. This experience may have been a factor in her becoming, after Frank had died in 1977, our only woman Pioneer in a long-term same-sex relationship. Her partner Jennifer Lorch warned our interviewer in 2003 that *Meg* 'says that she has two boxes labelled Banbury but has not had time to look at them. She has a special reluctance, because the Banbury study provoked a lot of controversy'. Those two boxes had sat there for a good 40 years.

Others were more openly reflective. These include *Stuart Hall* describing the impact of feminism on his marriage with Catherine. Another example is *Raymond Firth*, who married his anthropology student Rosemary in 1936, describing their 60 years of marriage: 'although, temperamentally, we're very different, and this sometimes comes out in vigorous arguments, even bitter arguments sometimes, fundamentally there's a very real affection. And she has had a most important influence as a stimulus and a critic'. He explains how they like different types of music, and how in reading, while he is 'omnivorous', Rosemary reads 'only good work'. Hence, 'she thinks I write too much, and that my style could be improved. And we argue a lot about words. She has always been very interested in the precise use of words.' And, indeed, these clashes came out in our first interview session, which she also attended, denouncing Raymond's stories as 'old rubbish' (pp 101–103).

Not surprisingly, the most romantic presentations of married life come from those who experienced lifelong couple relationships, such as *David Butler*, *Stuart Hall* or *Hilary Rose*. *Michael Redclift* describes Nanneke from the first moment when they met on the steps of the University of Sussex Library as the 'light of my life' (p 119).

Yet *Peter Townsend*, although by contrast twice divorced, also recalls with balance his long relationship with his first wife Ruth. They had fallen in love when he was 17, and were together for 25 years. He sees only the very last years as unhappy, shaped by diverging interests. He describes his active but lesser role in the home, how she initially shared in his researches, and how later on commuting to Essex brought a separation between them. 'I was lucky, enormously lucky, to have had someone like Ruth to give that form of security and basis for family existence.' But after 20 years they had both changed. He asks whether marriages 'should be forever or not. I'm saying, "No, it doesn't have to be". Sometimes marriages are matters of chance, matters of the moment, or the year, but they can be honoured and appreciated.' After a new marriage it is not easy 'to then give any objective view about the preceding experience. So I think all I can do is say that we were very happy, in my opinion, for the first ten years of our lives together' (pp 204–205). None of the separated women Pioneers are as generous about a former partner.

In terms of ethnicity, of our five non–white Pioneers all but one had lifelong partners, and four of these partners were of a different ethnicity. With *Elizabeth Thomas-Hope* this reflected a long-standing family tradition, for both her Jamaican parents and her maternal grandparents were mixed couples in terms of colour.

As regards social class, both men and women almost all married other professionals. But only eight couples – four of anthropologists – chose partners in the same academic discipline. Men seem to have been particularly attracted to psychologists and psychotherapists, perhaps unconsciously seeking an expressive relationship in an era when men were taught to keep their emotions to themselves. Two men married into wealthier families with more contacts which brought career advantages.

Of the wives, nine worked at least briefly with their husbands, and also one woman Pioneer, but mostly in subordinate rather than joint roles – interviewing, keeping a research diary, organising fieldwork, computing and so on. More typically, especially with our younger Pioneers who were powerfully influenced by the onset of Second Wave Feminism at the end of the 1960s, they supported each other as fellow professionals, whether working together or independently. Thus, Jan Pahl co-authored *Managers and their Wives* (1972) with Ray Pahl, broadening the study to focus on marriage and family life as well as men at work. *Hilary* and *Steven Rose* worked very closely together and published jointly on the sociology of science. Steven was a very exceptional partner, prepared to lose his job for insisting on leaving his Oxford biology laboratory to pick up their son from playgroup. By contrast, *Raymond* and *Rosemary Firth* had earlier gone together to research Malay fishing communities, but published two separate books, his on the men and hers on the women and family, not at all integrated – but reflecting their own strictly separated marital roles.

But mutual involvement in fieldwork could be dangerous. At least three divorces sprang from fieldwork, either from bringing wives out to the field or from leaving them behind, struggling to bring up children on their own.

Parenting and grandparenting

For women Pioneers[2] marriage – in most cases in their early twenties before their careers were established, and soon followed by the birth of their children – was much more challenging. Seven women, of whom five spoke of very supportive husbands, continued working throughout. *Sara Arber* describes how in the 1980s being a mother was not thought compatible with a serious research career, so she kept her life with her children as secret as she could. For anthropologists working abroad, like *Ruth Finnegan* and *Sandra Wallman*, working was much easier while their children were young because paid help was so readily available and socially acceptable. Sandra also emphasises the support of her Trinidadian husband Wally as 'amazing, because he likes to cook, and he likes to talk, and so his involvement has always been very positive'. Sandra also observes that if she had not brought up the children she would have been 'a lesser anthropologist' (pp 49, 52).

By contrast, six of the women Pioneers ceased paid work altogether for a period of up to ten years. While the older women, born in the 1920s, seem to have accepted this as a normal situation, all of the younger women recalled it as a restless and challenging phase, cut off from colleagues and with no clear career hopes ahead. Thus, for the historical sociologist *Leonore Davidoff*, married to a rising Cambridge lecturer, it was 'a really difficult time'. She felt 'very very isolated' (p 44).

Nevertheless, for some it proved possible to turn this adversity into advantage. Thus, *Janet Finch* married a clergyman and then wrote her thesis on clergy wives. *Marilyn Strathern* wrote in Papua New Guinea, *Women in Between: Female Roles in a Male World* (1972). Then once back in England she chose to work from home, with no new fieldwork of her own, on the secondary analysis of interviews independently recorded earlier for Audrey Richards in the Essex village of Elmdon. Still more explicit were *Ann Oakley* and Mary Douglas. Ann felt lonely and isolated, and was diagnosed and treated as depressed. Eventually, one day she had her 'conversion moment' while dusting the sociology of work books on her husband's bookshelves. She thought, 'What I am doing is work' – and before long had launched into her first major study, on *The Sociology of Housework* (1974) (pp 11–12). *Mary Douglas*, by contrast, fell back on more traditional revelations. The outbreak of civil war in Congo had blocked any hope of return for more fieldwork. So she turned instead to theory – but inspired by her personal domestic situation. She set about satisfying her husband's expectations for a clean house and regular meals. But that in turn led her to question how cultures define dirt – to *Purity and Danger* (1966).[3]

A traditional gender difference may also be spotted among those of our Pioneers who had retired. Many, of course, have carried on writing as if they were still employed. *Jack Goody* was still publishing a new book almost every year when he was in his nineties. But among women particularly, a new involvement could come from helping with grandchildren. *Sara Arber* commutes from her Surrey home to a second home which she has bought in Northamptonshire specifically to be able to look after her grandchildren in her own home. Grandparenting is rarely mentioned with similar enthusiasm by men. Thus, *Meghnad Desai*, who sees his grown-up son and daughter once or twice a year, comments: 'I've got far too many things to do, to babysit children' (p. 12).

Family, social change and careers

So how did these diverse peronal life experiences shape the research lives of our Pioneers? Firstly, it is important to note that some of the key factors which brought them opportunities were due to national social changes and international events. They came overwhelmingly from middle class families, and from the small families typical of their era. Their parents were supportive. At their schools they learnt to work hard and consistently. They were encouraged by good teachers, who in later decades would have moved to university teaching. But they themselves were also brought important work opposrtunities through the rapid expansion of universities from the 1960s onward. And the older generation generally benifitted from Second World War experiences which took them out of their social class cocoon. All this gave them both opportunities and confidence. Our Pioneers were fortunate men and women.

We discuss their changing intellectual concerns in other chapters. But their capacity to innovate shows up especially in challenging ways. Most chose to explore other cultures rather than to research their own communities. But early anger at social class injustice, and still more powerfully the experience of racism, could shape lifelong research concerns. With women Pioneers a parallel anger at gender injustice broke through in the early 1970s, and then gay liberation. These were public movements. But the crucial point here is how our Pioneer researchers responded to their own difficulties. They were resilient, but above all, they proved to have the creative ability to turn the problems upside down, and use them to develop their own thinking.

VOICES 2

Beginnings

Here we glimpse how the personal and family lives and their education and work experiences of our Pioneers helped to shape their research interests.

Childhood: class and Empire

Researchers often had sharp ears and eyes early in life. Those few, later to be professionals, who grew up in working-class families, could be brilliant observers of their childhood communities, vivid and perceptive.

John Goldthorpe: a Yorkshire mining village

My father came from a mining family. His father had been a skilled miner, who was then promoted to mine supervisor, or Deputy, and then to Overman, which is, as it were, the highest supervisory level before you get to managers who needed a professional mining qualification. My father's brothers went into mining, and some of his sisters married miners. My father, himself, worked all his life as a clerk at a colliery in the next village – spent 50 years in the same office as a wages clerk, and then a cost clerk. And my mother came from a rather different kind of family. She was one of four sisters: two of her sisters married mineworkers, so we were, in part, a mining family. And the community that I grew up in this little village the majority of men in that village would work in the mine by the village, or in neighbouring mines...

There was a pathway, a bridle path, and then another footpath close to our house, that miners would walk from the village to the mine and back again. So you saw them coming back, black-faced, and so on – it's the kind of thing that I suppose a young child asked questions about. Then, of course, my father would talk about what was happening at the pit, and my uncles would always be talking about mines. So you just grew up with the idea that that's what work meant – working down the mine or at least in the colliery in some role or other...

Very very low rate of women working. They were housewives. Very busy, because an enormous amount of washing and cleaning to do. No, women in that village worked until they married, typically. Some even didn't work before they were married. They might be daughters helping their mothers if it was a big family and there were three or four miners in that family – father and then sons – working different shifts of course. Because it was all shift work, then you probably needed two or three people to do the housework and the cooking and the washing. Just the whole time. (pp 5–6)

Dennis Marsden: family and the complexities of English social class

Again from Yorkshire, Dennis Marsden has remained particularly reflective on the subtleties of English class distinctions:

I had only one grandparent alive, and that was my mother's mother... She was from Parton in Cumberland, a little mining village, and all her relatives were miners... That really was working-class, because it was different working-class from the one in Huddersfield. They were miners, council house dwellers. The house we used to go and stay in, it was a tenement block, it was a tall, thin stack of rooms, one on top of the other, and very crowded, I remember. And I think my grandmother used to live with her son and his wife and child...

So that was a big difference. It was not being home-owners, and... I think drink was one of the differences... And my mother's sister, older sister, she wasn't particularly poverty stricken, she was actually slightly better off because she ran a little shop in the front room, but it was a constant fight because Uncle Billy always used to like to go out and have a drink. He was a miner, used to come in puddled on Friday night, and there was a kind of ritual encounter between them, where she would threaten the rolling pin! But they had very, very powerful women who hated the drink...

Thinking back, it's a bit difficult, but they were all injured, they were all ill – the men. I remember my cousin married a miner, one of the daughters of my mother's sister, married a miner, and he dropped dead in his thirties, leaving her with two kids. Uncle Billy didn't last ever so long, I think he got up to about his fifties. Uncle Joe had an accident – that's my mother's younger brother – had an accident and never worked again...

The other thing, if you look at the Huddersfield end – my father's end – they were rather churchy, rather proper. My father, the most drink he ever had was – he wanted, I think, to get out of the house, because the house was kind of small and claustrophobic, he used to go down to the Liberal Club at the end of the road, and have what he called 'a gill', which I think was half a pint, with the newspapers...

It always struck me that my mother was extremely intimidated by his family...

They were extremely powerful women, and I think he'd been totally dominated by these sisters, and my mother was, I think, extremely dominated by them. She came into service when she was 16, by pure accident. Her friend... had a place down in a big mill owner's, well, it wasn't a mill owner, there were two spinsters and two mill widows, who lived together in this big house called Buckton Mount, I remember, with a cook and a gardener, and four under-maids, of whom my mother was one... Well, we used to go there, when we were children, and used to get invited to tea and things, and it was very splendid, yeah! It really was! That was all mixed up with the church as well, that was mixed up with Methodism... They used to be strong churchgoers, and the servants went to church, which was where my parents met. (pp 1–4)

So it's quite a successful upward mobility for that family... I was the next but youngest of 13 cousins, and I think about 11 of those went to Grammar School. (p 7)

Janet Finch: a very female family

Janet Finch was brought up in another working-class family, in Liverpool, in which the key figures were all women. Here was the first seed of her interest in gender:

My family was really a very female family, actually, and a very kind of happy, fairly large female family...

My mother was an only child. But her family was enormous. Her mother was the eldest of seven children. They all lived in relatively close proximity, and they had a family grocer's shop, which they still had when I was a child. So my grandmother and one of her sisters, and one of her brothers, ran the shop, and we lived very close to that, and that was very much the centre of family gatherings on a regular basis... Until I was seven, we actually lived with my grandmother, who lived almost next door to the shop... So my maternal family's grocer's shop, itself, was the centre of family life. (p 1)

David Butler: deep academic roots

In sharp contrast, none of our Pioneers was more rooted in the traditional male English intellectual elite than David Butler:

> My father had been a Mods Scholar at New College, and then he succeeded A.E. Houseman as Professor of Latin at University College, London, in 1911. During the War, he married a student of his – my mother, Margaret Lucy Pollard, daughter of A.F. Pollard, the historian – and he bought a house just off Gordon Square, three minutes walk away from the University [of London]. They raised four children there in the inter-war period, we just didn't move house or anything. And it was a very solid background. (p 1)
>
> Well, obviously I'm from [an] overwhelmingly academic background. My great-grandfather, George Butler, was born in 1774, before the American Revolution, and he became Headmaster of Harrow at 25 years. He had four sons, two of whom became headmasters and dons, and my grandfather, A.G. Butler, went from Rugby to Univ, and then became a Fellow of Oriel and stayed there for 60 years, but broke away to be the first Headmaster of Haileybury in the 1860s, for five years, and then he came back to Oxford. Because dons couldn't marry, he didn't get married till 1877, and my father was born in Oxford, in 1878 – before the internal combustion engine! His father had been born before the Great Reform Act.
>
> So we stretch back a very long way, academically, and really, there were no near relatives who weren't dons. Two of my father's three sisters became Fellows of St. Ann's, and being an academic was a solid part of the background. (pp 1–2)

Pat Caplan: foreign travel in the family

The Empire created a space for travel and work opportunities through which some of our Pioneers came to Britain, but others moved outwards. For Pat Caplan this felt part of the family spirit:

I guess I was a child of Empire. There were so many members of my family who'd travelled very widely – not because they were well-to-do and doing the Grand Tour, but because they had been soldiers or they were migrants. So, for example, my maternal grandmother was born in Australia because her family had migrated there, presumably because of poverty, although they did eventually come back. But there remained an Australian branch, and people would appear from time to time from Australia and other family members would go and visit in Australia. And then my mother's older brother, who had travelled a lot during the War – he'd been in Ethiopia, for example, in the Second World War – he migrated to South Africa when the War ended, and he came back and got married, they went to live in South Africa. So that they'd come on visits, or they'd send photographs, and bring objects. So I always remember all of these houses having lots of objects which were from somewhere else – you know, Indian: both my paternal grandfather and his younger son had been in India – he in the First World War, and my uncle just after the Second World War. So the idea of travelling to places that were very far away didn't seem at all strange. In fact, it was quite enticing. So I guess I got the travel bug early! (pp 1–2)

Stuart Hall: colour, class and family in Jamaica

By contrast, the shadow of Empire could be lastingly negative. In Jamaica social class and colour were inextricably intertwined, not least in Stuart's own family. This led to a tragedy, a turning point. He never returned to Jamaica to live:

My grandmother could pinpoint people's racial background, you know, to a T. She would run the combinations of skin colour, education, straightness of the hair, European features, on and on and on, she'd say, 'A touch of the tar brush there!' So that's what they talked about. We used to have rum punch parties on Sunday and some expatriate people would come, some of my father's business people, old family friends from Port Antonio, etc., the grounds would be full of these people drinking my mother's rum punch and chatting. They were chatting about affairs, and about class distinctions. And the class distinctions were always mediated through colour. (p 5)

My sister went to work – and fell in love with a black student. The University of the West Indies had just started, and a black Barbadian student, medical student was there – very educated, etc., etc., but black. My mother said, 'No! It will not happen. Not from this house. Absolutely not'. She forbade it. They broke it off. My sister had the most tremendous mental breakdown within two months. She was given shock therapy, bouts of it, by ordinary GPs, because there were no psychiatrists, blitzed her mind, cleared her mind of these funny ideas she'd somehow gotten hold of! And I suddenly saw that the whole microcosm of Jamaican society and its problems and intricacies, were being mirrored inside the family culture, you know? She was the victim of colonialism! I don't know any other way of putting it. She was sacrificed to the social system...

I just looked at her, and I thought, 'Now, this is a certain kind of emotional death, and if you ever get a chance to leave here, don't come back to it'. (pp 12–13)

Opening minds

As we see here illustrated, the stimulus to independent thinking might come from within the childhood family's practices, as with *Pat Caplan*, in this instance both autodidact and religious. But for others, such as *John Bynner*, it was as a reaction against the intellectual tensions within his home.

Pat Caplan: writing and speaking in the family

I guess [there was] the notion that people were always writing in my house. My father knew how to type, he would sit at home typing the extra articles he did, to make a bit of extra money to kind of keep things afloat. And, of course, my mother also was a very good typist because she'd been trained as a secretary, in fact she typed my Ph.D. thesis for me, bless her! So this notion that you wrote and you wrote things on typewriters, was just there all the time. And then because my maternal grandfather was a Methodist local preacher, he wrote as well. He wrote sermons. And he had been a member of the 'labour aristocracy', he worked for the *Liverpool Post and Echo* as a printer, and, of course, in those days, the days of hot metal presses, printers were highly skilled and not too badly paid. But he too had a family to support, and so he would make money by writing little articles. So he wrote as well. So even though none of them were famous writers in any sense, this notion that you wrote, and you spoke.

That was the other thing, because, of course, I was brought up as a Methodist, and went to church at least once, often twice, on Sunday, so I must have listened to more sermons than I care to remember, and so the notion of standing up and speaking in public – some of them were ordained Ministers, some, like my grandfather, were local preachers, and others were just members of the congregation who would have something to say. I think I gave my first public speech in the Methodist Central Hall in Westminster at the age of 14. You know, it was just something that people did. I didn't think it was extraordinary! You just did it! (p 5)

John Bynner: pulled between intellectual perspectives

My mother had been an artist working in Chelsea, actually, until she met my father, who, being of his day, couldn't imagine a wife working when her husband could support her. He had joined the Prudential Insurance Company at the age of 14 or 15, and spent his whole life in that career, but forced to retire early through an hereditary sight problem... He was an avid reader, and collected huge collections of books and first editions – you can see a few of them next door. And very active politically, originally ILP [Independent Labour Party], in the Labour Party, but also mixing this with a great interest in theosophy, Spiritualism, and all that side of life – an odd, not exactly a contradiction, but I grew with both those massive intellectual contexts, if you like, and they had very different reactions on me! One, political and on the Left, and on the other more philosophical, or, more religious almost, which was the theosophy – the Theosophical Society...

[Being active in a Theosophy Society] meant going to meetings and holding meetings at our house – had a big house in Ealing – and it was, and having garden parties and all this kind of things where people would give spiritual – it was linked to Spiritualism. Because it was all-embracing in terms of alternative types of religion, then the Theosophical Society could bring in things like Spiritualists, or mediums. Mediums were strong and they would give people advice at these parties. I grew up with all of that, and I reacted, oddly enough, quite strongly against it. I began, increasingly, as I grew up and moved very much towards science,

I suppose, in what I studied, I increasingly became disillusioned with all this, and thought it just didn't stand up... And also, I wasn't very close to my father, ... I didn't feel in his own personal life he was actually exemplifying a lot of that! (pp 1–3)

George Brown: bookshops as an intellectual opening

For George Brown the crucial stimulus came not from his unsupportive family but from a local bookshop where he worked quite briefly:

I was out of a job, and one of the big influences in my life is that I was in Notting Hill Gate, and I saw a placard on a second-hand bookshop, saying, 'Boy wanted, for 30 shillings [a week]'. It was [run by] Peter Eaton, who became very well known later on, very rich... It was in Church Street, there was an old fish shop, and they would throw the books on, shilling and sixpenny books, on a big [marble] slab. And I went to work there for three months.

It must have been one of the key experiences in that in some way, I began to get turned on. I met David Glass – in fact, people would come in. I must have seemed quite an interesting chap, because there was an inner office, and they would come and confide in me. So a prostitute came in, and a businessman, and so on, and they would talk to me. And David Glass, saying he was highly critical of American sociology, and he brought in a lot of books on populations, he didn't really want them...

The other experience, at that stage, was a Times Book Club, a wonderful bookshop, any rate, which has now gone, in Wigmore Street. I would look in the window... And then – this is the key intellectual occurrence of my life, I saw a book by Will Durant, *The Story of Philosophy*, American, which I got... When I read this book, it just transformed me. I actually started taking notes. And I think it's the first time, and I was 18, that I'd been intellectually turned on. It quite transformed me. (pp 14–15)

Mary Douglas: schools, hierarchy and doctrine

Our Pioneers' school experiences varied greatly, but some schools or particular charismatic teachers did open paths to original thinking. But while for *Michael Young* school was the start of a lifetime as a social entrepreneur, for *Mary Douglas* it was through her introduction to the formal orderliness of doctrinal thinking:

The first school was called Studley Knowle in Torquay, and the nuns were a little French Order, recruiting Catholic nuns from Ireland, so it was French and Irish. And at that time, as you might know from social reading, there was a very strong, sectarian attitude in the Catholic Church, you were inside or you were out, and Heaven was only inhabited by Catholics and the rest had to look out for themselves! ... But I loved the School, I really enjoyed it very very much. And obviously I was very well taught.

When I left at 12, when my mother died, before she died, she handed us over to the school that she had been at, which was in London – Roehampton... We were prepared for exams, but they weren't terribly important compared with singing, music and practically nothing else, really! Religion. Doctrine was terribly important. And they so loved teaching us theology that we enjoyed it very much. All the children did.

It was a Jesuit education, actually. All my life I've continued to come across the problems they talked about and find that they really were very far ahead on the theological solutions to enigmas and mysteries and problems. And we did get the subtle theological – the casuistry, which is so important, I think... Absolutely crucial. Yes. I know that the doctrine was, because of all the metaphysical questions it opened up for one, and ways of talking about them too. But the strong confidence of faith, because they had warned you against what belief meant, and what unbelief meant... I really loved the orderliness of the life, and I loved the hierarchical protections that they provided for each other, against each other. (pp 9–11)

Michael Young: the fostering of individual creativity – Dartington

Well, [Dartington] was wonderful from the very start... Maybe one of the best schools in the world. Anyway for a person like me... There were only thirty children there... And we were all in the main courtyard at Dartington in a sort of converted barn. There were no qualified teachers, but they were all an interesting lot of people that had been brought together. Who could vaguely teach something or other. But that wasn't the important thing. The important thing was that they were nice people who believed in the experiment.

The experiment was there was no teaching unless the children wanted it, so there were no classes you had to go to unless you wanted to. There was no pressure to learn anything, not even reading and writing. You could make up your own programme.

The estate was thought of as a giant classroom. And so different bits of the classroom were the sawmills, the forestry, farms in their different compartments. The woodturning shop and the carpenter's shop and a little later on the architect's studio in which I worked for nearly a year, half-time. Fruit farm...

Then I started a poultry business. And had two hundred hens with some other children. And we sold the eggs in Totnes market and supplied the school and all the kitchens on the estate with eggs. And kept the money, amazingly! ... We had to keep proper books and we learnt about double entry bookkeeping and so on. We had to get up very early in the morning and look after these hens. I could do everything except kill the damn hens, that I couldn't do!

There was a real poultry farm on the place. I mean a commercial one which is another sort of department. And the chap who ran that came and gave us lessons. And when we had trouble with disease or something we could go and ask him what we should do next. And he gave us quite a good deal of advice on the side. And, I ran a greengrocery business. Growing vegetables and selling them too. And also a secondhand motorcycle business. At the age of l5. And we bought and sold old motorcycles for about thirty shillings each. (pp 19–21)

Partnership and marriage

Hilary Rose: misogyny in biology's research culture

Lastly, inspiration can come as a couple. Here are two distinctly different instances:

> If I tell you [a story] about Steve, you'll see the reasons why I'm so devoted to him – love him to bits! When we married, he'd got this grand Fellowship at Oxford. As a lab scientist he has to live near the workplace, because you're in there, it's like being in a kitchen, cooking doesn't happen unless you're there. So I left my beloved London to live in Oxford... We got married, and we went there. Steven is quite a bit younger than me – three years younger than me – and remember, I was a mother at 20, so he's 17 years older than our son. His boss [Professor Krebs] was a very grand Nobel Prize-winner, who took a very dim view of Steven

taking off from the lab at three o'clock, two days a week, in order to pick up Simon from nursery school, and Steven explained that that was his share of childcare. Now, for this professor, you were married to the lab. You know, your family was so far down there, and he was completely, Steven just stood his ground, and said, 'Oh no, no, no, that's my obligation'. So that led to him needing to leave that laboratory. (p 29)

Mary Douglas: marriage and writing – James Douglas

And to what extent has he been an influence on your work?
Very strong, because first of all, I would never have written at all, but for his requirements of punctuality and mealtimes and an orderly life, otherwise I would never have done anything, you know! And he also has very high standards of work. He didn't see why his supper should be late if I wasn't doing well, if I wasn't doing proper work, writing properly! (p 42)

CHAPTER 3

Contexts: Empire, politics and culture

All research is shaped by time and place, history and generation. Through listening to the experiences of a few of our Pioneers, this chapter will reveal something of the social, economic and political contexts in which they worked. It gives us glimpses of the changing twentieth century and sets the background for later chapters. It sets the scene.

From the outset we are dealing with a fundamental dilemma: how to link individual lives with their wider changing context, when both are moving in time, and not to a common tune – indeed, very often at differing speeds or in differing directions. In terms of family life the concept of generations gives a very useful basic structure based on parenthood, which is only roughly linked to time. Here it may help at the outset to think of researchers as also located in wider 'generations', in terms of specific age cohorts, with each generation broadly lasting some 20 to 30 years. All are moving forward into the mists of time, so that in the long term only the most remarkable individuals still stand out. Thus, our Pioneers were preceded by earlier researchers, earlier pioneers: Victorian, or post-Victorian, from the interwar years. And they are also already being succeeded by younger generations of innovators.

Our Pioneers can be seen as a double generation, divided by whether they experienced the Second World War as adults. Most of them published the prime of their work between the 1950s and 1980s. They lived through the post-war rise of the Welfare State, the left-wing political optimism of the 1960s, the decriminalisation of homosexuality, the rise of migration as a political issue, and the later growth of post-colonialism, neo-liberalism and Thatcherism. Less dramatically, they could see the growth of cities and the decline of traditional rural life, and the ebbing of Christian religious practice. And their own lives were especially influenced by sharing unusually open opportunities brought by the dramatic expansion of the universities and unprecedented growth of social science research and teaching. In this sense they were a founding generation of modern social research.

Research under colonial conditions

In 1901, Britain was at the height of its imperial and colonising power and influence around the world. The final phase of this Empire came after 1945 as the colonies successively became independent, the former Empire became the Commonwealth and slowly awareness grew of many of the problems generated by past and present connections – the post-colonial critique. Researchers in the Empire were throughout typically anthropologists: mostly English-born and white, but with a scattering – not all white – who grew up in the colonies. After 1945 they were active especially in the Caribbean, India and, above all, in Africa. Their interests were led by Western intellectual debate – in that sense a 'colonial gaze'. But they were also closely tied into the colonial system through their funding and fieldwork: it seems more so than in the interwar years.

Raymond Firth is our prime example. He grew up on a New Zealand farm, son of an immigrant, climbed a scholarship ladder and came to study at the LSE under Malinowski. But he had already developed his own interests in Polynesian culture in his early years through his contact with the Maori. Equally important, when in 1928 – as he describes in Voices 5 – he set out for his epic journey to the Pacific island of Tikopia, he was a lone researcher, and for months completely out of contact with the western world. Firth contributed himself to the changed system after 1945. He had returned to the LSE, succeeding Malinowski as professor and head of department, and when the Colonial Social Science Research Council was set up in 1945 to award scholarships he became its first Secretary. His policy was to encourage research with practical implications:

> I conceived it was my job was to try and get people out into the field, as much as possible, on significant problems. So I accepted the post... I think, initially, the thing was to identify the problem. And for that purpose, I looked a lot at files out in the colonies themselves, I talked to Agricultural Officers, to District Officers, and to anybody I could talk to, to find out what kinds of problems. But the real thing was, the Governments had been asked what kind of problems they wished research on. Almost no reply was received. That was why I went out, to try and stimulate things. And so that meant that the Colonial Office could take the initiative, and say, 'Here is a problem. We will send somebody to look at it'...

And in 1945, I went to West Africa as one of the principal colonial areas, so to speak, regions. I visited the four colonies – Gambia, Sierra Leone, Gold Coast, as it was then, and Nigeria – travelling around. I spent, in all, about three months, finding out from officers and local people what kind of problems they were concerned with – agricultural, economic, social, and so on. And I published a report on that. And, as I say, from the anthropological point of view, regarded it as my job to try and get as many anthropologists into the field as possible. And I think I started that process, which was later carried on by others. (p 136)

Thus, the colonial system was more tightly controlling who went out to research, where, and what it was about. And once there, as *Jack Goody* so vividly describes in Voices 3, they were settled in and guided by the local colonial administrators.

The image of Empire in its final phase, projected by government and accepted by most British people, was of making a progressive educational and economic contribution to newly developing nations. This was the spirit in which *Pat Caplan* at the start of her life story describes herself as a 'child of Empire'. Her family members had lived at times in Australia, South Africa and Canada, and four generations, including Pat herself as a researcher, spent years in Madras. A 'famous object' in their childhood family home was a camel stick brought by an uncle from Ethiopia which she and her sisters used for protection (pp 1–2). By contrast *Maxine Molyneux*, living in a 'colonial bubble' in urban India, became directly aware as a child of the contradictions in colonialism:

It was a very segregated sort of life, and my parents lived in this ex-pat bubble. They and I spent a huge amount of time in 'the Club' – a big swimming pool, my mother sat under an umbrella all day, drinking gin, as far as I can ascertain. And I would come from school and have a swim.

So there was that world, and then the world of India, which was very different... My memories are to do with things like seeing lepers, to do with riots in the street – there was a kind of generalised fear of civil unrest, because there was quite a lot of it in Bombay. And one had this sense of a slightly risky world, that was outside of the bubble of the compound, or the ex-pat world – which was much more exciting than the languors of the swimming pool. This is why being able to escape that world and somehow get out of it – and there were ways one could do that, one could just go and talk to people in the street. One could. I took huge risks, looking back on it now, about where I played, or where I went. I never had any experience of trouble, but I was constantly fascinated by and wanting to know more about the land that lay beyond the four walls of where we were all interred, so to speak! And that, I think, stayed with me – that sense of fascination. (pp 8–9)

Over the lifetimes of our Pioneers the image of colonial progressivism has been increasingly sharply challenged. We know now, thanks to Ian Cobain's *The History Thieves* (2016),[1] that the official records were being thoroughly weeded to give a more positive image of British rule. We can also see how reluctant the British state is to apologise for its worst mistakes: thus, in 2019, a century after the military murder of over 300 Indian civilians in the unprovoked Amritsar massacre, the British prime minister can express regrets, but not a straight apology. We still need to ask other questions which have been strangely forgotten in national memory. Were we not the leading slave traders and slave plantation owners in the Caribbean? At emancipation, why did Britain compensate the former slaveholders but not the slaves? *Stuart Hall* has consistently answered:

Colonialism was founded on, and continues to work, not through its gifts but through the conquest of land and resources, the violent exploitation of labour, the imposition of foreign rule, the subjugation of peoples and the destruction and marginalisation of those cultural traditions which are perceived as inimical to colonial authority. Its interventions broke up historic old civilisations. It represents one of the most far reaching, brutal ruptures in modern history equivalent in depth to the Holocaust, although – surprisingly – this is a comparison that is not often made. It irreversibly shaped individuals and society.[2]

Times of war

War dominates the early twentieth century: explicitly through mass killings, and implicitly through memory or its repression. The First World War is remembered for the millions who died in the frontline trenches and mud. The Second World War allowed a second mass killing of millions in the Holocaust. But for soldiers it was a more mobile war, less lethal, with more proud moments. And many of our Pioneers were touched by it.

A striking example is that of *Jack Goody*, born in 1919, who fought in North Africa in the Second World War, was captured, and spent three years as a prisoner-of-war in Italy, in camps, and for six months escaping in the Abruzzi. When he returned to Cambridge to complete his degree in 1945 he transferred to anthropology. He had been inspired by books in the camp library, but also crucially by people he met when an escaped prisoner in 1943–44:

> You were thrown up against people in very close contact, and in the group that I was in, they came from my Regiment, and we'd all been taken prisoners together... When I escaped, I escaped for six months, even more so, I mean, I was in a cave... later on with some South Africans and two guys who, I think, were Nottinghamshire miners. But anyhow, people who were in a completely different way of life... Because all the things that I've been describing to you – you know, school, university – you were simply somebody concerned with books and books and books, you weren't concerned with doing things like cutting up meat or even acting on the stage, so it was very different in that way. So I think you met a lot of people with a lot of different experiences. Particularly, as I say, many of the people in my regiment I met then and afterwards, were Nottinghamshire miners, who had joined the Regular Army because they were out of a job... This was the sort of person that you were meeting.
> *But you were also coming across very different cultures, weren't you?*
> Of course, if you were in a military camp, it didn't matter whether you were in Iraq or Afghanistan, you didn't learn much about what happened around you... It was more particularly... after I'd been in Italy, at the end of the Armistice there when I escaped for six months. Then I was with villagers... and lived very close and had to live in houses, in villagers' houses, to get food and to get a night's rest. (pp 23–24)

Many other 'war stories' can be told. *Margaret Stacey*, graduating in 1943, went to work in a war factory on the Clyde for a year, intending to be trained as a personnel manager, working with communist shop stewards, and active herself in the Labour Party. In 1944, she became an Oxford extra-mural lecturer, living in Banbury, where it was thought important to educate the new aluminium factory workers, teaching them sociology. Banbury was then to become the site of her major fieldwork.

Mildred Blaxter tells of being evacuated:

> My brother and I were sent off, on, in fact, the last ship which left as an evacuee ship from Britain. Because the ship afterwards was the *City of Benares*, which sunk with all the children on board, and most of them drowned. So there were no more. So we were some of the last to go across the Atlantic as evacuees. And we lived with an aunt, and it wasn't a great success, and I must have been a terrible trial to her... In Winnipeg. And I was very homesick. (p 6)

Some 'war stories' were far from straightforward. *Claus Moser*, for example, had been born in Berlin in 1922 and came to England in 1936. His father was hoping that he would follow him into banking, or at least into commercial work. Although Jewish he was nevertheless interned as an enemy alien in 1940 at Huyton Camp, Liverpool, where he found himself helping a mathematician internee, Landau, who had set up a statistics office in the camp. This experience inspired him to see the potential of a life in statistics.

Peter Townsend captures the feel of living through the war in London:

> I was only 11 when the War started, and it had a very big impact on me as everybody else... It is a vivid theme in my early life, and, of course, just to underline it, in the early part of the War years, I was living in Belsize Crescent, first in an attic flat, and then in a ground-floor flat, and, of course, we had air raids, and we had to hide under the bed, an iron-framed bed, in the basement, or on the ground floor. There were all sorts of occasions when it was very risky, which I can say more about, but essentially, the important thing of all, was sociability and the way in which I, even at the age of 13, I was an Air Raid Warden, and helped shovel one or two incendiaries off the roof tops of the street, and was sitting with mugs of tea, around the clock, into the night shift sometimes, with other people from the surrounding houses. And people met each other through hiding in air raid shelters. (p 9)

He was also influenced by meeting people from different backgrounds during his National Service:

> And, of course, later, my Army experience. When I became 18, there was still compulsory service after the War, and I remember vividly that, in the next two beds to me, when I was doing my compulsory training in the first months at Yeovil, Somerset, to which I was recruited, the two people on either side were Geordies, who were illiterate, and where, regularly, I wrote their love letters home to Newcastle. And, of course, that was a very vivid experience of actually meeting people and being in conditions where one both understood them, but became quite familiar with the problems that they had encountered and the lives they'd experienced, and this was, I think, one of the formative experiences in my life. (pp 8–9)

Nevertheless, he finished his two years with a very 'negative' view of army culture. It did bring him a new insight into the British social class system, experienced in the Army context. But about the skills he was taught in the Army he simply said, 'I learned about all those skills which I didn't really, personally, want to possess… Square-bashing. Shouting, shouting, becoming a sergeant-major, and shouting at troops, and getting them up at 5.30 in the morning. All of those sort of things. (p 19)

Shifting politics and professionalisms

How far did our Pioneers see a conflict between holding political values and maintaining professional research standards? On the one hand it is clear that not only in private but also in their professional fieldwork both sociologists and anthropologists were willing to take sides in local politics. Thus, *Colin Bell*, whose explicit role in the Banbury re-study was to investigate the local Labour supporters, recalls that he was not just 'observing' – 'they were close mates of mine, really close mates. They even allowed me to go to caucus meetings… and they would vote in the caucus, and I was expected to vote!' (p 64). Looking back, he felt that this had been questionable practice. By contrast, *Jack Goody* had no regrets at all for joining a local political party when he was in the field in Ghana:

> I did join a local CVP [Convention People's Party] which was Nkrumah's Party. I did join that, yes, because I was in favour of independence for these countries. But I didn't really do much else. I wasn't very active… Well, I didn't think it would make much difference.

But anyhow, at the time I thought it would be useful to attend these local meetings... I was interested in seeing what was going on. No doubt if the opposition party had also been there, canvassing the area, I might have joined that as well! But my sympathies were more with the CVP.

Yes, I think that if you're in a political situation, which was very divided, you would be better to remain apart in any quarrel. But you hoped to take that with a pinch of salt in that, unless you get in a little to whatever the situation is – domestic or national – you aren't going to learn anything. (pp. 45–46)

There is certainly a significant strand of people who claim to be as scientific and neutral as possible: we encounter them mainly among the more quantitative kinds of researcher, and especially those working with national statistical surveys. But even here, we soon heard many of them speak passionately about their political beliefs outside the study. And a very large group of our researchers continue to be as empirically neutral as they can in their research, while at the same time being members or supporters of political parties – usually the Labour Party. There is a very clear broad liberal left politics attachment behind very many of our researchers. They were outstanding researchers, but they carried out their work with passionate political engagement.

Peter Townsend is the obvious case. He was manifestly concerned about poverty and his research had ultimate policy goals: to reduce poverty and inequality. Likewise, while *Stuart Hall* gave great emphasis to developing a serious and deep theoretical understanding of culture, he was equally engaged with political and theoretical Marxism and the cultural formations that are generated through dominance. This included Thatcherism, a term he coined. *Maxine Molyneux* hoped to mitigate the domination of women by the patriarchal structures of the Middle East. *Stan Cohen* was concerned with the plights initially of the young delinquent and what is now called 'the stigma machine', then with the rights of the prisoner, and ultimately with the struggle for human freedom and decency in the conflicts in Palestine and Israel.

And so on. Some became frontline activists. *Hilary Rose* worked with Claimant's Unions; *Avtar Brah* was a founder member of Southall Black Sisters. In *Judith Okely* we find a concern with the suffering of gypsies; in *Ken Plummer* with the development of a LGBT/queer politics. And when we look broadly at the many women among our Pioneers, we quickly find a widespread concern with the generation of a feminist standpoint and a feminist politics. For many of our Pioneers, research was at least an art structured by a political passion: and this set many of the novel questions.

There are also many in our sample who will reveal their political characters by taking on major tasks within the university administrative hierarchy. *Howard Newby*, for example, was knighted in 2000 for his services to education. He was then Chairman of ESRC. He had earlier been been director of the UK Data Archive at Essex. He went on to successive adminstrative roles as Vice Chancellor of Southampton, chairman of the funding council HEFCE, and Vice Chancellor of the West of England and then of Liverpool. There are a number of other researchers in our sample who will move to hold high positions like vice chancellors in the rapidly growing university sector, such as *Colin Bell*, *Sir Ivor Crewe*, *Dame Janet Finch* and *Sir Peter Hall*.

Post-war reconstruction and the rise of the welfare state

Labour's 1945 election victory led not only to decolonisation abroad but also to major change and reconstruction at home with the initiation of the welfare state. It was the time of the creation of the National Health Service, the setting up of a National Insurance to provide sick and unemployment benefits, a free tripartite system of secondary education, and the nationalisation of public utilities including the railways, and also some industries. This drew intellectually on the ideas of earlier Fabian socialists and also especially of John Maynard Keynes as an economic theorist who argued that to achieve social goals like full employment governments had to actively manage the economy, in part through public spending. The need to staff the new institutions was partly met through encouraging – as with those aboard the *Windrush* – the first big wave of worker immigration from the former colonies. Sustaining these changes and taking them forward was a key hope of many of our Pioneers.

We can take *Peter Townsend* (1928–2009) as our first emblematic Pioneer of this period.[3] Indeed, he is now considered internationally to be one of the twentieth century's leading pioneers of innovative research on poverty, ageing and disability and a public campaigner for global social justice for the underprivileged. He followed in the grand tradition of early twentieth-century research into poverty in British cities by Charles Booth and Seebohm Rowntree, who had found between a quarter and a third of the populations to be living below the poverty line. After studying anthropology at Cambridge,

Peter started his career by writing reports for the independent research centre Political and Economic Planning (PEP) – which proved a brief but influential experience:

> The very first pamphlet I did, was called, *Poverty: Ten Years After Beveridge*, and that actually appeared in 1952. And the second thing I did, which was equally important, was that I went to Lancashire, in a recession in the cotton industry, and visited several of the cotton towns and interviewed unemployed, mainly men, and visited the various Employment Exchanges, as they were then called, to talk to people in the queues, waiting for Unemployment Benefit. And this was a very deep and absorbing experience, because I went to places like Nelson and Rochdale, and Oldham... I tended to get bed and breakfast at local pubs when I could, and I remember, at Nelson, being woken up at 4.30, I think it was, or 5 in the morning, with the clatter of clogs on the cobbled streets, which is intriguing, as a memory of people still alive, as it were!
>
> The clatter, it symbolised the collectiveness of working-class life, in many respects. I'd seen in it in the docks in London, when you can easily get to a meeting, or could do, in those earlier days, in the forties and fifties, for 10,000, 5,000 men. And similarly, in other parts of Britain, you had these experiences of many working-class people getting up at the same hour, trailing to the factories, to settle into work. And, of course, there were many hands plying their way at the spinning wheels and the machines generally. And I remember seeing some of them where they were, literally, using, in the early 1950s, machines that had actually been installed in 1840, and things like that. And I haven't forgotten that particular experience, because it just reminded me of the kind of sheer boredom, but also the drudgery, and extreme physical stress of working like that for, well, ten hours, often, a day. Because in those days 70 hours a week was quite common. Sixty hours a week was also quite common.
>
> So that experience of doing the first pamphlet about the meaning of poverty, and the poverty line, and in the second pamphlet, about the actual experience of it, those who suddenly, not long after the War, who'd enjoyed a few years of full employment, but then experienced a sharp cut-back in the recession, which reminded everybody of the pre-War

mass unemployment. That was a very valuable experience to me. (pp 27–28)

He went on to join the new Institute of Community Studies in East London, which had been recently founded by *Michael Young* (for more on Michael, PEP and the Institute, see Chapter 4). Peter moved to be a lecturer to the London School of Economics (LSE) in 1957, working alongside Richard Titmuss, who like Michael Young was already a leader in policy research. Then in 1963 he became one of the founding professors at the new University of Essex, part of the programme of massive university expansion that was then taking place. As first Professor of Sociology, he was to stay at Essex for nearly 20 years, building up a notably strong department with a wide span from social policy to social history and anthropology. He also had to confront and find a path through the storm resulting from the worldwide of student unrest of 1968, the 'troubles', when Essex became notorious as a radical university. Later he moved to Bristol in 1982; and ultimately returned to the LSE.

From his earliest writings Peter helped to reopen a wide range of social and welfare concerns – around poverty, unemployment, ageing, health and disability. He pinned these key issues on to the political agenda, particularly through nurturing strong connections with the Labour Party's leaders. Throughout his life he was a tireless campaigner for the disadvantaged, breaking down the often-assumed boundaries between the objective social researcher and the activist. Most notably, he founded and chaired the Child Poverty Action Group from 1969 and the Disability Alliance from 1974. He also carried out major policy research in the 1970s for the Black Report on *Inequalities in Health* (1980).

Peter's eloquent and moving Bethnal Green study of *The Family Life of Old People* (1957) became a widely read paperback. This first classic was followed by his national study of old people's homes *The Last Refuge* (1962), again combining surveys with vivid qualitative fieldwork, much carried out personally. And then at Essex, he built up a research team for his third classic, *Poverty in the UK* (1979). Peter now focussed increasingly on innovative computer-based analysis, and the development of new measures for poverty and disability. But he remained committed to mixed methods and used qualitative fieldwork in his own growing international work, for example in Kenya and Georgia. Thus, his many later publications include *World Poverty: New Policies to Defeat an Old Enemy* (2002). From originally focussing on a local East London base, his research first had become national, and then increasingly international in scope and commitment.

Essentially, the post-war reconstructive phase linked to political progressivism, believing a juster and more effective Britain could be built, lasted into the 1960s. *Peter Hall*, London-born geographer turned town planner, widely read author on cities, re-invokes the atmosphere in his parallel field:

> I was getting more and more tied up with Labour Party politics – it was then '62/'63, the last years of the long Conservative Government of '51 through '64, gearing up to the inevitable General Election. I joined the Fabian Society... and then joined the Fabian Executive, so got very tied up with all the leading people in the Labour Party at the time, including the disastrous George Brown. So we started helping George, and involved in his leadership bid, which failed.
>
> But then, of course, Harold Wilson made him his Minister for the new Department of Economic Affairs... It was felt that the Treasury were an obstacle and that this new Department would do what was necessary to do planned economic growth. So it was to be a national plan, French style – French style planning was very big – and with it, within it, regional plans for each region of the country.
>
> So they decided to set up regional Economic Planning Councils with boards of civil servants, and in late '65/early '66, they asked me to join the South-East Planning Council... So I got very heavily involved, directly, in shaping government policy in those early years of the Wilson government, in particular these questions of the growth of London, and whether you could seek to, in any way, control the growth of service industries... I was directly in the middle of that.
>
> There was idealism all right, but it was very much associated with a spirit of the time – zeitgeist – which is difficult to capture now. It's almost captured in the history books by Harold Wilson's famous statement about the 'white heat of technology'. Labour presented itself, in the '64 Election, as 'the Party of modernisation', as 'the young Party', 'the serious Party of the new class of the technocrats'...
>
> The country was then and had been, very very physically flat out in a way that is difficult for anyone to imagine... London was filthy, shabby, basically Victorian, and there was a feeling that all this had to be swept away and created and replaced by

a 'New Britain'. The cities had to be rebuilt totally... We were all deeply committed to that, to a notion of modernisation, including physical modernisation. (pp 21–23)

The spirit of 1968

1968 symbolises both a zenith and a turning point: a moment of great optimism and enthusiasm for radical change, led above all by students. It was heralded by new cultural styles, new music, and in Britain by new legislation around social issues, such as abortion and homosexuality. This was the time of the 'summer of love' as well as the protests against the Vietnam War. But certainly American student protest was crucial in the withdrawal from Vietnam. The barricades of French students nearly brought down the right-wing government of General de Gaulle. And in Britain there were lesser echoes of this with protests and sit-ins across the country, notably at the LSE and Essex. *Peter Townsend* again captures something of the mood:

> You have to look back at the context, the social context within which this operated: the whole cultural transformation, well, the Beatles phenomenon, plus the young people's search for liberty at the time, these things go together. After all, we had too a very progressive development in abortion and homosexuality, this was going on nationally. That struck a chord with the mood of the times, which was for expansive release and individual liberty par excellence. And this mood existed, this almost Evangelical mood among young people existed, and would have existed at Essex in whatever circumstances... There was this radical spirit. (p 169)

Maxine Molyneux felt a similar spirit through her involvement in the art world:

> I wasn't involved at all in the Student Movement of '68, but the experiences of the changing social climate were very profoundly felt by my generation. You couldn't not be aware of the politicisation of everyday life, if you were young. And in the art world there was a lot going on there with the Situationists, there were all kinds of art movements, I was very interested in that. And I was becoming, I'd always had a radical rebellious streak, I was in CND when I was 13, and anti-apartheid and all these kinds of things, and the Women's Movement later, of

course. But the art world was quite political and I was getting very interested in all of that as well. (pp 13–14)

1968 touched many others. At the LSE, from the staff *Meghnad Desai* became a famous chair of mass meetings, while *Stanley Cohen* had arrived from South Africa where apartheid had deeply troubled him and was researching for his PhD work. He was studying the much-publicised seaside riots between the Mods and Rockers youth groups, and went on to publish in 1970 one of the classics of British sociology, *Folk Devils and Moral Panics*. Here he captures something of this moment as not only exhilarating, but also a turning point in ideas, an intellectual inspiration:

> The LSE political events, the Walter Adams year, Rhodesia, the sit-ins, this was terrific for me. I mean, I – I threw myself into all that! At last the myth had come true. Going to hear Tariq Ali and Robin Blackburn and the people of the LSE was exciting. So I think my political commitment was strengthened by the events, in a sort of anti-authority direction, very anarchic anti-authority direction. (p 36)

He had himself been studying rebellious youth, powerless people at the bottom, but now he thought 'the kids are all right, it's the authorities. It's the labellers, it's the social control agents, they're the ones to look at.' His new focus was on the labelling process, the media and 'moral panics'. In retrospect he sees

> in the clearest way, the simple idea of labelling theory, and the anti-authoritarianism that I picked up from the LSE sit-in days, and the spirit of the excitement of being anti-authority, reinforced for me the idea that I could find some connection between political commitment and intellectual life, which was one of the sixties themes that emerged – bearing all the myths, or problems, that we later saw. (p 36)

Paradoxically, after 1968, partly from disappointment, the broad progressive wave fragmented, making the connection hard to sustain. Political activism became more focussed on rising sectional campaigns, heralding new social movements – notably, the women's movements, the gay and lesbian movement, the environment movement, and in the US the Black Power movement. And the connection withered. As Stan remarks later:

> I think the sixties, and up to the end of the sixties, was that
> time when that integration was taken for granted. That your
> intellectual theory, your political commitment, your position as
> a teacher in a university, all these gelled together, and you were
> looking for integration. And now, not that I accept the label in
> any way, I think the post-modernist insistence on some form of
> fragmentation is actually much more realistic, in the sense that
> those worlds just don't cohere. It is very hard to find a master
> political analogy, and then a master epistemological one, and
> it's certainly impossible to find it in life in universities, which
> is just, you know a Darwinian struggle for existence. With no
> ideology left in it whatsoever. (p 56)

Here, then, is a hint at the times to come – the postmodern times.

Encountering gender

Another major background for our pioneering researchers was the
gradual growth of both feminism and gender issues. Among the lone
earliest names as a female sociologist is Harriet Martineau (1802–76).
Our Pioneers, who were born much later, too late even for the first
wave of activist feminism from the late nineteenth century until the
1920s, were to become the pioneers of the Second Wave Feminism of
the 1960s and 1970s. While through the work of the suffragettes the
first wave brought not only the right to vote but also significant social
change, very few women were then to be found in sociology, and only
a sprinkling in anthropology. Social research was still a rare pathway
for a woman. There was little discussion of gender in early sociology.
Among the first-wave names we could spotlight how Beatrice Webb
played a prominent role through her activism, research and writings.
Not least, she was also one of the founders of the LSE. She actively
encouraged both social research and social reform – much as Jane
Addams did in the US. There were a few others.[4]

Substantial change was only to begin with the university boom of the
1970s. The oldest woman Pioneer in our sample was *Mary Douglas*: but
she was critical of feminism. All of our other women Pioneers become
prominent as researchers from the late 1960s and active feminists in
the 70s and 80s. Here, *Pat Caplan*, anthropologist, talks about how she
first encountered feminism and clearly suggests its impact:

> I remember being in Surkhet [in Nepal] and staying in the house
> of a Peace Corps guy, and he said, 'Oh, there's this new book

everybody's talking about. Have you read it?' Betty Friedan's *Feminine Mystique*. And I said, 'No, I've never heard of it'. And he said, "Here. Read it'. So we got stuck in Surkhet, and I started to read *The Feminine Mystique*. I think up to around that time – and don't forget, when I got back a few weeks later I found I was pregnant, and I was surprised, because I suppose it was like most babies, a half-planned baby, let's say. Up to that time, I'd always thought it was kind of the world is my oyster, so although I was aware that being female had certain problems, I thought if you were good enough and clever enough, and you worked hard enough, it wouldn't be an issue.

And, of course, once I had a baby, I realised – well, I mean, I'd realised it, to some extent, becoming a wife, but even more so becoming a mother, that it did put a lot of constraints on what you could do, but more importantly, how people saw you. Then I'd had this period that I talked to you about, where my mother and my uncle both were very ill and died eventually, and then I had the care of my very elderly grandparents, as well as having two small children to look after. So I realised that the female lot, in all of these circumstances, which is having children, giving birth, looking after the elderly and so on, is very time and energy consuming. It needs to be done with more support from all sorts of people.

But I think I was probably very receptive to the message of feminism, as I could feel myself getting pushed into a sort of wife/mother/housewife role – these were the sort of pressures that were coming, and I didn't like them. I recognised that all those things needed to be done, and I didn't resent doing them one iota, because I'd made the choice to have children, I was happy to have children, I was not happy about what happened to my relatives and their illnesses, but they needed looking after, and so that was okay. But the kind of messages that feminism gave, I think, resonated very strongly with women like me, who'd been very highly educated and who thought that there were no barriers to whatever we wanted to do, and suddenly we discovered with the rude shock of, 'It's not quite like that, actually!' (p 51)

This same life phase recurs as turning point among our women Pioneers – a phase of not only difficulties, but also of revelation and potential. We can take *Ann Oakley* as an exemplar of this time. She is a pioneering and prolific feminist, writing over 30 books, a major influence in sociology as a researcher, but also as an autobiographer and a novelist with a much wider public audience – such as through her televised novel *The Men's Room* (1988). Born in London in 1944, her father was Richard Titmuss, himself a leading figure in social policy research at the LSE. She has written a telling biography of her father, *Father and Daughter* (2014), which shows how she was immersed at early age in a life of politics, university, gender and the LSE itself. Like most of our Pioneers, her education led her eventually to university – to Oxford where she read Philosophy, Politics and Economics (PPE). In 1964 she married Robin Oakley, and then had her first two children, working in social research and experimenting with writing fiction. And in 1969 she signed up for a PhD at Bedford College. But she recalls this as a bleak phase:

> I signed up for the Ph.D. in 1969. I had my first two children in 1967 and 1968. A boy and a girl. And we were living in West London, and Robin was teaching at Bedford College – teaching sociology at Bedford College – and I was pretty much a full-time mother, although I was always trying to do something else. I wrote some scripts of children's television, I did some very tedious work for some catalogue of businesses in the East End, which involved me sitting in the playpen to make the phone calls, and giving the children the run of the house – it was the only way I could do it! I was quite isolated because I was the first of my friends to have children, and in those days it was much more difficult, there weren't these networks of young mothers that you could plug into, so I think I was probably quite lonely. I, of course, got a diagnosis of post-natal depression and was put on various anti-depressants and it was a difficult period. It was nothing to do with my feelings about my children at all.
>
> A lot of my work, subsequently, has interrogated this whole notion of post-natal depression, which most of the time is actually a label for women who are chronically exhausted and sleep-deprived, and just have too much to do, and I think that was probably my situation. (Part 1, pp 10–11)

Nevertheless, this proved the context for her key moment of intellectual discovery. 'I remember there being a sort of conversion moment when I was dusting bookshelves in Robin's study and found these books on the sociology of work, and I thought, "What I'm doing is work".

And I looked in these books, and I looked in the index of various books, and there was nothing about housework' (Part 1, pp 9–11). She focussed her thesis on housework conceived of as work, published as her influential books *Housewife* and *The Sociology of Housework* (1974). She went on to broaden the scope with her widely read Penguin book, *Becoming a Mother* (1981). And in these years she became a crucial figure in the whole field of feminist research. She published *Sex, Gender and Society* (1972), which introduced the term 'gender' into social science and then into general use. And with Juliet Mitchell she edited the flagship volume *The Rights and Wrongs of Women* (1976). She is still working broadly on women's issues, and especially with those linked to health, and experimenting with innovative methodological approaches, including both qualitative data and randomised controlled experiments – explored in *Experiments in Knowing: Gender and Method in the Social Sciences* (2000). She has explored how gender divisions and the differing behaviour of men and women impact on the environment in her wide-ranging *Gender on Planet Earth* (2002).

From the 1970s onwards Ann has worked especially on women's issues in health, including notably childbirth (*Women Confined: Towards a Sociology of Childbirth*, 1980) and antenatal care (*The Captured Womb*, 1984). In 1990 she became founding director of the Social Science Research Unit, experimenting with innovative methodological approaches. Looking back on her earlier work, she now sees it less as reflecting feminist activism but rather as driven by a fundamental need for re-balancing:

> I thought I was redressing an imbalance in the research. Most of it had been from a masculine point of view and had reflected – the vast bulk of sociology was about these really important issues to do with power and occupation, and social class defined in male terms, and there was simply an enormous gap. You didn't have to call yourself a feminist in order to do that, any more than the men who did the rest of it called themselves masculinist. It was simply something that needed to be done. And the way in which people talk about feminists and feminism is always to imply that people who identify themselves as feminists are, in some sense, biased, and, of course, they're no more biased than people who aren't feminist. A lot of my research and writing has been informed by my desire to put women back on the centre stage along with men. But a lot of it has also been on a more general level about the uses of research to inform public policy, and women are recipients of public policy just as men are. (Part 1, p 33)

Nevertheless, it is clear that 'redressing' only became possible because it was driven forward by the activism of the second-wave women's movement. This activism pervaded the movement and is frequently recalled in detail by our Pioneers. Ann herself speaks of the earlier years:

> I was active at the beginning stages of the Women's Liberation Movement, Second Wave Feminism. I was in a workshop, and I was involved in various activities like providing pregnancy testing in people's front rooms, in West London, self-examination – a lot of health issues. But, I wasn't an organiser. In theory, the Women's Liberation Movement didn't have organisers, but, of course, it had some people who were better at that and had more time to do it than other people! So in that sense, I was involved, but, no, I had children and a full-time job, and had to earn money, so time was limited. But the commitment was always there. (Part 2, p 11)

Pat Caplan recalls local women's consciousness-raising groups and book-reading groups as her first feminist connection. She also became a founding figure in the London Women's Anthropology Group. Like *Leonore Davidoff*, Pat was a volunteer with a new women's library in London, the Women's Research and Resources Centre. Others like *Janet Finch* and *Diana Leonard* worked closely with the British Sociological Association's (BSA) Women's Caucus.

Equally important, the women's movement succeeded in raising very deep issues, both public and private. Thus there were public campaigns, most famously to win better work conditions for London's night cleaning women. But its challenge to authority could be profound, even shocking, at a double level, public and private. *Stuart Hall* felt that shock to the core. He and Catherine Hall had fallen in love after meeting on an anti-nuclear Aldermaston March. Since 1964 he had been leading the intellectual development of the new Centre for Contemporary Cultural Studies in Birmingham, becoming director in 1968. In retrospect he describes how unbalanced their relationship was at first, romantic and poetic, but unquestionably as the older partner, already a leading innovative academic, he was setting the tone. And soon Catherine was 'locked up at home with a young baby, starting a Mediaeval History Ph.D., and I'm teaching my life out at the Centre'. But with the arrival of the women's movement she was far from alone:

> Lots of other people like her – those mothers with academic, or husbands, or people who worked elsewhere, who are locked up for the first time, at home, with children – got together. So

Birmingham started a crèche, and a school, and jointly parents looking after other children, and the whole neighbourhood became a kind of feminist network... They set up this group – a lot of our friends were involved, and the men were all helping, while the women had discussions, the men were helping with the kids, and helping at the school. And we had six children for tea, we would have them... A big network in which neighbourhood feminism, feminist politics, and academic interest overlapped...

So it's a period of huge turbulence. And because Catherine was involved in all of that – very actively involved – it was a matter of in the home as well. How do you bring up the children? Do you give the boys guns? I had always had guns, I grew up with holsters and air rifles at home! Yes, but what does that mean? Why don't they have dolls? Dolls? What about the girls, read them cowboy stories, etc.! So, in every detail, we had to re-think the whole of that. (pp 53–58)

At the same time they had to redefine their own partnership – and that was

a big transformative moment for us. It took quite a long time, and by the end our relationship was very different... What I discovered from it is that you change your ideas, but your practice is much more stubborn. So, of course, I was in favour of this equality. Of course! So obvious, you know! Men bossed them about and tell them what to do, as I have done with Catherine – so this has to stop. But what was an alternative way of relating to one another? (pp 53–58)

And perhaps most challengingly of all for Stuart, whose influence hinged on his exceptional skill with words, both in public and private, he found himself silenced:

You'll almost certainly remember, the beginnings, the early stages of Second Wave Feminism, they didn't want to hear from me! 'Shut up! We're going somewhere else. To have our conversation, listen to our own voices for a change!' (pp 53–58)

Cultural studies, migration and Thatcherism

Stuart Hall (1932–2014) is a pivotal figure in the changing context of social research from the 1950s onwards: pioneering a new agenda of interconnected issues encompassing popular culture and the media, immigration and racism, neo-liberal economies and the transnational diaspora. He was brought up in Jamaica in a highly colour-conscious middle-class family (whom we have encountered in Voices 2). Stuart came to England in 1951 as a Rhodes Scholar specialising on Henry James, who he saw as dealing with the problem of living across two cultures – Europe and the US. This was the start of Stuart's lifelong concern with culture and with living across two (or more) cultures. He recalls how he was set thinking by encountering outside a London railway station a crowd of migrants who had arrived from Jamaica, but unlike him, not to study but as workers:

I saw this stream of ordinary Jamaican people coming out of the station, and I thought, 'Who are these? Where are they going? These are not middle-class travellers, these are ordinary working people from Jamaica. What are they doing here?' Well, of course, it was only two years after the arrival of *The Windrush*, which is 1948 – two or three years – and the migration was just beginning to build up. Well, that was a very strange experience to me, because I regarded coming to England as a kind of escape attempt. I couldn't come to terms – I wasn't the person my parents wanted me to be. But somehow that formation prevented me also from identifying as an ordinary Jamaican boy. So I felt blocked in both directions...

But there they were. There was my problem! On the station forecourt, all there, all in England. What were they doing here? Where were they from? A lot of them were from the countryside and never been in Kingston, though it's been a bit exaggerated how unskilled they were, it's turned out. But, nevertheless, they'd scraped together and found the wherewithal to travel, and here they were, in their brimmed felt hats and their brightly coloured jackets, and their baskets – an incredible sight! I thought, 'Well, what will happen to them? They're not going back right away, they've come to work. Can they find work that isn't available in Jamaica? They'll have to live here. They'll have to live somewhere. Where? What relationship will they have with the people that they're living amongst? What kind of jobs will they find?' But more especially, 'What sort of Jamaicans will they be in ten years? They'll be habituated to something else'... What I realised is that they would never be the same as they'd come, as this experience would transform them. I couldn't see in exactly what ways, but they could never quite go back. In that sense, they, and I, couldn't really go home again... So for the first time, their fates and mine were sort of the same!

That's where I learnt to see life as a diasporic subject – as somebody who's living the in-between life there and here, between cultures, between temporalities, between forms of authority and power, and finally decide, 'Could you make a home here when you really thought of that as home? But if you went home, you could never make a home there.' You'd always be thinking about there. Well, that is what diasporic subjects are like. They're going to be them, and so am I. So it's a critical experience for me, because suddenly I saw myself from some other person's place. (pp 26–28)

We see the forming of many ideas that were to help him shape a radical research project for the next 50 years. Initially, the context was the emerging broad political and cultural New Left movement, encompassing the Campaign for Nuclear Disarmament, the rediscovery of a more humanistic socialist theory through Marx's early writings, political activism typically within the Labour Party, encouraging working–class autobiography in local history workshops, and enjoying jazz and coffee. Its London centre became the Partisan coffee house off Soho Square, which was launched in 1957. Stuart soon became a leading figure. In 1958–61 he became a founder-editor of *Universities and Left Review* and briefly editor of its successor the *New Left Review*. During this time he gave up his thesis, and instead began to focus his intellectual interests on popular culture, both British and Jamaican. He found a new focus for thinking about problems of class, culture and education in Richard Hoggart's *The Uses of Literacy: Aspects of Working Class Life* (1957). He recalls how in this time he and his New Left colleagues were

massively preoccupied with the question about culture, and Hoggart's *Uses of Literacy* was published in that period. Massive debate. And the debate was about what was happening to working-class culture after the War: would it be affected by the American models, and American mass culture? Television and all that was coming. Was capitalism the same as it had been before? Was this new orientation to affluence and consumerism and so on, did this represent another stage or phase of capital? We had to debate that. Well, could class be interpreted in the same way as it had been in the high industrial period? What was the equivalent of the cloth cap working class in 1950?

So when I say 'culture', I don't just mean that it was about cultural questions, it was about culture in exactly this broader sense that I'm talking about. But it was also about culture in another sense. It paid attention to the cultural dimensions of politics, of the political, and therefore it was from the inception in my head opposed to the narrow base/superstructure model that prevailed within classical Marxism, which gave culture, and literature, and the symbolic dimension, a dependent status. It depended on, [was] reflexive of everything else. We just were not able to think about that in that way.

So there's a theoretical thread going which leads all the way through cultural studies, and there's a political thread going of a position in between the major currents and tendencies. (pp 38–39)

As Stuart points out, this was not just a private debate:

We didn't generate this debate, everybody was talking about that! I remember the 1959 Election, Gaitskell's speech to the Labour Party Conference was, 'What will happen to the Labour vote in the light of the coming of the small motor car, the washing machine, the fridge, and the television? Will affluence undo all of that?' Well, Hoggart had said, 'Well, no, but it will change it. It will change it'. (p 39)

This interest in culture led to Stuart becoming the first staff member of the Centre for Contemporary Cultural Studies at Birmingham University, founded by Richard Hoggart in 1964. This was the key moment when cultural studies moved into its academic phase. Here, Stuart played the leading role in developing its research and teaching, and from 1968 succeeded Hoggart as Director. He led the design and writing of the new courses, and focussing in particular on the links between sociology, politics, race and culture. The Centre proved highly influential, with cultural studies later becoming established in many other universities across the world. Teaching at the Centre was also innovative, centred on group work and group discussion and publication. From a literary starting-point Stuart developed new interpretative approaches for analysing popular culture, such as his concept of the dual process of 'encoding' and 'decoding' cultural messages. He always retained a crucial interest in the political implications of culture and cultural change. Crucially, he expanded concepts of culture to include issues of race and gender. Among very many publications he was co-editor of two outstanding examples of co-authored books from the Centre, *Resistance Through Rituals: Youth Sub-cultures in Post-war Britain* (1976), and *Policing the Crisis* (1978), a telling prophesy of the Thatcher era.

Stuart stayed at the Centre until 1979 when he left to be Professor of Sociology at the Open University. He pursued his analysis of Thatcherism in later work such as *The Hard Road to Renewal* (1988). He can rightly be seen not only as an early visionary of cultural studies, but also continuing as a major and valuable commentator on the politics of the whole period. But he is particularly remembered for his key ideas on the birth of Thatcherism. Stuart again captures the moment well:

> *Policing the Crisis* was written and conceived at the moment between two conjunctures. On the one hand, the social democratic Keynesian Welfare State, more egalitarian redistributive moment, which comes apart in the seventies, the coming apart is the crisis in the title of the book, and more or less is ushered out in '79. Mrs. Thatcher comes in, and Thatcherism begins, and a quite new conjuncture – the newer liberal free market forces, privatisation, marketisation, restitution of the power of private capital, all of that comes in – another conjuncture.
>
> We published in '78. Mrs. Thatcher had already emerged, but was not elected until 1979, but anybody who read *Policing the Crisis*, or who understood what *Policing the Crisis* was about, and how its analysis was developed, knew that what was happening was not a mere twist in the electoral pendulum, but was a new conjuncture, a new phase altogether. And since we were looking at the impact of Conservatism and the anti-Welfare State consensus position, at a popular level, we said, 'If you find a populist Tory, who is able to put these new interests and concerns into a popular language, they will be elected'. They will be elected, because the old system has been coming apart at the seams. It can't hold any longer. (p 127)

Transnational and intersectional times

Cultural studies has influenced changing interdisciplinary approaches to researches on ethnicity and race, which now include transnationalism as a strand of global culture – for example, in the work of another Jamaican-born researcher, *Harry Goulbourne*. We will return to the issues of ethnicity in Chapter 7. But for the moment we choose to close this discussion with the story of *Avtar Brah*, a feminist sociologist who investigated issues of migration, borders and creolised/hybrid cultures. Her life begins framed by the last years of British colonial power, to which we can now return in full circle. While our earliest researchers wrote about other cultures from positions of imperial dominance, nowadays such work looks for interconnections and power relations between cultures. Avtar's work, exemplified in her *Cartographies of Diaspora* (1996), fuses sociology, anthropology, cultural studies, psychology and literature and marks the ways in which much late twentieth century has become more interdisciplinary, more critical and more global. She says on her website, 'I have lived on four of the five continents of the globe – Africa, Asia, America and Europe. These experiences of displacement and dispersal have rendered questions of difference, solidarity and identity central to my work'.

Born in the Punjab in northern India to a Sikh family in 1944, Avtar grew up in Uganda, where her family had a sawmill business. The family spoke Punjabi but from the start her education was in English, beginning in racially segregated Government Schools, part of what she calls the 'Colonial Sandwich' in pre-independence Uganda.

> We had the white at the top – we were called 'Indians' rather than 'Asians' at the time – the Indians in the middle, and the Africans at the bottom. So it was very much a hierarchical society. At home we had servants who were Africans, and my first encounter with Africans as equals was in my A Level school, because we had, but not many, I think in our class of about 20-odd we had maybe two or three African students. So that was my first encounter with people who were fellow students rather than servants in the house. (p 5)

Troubled by the social restraints there on young Asian women, she won a scholarship to study at the University of California in Davis, moving on for an MA in Adult Education at the University of Wisconsin in Madison, where writing her dissertation on Ugandan education proved a radicalising turning point. Coming to Britain for a brief vacation, she was unable to return to Uganda because of the 1972 expulsion of Asians by Idi Amin, in which her family lost their business and she herself became stateless. In the event, she stayed permanently in Britain and worked in a succession of activist research projects with young people and women: at Bristol University's Ethnic Relations Unit, Leicester University's Centre for Mass Communications, and in between as a training officer with young people in Southall for the National

Association for Asian Youth. The 1980s were a period of dramatic political tension in Southall, including notably the death of Blair Peach in 1979 and the subsequent Grunwick Strike by Asian workers.

By now a feminist activist, Avtar set up Southall Black Sisters, bringing together militant black and Asian women, with parallel groups in Bristol and Leicester. The Southall group has survived, principally as an advice and refuge organisation for young Asian women. She felt ambivalent about the white middle-class feminist movement, but found ways of working with it. From 1982 Avtar went to the Open University as manager for the Minority Experience course, and then from 1985 to Birkbeck in the Centre for Extra-Mural Studies: her working base for the remainder of her career, at last giving her space to publish much more frequently. Now retired, she was awarded an MBE in 2001 in recognition of her research. She captures the dynamic period well:

> I came here in the early seventies, and I was in Bristol, and one of the groups I got involved with was the 'Consciousness Raising Group'. In the early seventies we had Consciousness Raising Groups, and I remember becoming a member of a group in Clifton, which is where I lived, and this was a predominantly middle-class group of white women. I was the only person of colour there. But we were together as women, and so it was thinking about issues to do with patriarchy in general, rather than Asians specifically. And I remember attending some of the early conferences, the national feminist conferences, what used to be called the Women's Liberation Movement – it wasn't called a 'Feminist' movement as such. So I was a member of the Women's Liberation Movement, and attended some of the conferences at a national level...
>
> Before I came to Southall there was an organisation called the – OWAAD, it was called – Organisation of Women of African and Asian Descent, which was actually a national body to which local groups were affiliated. So we had formed, in Bristol, we had a Bristol Branch of that OWAAD.
>
> And we formed the Southall Black Sisters, we formed the Bristol Black Sisters. Later I moved to Leicester, and we formed a Leicester Black Sisters Group, so these were three solidarity movements. (p 21)

She describes her enthusiasm but also the problems she continued to feel after joining the editorial collective of the *Feminist Review* in 1988:

This was a socialist feminist project, so I was very pleased when I was invited to join the Collective. But even within that Collective, we were again, women of colour were in the minority, and although this was an intellectual project, we felt that issues to do with race and ethnicity were not taken fully on board...

So there was the intellectual project, but also we felt that as a group of women working together, we felt that, again, was a question – there's the intellectual dimension of this, but then there's the interpersonal level dimension as well, and we felt that there were certain sorts of issues that were not taken on board. The psychic impacts of racism and ethnicity, and how those mattered. So we actually said to the women – they were very sympathetic to what we were saying, not all of them, but many of them – so we said that, as women of colour, we were going to leave *Feminist Review* for a period of time, and we wanted the white women to get together and address these issues amongst themselves, and then, at a certain point, if we felt we could work together, then we will come back. So for several months, I think, it might even have been a year, we women of colour moved out of *Feminist Review*, and the *Feminist Review* women did genuinely make an effort to address, raise these issues amongst themselves. And then we went back, and since then the journal has been thriving, basically. I'm still a member after all these years. I'm the longest standing member as you can well imagine! But I love the journal. (p 22)

She sums up her overall position:

Some people would say that we were separatists, but I don't think we were separatists. The way we operated was that we felt we needed a space of our own in which we, as black women, could address issues that affected us specifically, but then when we were dealing with patriarchy in general we worked with white women's groups, and when we needed, when we worked around the issues of racism, we worked with anti-racists of all backgrounds. So that was the kind of politics that, that influenced our thinking at the time...

The differences really were based around the fact that – I said to you I attended some conferences, national conferences with the Women's Liberation Movement as part of that – but I realised, earlier on, that during discussion, basically they were all white organisations – all the speakers were white, and all the issues that were address were – I mean, they were not white issues, but they were issues that did not address questions of ethnicity or race at all.

And sexuality too, at the time. So I remember people raising gay, lesbian women raising issues of sexuality, and some of us women of colour, not many of us, but a few of us, raising questions around ethnicity and race. But we were often, we felt, were not listened to, that we were excluded from the ethos of these conferences. So we decided to form our own groups, which is how all that came about, as a black women's, called 'National Group'. So there was a huge – well, not a huge, but certainly a gap between white women's movements and black women's movements, as it became later on. (pp 21–22)

VOICES 3

Old boundaries, new thoughts

Any social research takes places in a social and political context which not only has been powerfully shaped by the past, but also has the first signs of possible future new directions.

Empire and war

Jack Goody's journey to colonial Ghana

Because his anthropological research was funded by the Colonial Office, Jack Goody went out to Ghana as a Colonial Officer. Despite his egalitarian social commitments, he found himself embedded within the colonial system:

> I went on the boat train up to Liverpool, and I was met there by somebody from the Dempster Line, who said to me, 'You do realise you're travelling with a lot of black gentlemen?' I said, 'Well, I suppose I'll have to get used to that, because I'm going out to study them'. So I was allowed to get on, and I got on this boat – it was rather depressing, right down in the hold – and we were allowed up on deck for what, half an hour or an hour every day. But I had very interesting company down there because the Africans I was with, one was going to be a lawyer, one was a doctor – I can't remember the others very much, but they're the people who were in my cabin, so I probably had a lot more intelligent conversation down there than I did up in second or first class with Europeans. (pp 34–35)

Jack was met as soon as he reached Ghana by a former Ghanaian student who like Jack had been supervised in Oxford by Meyer Fortes:

> The former student's name was Kofi Busia, who wrote a book on the Ashanti, and eventually became Prime Minister after Nkrumah, and he was Head of the Sociology Department in Lagos, and he looked after me... I suppose, through having been a prisoner-of-war, and also I felt my age was against me, I wanted to get things done as quickly as I could, so time was

very important to me, so I didn't spend long in Accra at that time, in the capital. I got my permits or whatever I had to do, got my kit together, and my food, made my arrangements very quickly – always did. I always felt the time-swinging chariot was hurrying near, even at that time...

I got together what I wanted, and wrapped them up, and had them in the back of the lorry that I'd got for a short time from the government, and took it up with me. But, really, all I needed was a bed, and some sort of bath, and a lamp – a pressure lamp – plus food, plus beer. (pp 35, 37)

So he quickly went on to Kumasi, the capital of the Division of Ashanti, where he met another contact from within the British colonial network, a local educational administrator in education, called Peter Cannon:

He fixed me up to go further on in a government lorry... He also found me a cook/steward from the area I was going to, which was most useful. So I went there with him, up to the North, and I stopped the night when I got into the Northern Territories, in a huge government rest house, built of mud, with sticks for a roof, but a vast place, where there was a man – that I remember to this day – the District Officer met me there, a very pleasant chap, and when we got there, said, 'Well, we'll have to go out and shoot something for dinner tonight'. So we went out and shot a guinea fowl, a wild one, and came back and cooked that.

Then I went on the next day to the next government place, to see the District Commissioner there. And his sister was married to an archaeologist in Cambridge, and he had a huge HMV gramophone – like one of these ones you see in these ads – which he turned up and played music on that, he was very proud of that! So I stayed there, and then went on, the next day, to the place where I was going to work. But even there, I stayed for a time in a rest house, a government rest house, before I went out to the village. (pp 35–37)

And how did he choose the village for his study? He took advice from two locally knowledgeable men. One was an Oxford man who had been a District Officer in the region. The other was a new contact, a local headmaster, who later on under Independence became a District Commissioner himself. So once again Jack was guided through the colonial system.

W. M. Williams: diverse experiences in military service

W. M. Williams came from a South Wales mining family and he served nearly five years in the army during and after the Second World War. He remembers strikingly different experiences. He first joined the Welsh Guards:

> I went into the Welsh Guards, and I hated it. I absolutely hated it. Because, for example, you weren't allowed to have any books or a newspaper, you weren't allowed any reading material. What you were allowed was writing paper and envelopes, and if they found a book in your belongings, you were put on a charge, because the Guards disciplined to ensure that you did exactly as you were told, and you did nothing for yourself. And although I admired it, and I could see what it was about, I decided I had to get out. (p 11)

But he succeeded in getting a transfer to the 'very hierarchical' Indian Army, where he had to adapt to having his own personal servant, 'an orderly, who brushed my boots and brought me tea in the morning. It was a servant, and I found this extraordinary, that there's a man here who's actually a servant! I'd read about it in books about Victorian England and so on!' But he revelled in the diversity of cultures which confronted him – in religions, in diets, in histories – 'they could just as easily have been in different worlds'. For him, service in the Indian Army proved an eye-openingly rich experience (pp 11–12).

New visions: books of the time

Most of our Pioneers speak of how their research was shaped by particular people, or by reading. Most often these were academic books found in a university library. Sometimes reading could lead to eureka moments and lifelong influences.

Stan Cohen on Howard Becker and labelling theory

> I was here at LSE, in the Library, and I picked up Becker's *Outsiders*, and I can still see, sitting in the Library, I remember reading that. There was the famous line there, 'Deviancy is <u>not</u> a quality of an act'... And I was absolutely knocked out by this! This simple idea would make sense of all the very pre-theoretical ideas I had. (p 37)

Robert Moore on Street Corner Society

Robert Moore twice insisted that William Foote Whyte's *Street Corner Society* for him was the nearest to a 'handbook' on how to do research in urban Britain. Later he repeated:

> When I started off in Sparkbrook [in Birmingham, working with John Rex on race], I think I mentioned *Street Corner Society*, but I think what I didn't mention, and it's very important, and has always stuck with me, was Malinowski's *Scientific Theory of Culture*. (p 72)

David Hargreaves on Erving Goffman

> But one of the most striking books that I read in the period that they allowed me to adjust before I started the work [an ethnography of a school in Hull], was Erving Goffman, who was just coming to the fore, and he'd published *The Presentation of Self in Everyday Life*, which was really an exercise in social psychology – 'micro sociology' as they were calling it – and *Asylums: A Study of Total Institutions*. And I think, probably, as I look back, in terms of how I was looking at the work, I think I was looking at it through more Goffmanesque eyes than, probably, say Evans-Pritchard or Max Gluckman or whatever they did with their structural functionalism!
>
> Yes, I think that was influencing how I felt, and I think it was the social psychological strand to that, and the fascination by the relationships which intrigued me. Of course, it related back to my own experience as a teacher, knowing that, as a teacher, you've two sets of relationships to master – those with your colleagues, and those with the kids – and if you make a hash of either of those, you're in trouble. (p 24)

But the post-war decades were also a time of many newer eye-opening books based on social research:

Daniel Bertaux on Oscar Lewis

> When I came back from Berkeley in October '63, and my mother was reading a book, which she lent to me – quite often she lent me books, she would recommend a book – it was called *Les Enfants de Sanchez*, by Oscar Lewis. I read it, I was absolutely

fascinated by that book, completely fascinated. Because I did not read the newspaper at the time, I did not know that Sartre and Simone de Beauvoir had also read about it, and were enthusiastic. It was a personal thing. I thought, 'That's what I want to do later on'. And I thought this was sociology, because it was about real people, real life. I didn't know Lewis was an anthropologist. I did not even care about it. I say, 'That's what I want to do', and I thought that was sociology. I registered in sociology. I got extremely disappointed, as I said, about the way they were teaching that discipline, sociology... But I stick with this idea that I will finish sociology and I will do, if I can, this kind of research. So the Oscar Lewis was very important in that time. (Part 1, p 70)

CHAPTER 4

Organising: creating research worlds

Before the twentieth century, there was very little organised social research in Britain. Now, the age of organised social research is on us. While we may like to see creative pioneering work as the product of isolated creative minds, it rarely is. For creativity and original research depend on the opportunities and social conditions that enable it to happen. Even in the time of Leonardo, it was heavily dependent upon sponsorship. Some of our researchers certainly experienced isolation in their fieldwork, particularly those anthropologists who in the early post-war decades, set out – usually not even speaking the local language – to report on community and kinship in remote territories: but in fact most were supported by the Colonial Social Science Research Council. By the 1980s, with the fading of Empire, the focus of anthropology itself had shifted towards working more often in Britain, sharing fields with cultural studies researchers and qualitative sociologists. And certainly in the contemporary world there are now deep structures of funding, research organisations and professional groupings that profoundly shape opportunities, and provide organised ways of doing things that make research more of a collective product. But not simply more co-operative: at the same time a field for splits and battles for resources. So in this chapter we look at the impact on our researchers of a period of unprecedented university expansion, a shifting scene of disciplinary divides, new research agencies and academic centres, and a big swing towards sustained long-term statistical surveys.

Expanding universities and shifting disciplines

In 1939 there was a tight group of 21 universities in Britain with 50,000 students, less than 2 per cent of the population. Most of our researchers started from the longest-established institutions – Oxbridge or the LSE. But by 1961 student numbers had already more than doubled. Following the 1963 Robbins Report, expansion accelerated with the founding of seven new universities – Sussex, Kent, York, Lancaster, Warwick, Essex and East Anglia – all of which took a major interest in the development of social research and social science. At the same time, a large new polytechnic sector was emerging with colleges of advanced technology (CATs) set up from the late 1950s, many of them becoming universities a little later – including Aston, Loughborough, City, Brunel, Bath, Salford and Bradford. Finally, in 1992, the Conservative government turned all polytechnics into universities. So, by 2017, there were 163 British universities with 2.3 million registered students. Of these, over 220,000 were in social studies.

Meanwhile, the profile of the disciplines was also transforming. Anthropology had long been the senior social science, but its imperial base was shrinking. Meanwhile, from the late 1950s there was a rising enthusiasm for sociology, fed by popular Penguin books and a thirst among younger people for social change. This backed the rapid expansion of sociology teaching in the universities. Stan Cohen recalls his first job at Enfield College (later Middlesex University) in 1966:

> Those were the heady days. I remember Roy Bailey just turning up in the canteen at the LSE, and I was sitting with Jock Young, who I'd made friends with at the time, and said, 'Well, I've got eight jobs in sociology. Is anybody interested?' And so we all got full-time jobs there, at Enfield in 1965–67. (p 42)

In parallel, there were new jobs at the top of departments. Between 1962 and 1965 the number of chairs in sociology at British universities had increased from six to 30. Very often the new professors had begun as anthropologists, but were now enthusiastic for sociology. There had been much earlier ethnographic work in Britain, especially focussed on poverty, such as Henry Mayhew's *London Labour and the London Poor* (1861). But there had been no sustained development to parallel the great advances being made by social scientists in the US from the 1920s onwards. This in itself created a moment of opportunity. As *Peter Townsend*, studying anthropology at Cambridge, reflected:

> The social anthropologist had practiced in poor countries – parts of Africa, or Latin America, let's say – and one can reproduce all kinds of people who have contributed enormously to our knowledge about that. I'm thinking of Margaret Mead, or Meyer Fortes, Radcliffe Brown, a whole variety of people who taught us a great deal. But... when it comes to Western society, two things have happened.
>
> One is that it's taken people time to begin appreciating that those societies deserve careful study and illumination, because too many things are taken for granted, or overlooked,

totally overlooked by people who live in them. Because
they're not strange events and strange relationships, as they
immediately feel like when you go to New Guinea, let's say, or
the southernmost tip of Chile. Yes, immediately you recognise
the differences, and you want to try and explain them, but we
can't identify the peculiarities of our own life so much. But also,
equally exciting, was the idea... that Western society, our own
society, deserved investigation and illumination, just as much as
some of the poorer societies, which the social anthropologists
had researched so industriously. (p 31)

Typically, alongside this intellectual interest went a progressive
commitment towards social changes aiming to better the lot of
disadvantaged and marginalised social groups. In the 1960s this
was an important part of the new appeal of sociology. But political
commitment also created antagonism and so made sociology more
vulnerable to public disapproval, especially after 1968. This set the
scene for a disciplinary fragmentation, with the focus instead on major
issues. Thus, the revived women's movement led to women's studies
and later to gender studies; oral history sprang from listening seriously
to older people; race riots and colour issues led to ethnic studies, and
also to cultural studies. We see the rise of media studies, queer studies,
environmental studies and many others, along with a proliferation of
new courses and new journals.

At the same time came another key development. In contrast to the
US, British social science had lacked a focus on research methodology. In
ethnographic work especially the traditional style was amateurish: jump
in and try to swim. However, survey work already demanded a serious
understanding of statistics. Hence, one of the first books was *Claus
Moser*'s very successful *Survey Methods in Social Investigation* (1958).
A substantial book with some 340 pages, it sets up a clear framework
of issues: planning surveys, what to cover, sampling and sample design,
methods of collecting – documents, observation, mail questionnaires,
interviewing, 'processing of the data' (editing, coding and tabulations)
and finally 25 pages on analysis, interpretation and presentation. In a
sense it depicts the 'state of the art' by the 1950s. Moser himself remarks:

In terms of publications as a statistician, obviously what I'm most
proud of is my book on survey methods... That was published
in 1957, and I was quite a young academic, but it remains a
standard book on survey methods now in 2012! I get royalties
all the time, it's unbelievable! ... And it is in several languages.

> I know exactly why it's been such a success: because... it's written in a language so simple, but technically absolutely correct... There are thousands of people who love to do sociology, or social science, or economics, who are not good at statistics, but you have to do it as part of that, and you have to know about surveys, and here's a book that makes it so simple. (pp 10–11)

From the 1960s a broader methods teaching became a major focus in its own right. Methods courses became a normal part of teaching, and voluminous methods books became standard recommendations. New degree programmes, professional associations and journals devoted entirely to methodology started to appear. Spontaneous inspiration was no longer a good enough start: it was improper for you to begin researching before you had trained.

Research agencies

While most of our Pioneers researched within the rapidly changing university contexts,[1] a number became engaged with wider research settings. Many were involved in running journals or with developing their professional organisations, such as the BSA. *Raymond Firth* became the first secretary of the Colonial Social Science Research Council when it was formed in 1946; *Michael Young* set up the Social Science Research Council (SSRC); *Claus Moser* became second director of the Office of National Statistics (ONS), and *Ivor Crewe* of the Data Archive. Here, these Pioneers comment on the stories of four such agencies in which they played leading roles.

Before this, however, we need to introduce *Michael Young*, whose name we have already heard. It will keep recurring. His prolific originality makes him is a unique figure among our Pioneers. Born to a wealthy Australian family who almost abandoned him, he found his creative home at Dartington School. In 1940, he became director of PEP. He went on to become research director for the Labour Party, drafting Labour's key 1945 manifesto. In 1954, he founded the Institute of Community Studies in Bethnal Green, which thereafter remained his base. He envisaged and helped to set up of the consumer magazine *Which?* He proposed the SSRC and the 'Data Bank' – now the UK Data Archive which is the lead partner of the UK Data Service – and became the Council's founding director. He remained a far-seeing social inventor throughout his life.

Political and Economic Planning and the Institute of Community Studies

PEP can be seen as one of the earlier non-governmental organisations (NGOs), a 'policy think tank' formed in 1931. (It eventually became the Policy Studies Institute.) Through meetings, discussions and pamphlets, it played a major role in the formation of the National Health Service, the Beveridge Report, the Welfare State and the changes in both education and work that characterised the post-war reconstruction. It was also concerned with the changing role of the colonies. Michael Young became Director in 1940, and here he comments:

> They [PEP] believed in planning but not from a socialist point of view particularly. You could do it then. A lot of people I believe did planning, planning everything really. Planning industry. But planning meant just sort of being sensible about things and government and industry working closely together...
>
> They got together groups of people who were expert on their subjects, volunteers, who were very carefully chosen, and gave them a free meal once a week or once a fortnight or once a month, according to how intensely they were prepared to work at it. And managed to keep them there until their report was produced. They produced a report that way on the National Health Service – a need for a National Health Service, that was published in l937. Way before it really got on to any political agenda. And a very good account of the things that were wrong in the Health Service of that day, based on the voluntary principle. (C 408, pp 37–38)

They also produced reports on industries – coal, electricity, building – 'a whole lot of big volumes. Substantial reports.' And a fortnightly broadsheet with 2,500 subscribers.

> I inherited this technique and had to keep it going by bringing in people - quite a lot of civil servants, but also academics and business people, journalists... It was very much into post-war reconstruction. So we took almost every field one after the other, housing, social services – and produced reports and broadsheets. We did much the fullest evidence I think than anyone did for the Beveridge Committee. We set out a sort of agenda for the Beveridge Committee before there was a

Beveridge Committee. We published a lot on the need for a National Health Service. The whole thing went very much to the left in the war, I mean as the country went, so it was much more agreeable to me. And it was something like working out a policy for a Labour government, only not with any party labels to it...

And it was on the strength of all that that I got offered the job of secretary of the Research Department of the Labour Party. Morgan Phillips offered me the job. (C 408, pp 37–38)

In 1954, Michael left his role in the Labour Party and set up the Institute of Community Studies as an independent organisation.[2] Essentially, this had similar aims to PEP. It did not in fact carry out overall multi-theme studies of particular communities. Its focus was on social and health policy issues, combining an anthropological perspective on kinship with a belief in local community resilience. Its work was later much criticised for using contradictory theories and rough methods. But their early publications, such as Michael Young and Peter Willmott, *Family and Kinship in East London* (1957), *The Family Life of Old People* (1957) by *Peter Townsend*, and *Education and the Working Class* (1962) by Brian Jackson and *Dennis Marsden*, played a key role in firing public enthusiasm for the potential of sociology.

Central Statistical Office

Claus Moser suggests why the Central Statistical Office (CSO) was founded:

> Because people are poor at maths, and don't worry too much about accuracy – numerical accuracy – that led Churchill, no other, led Churchill to set up a CSO in 1940. Churchill said, one day, 'I can't stand getting different figures on shipping, and getting different figures from there, that Department, that Department, I'm going to have a Central Statistical Office'. That's how it started, and that made an impact. But it's always been a bit of a problem... It was always slightly easier to get people interested in economic measurements, but stuff like crime or education or health, and that was my field, and that's [where] my first boss, Harold Wilson, told me to focus. He appointed me because I was a social statistician – that was my interest – and he gave me total support, and we did improve all those figures, and we improved public attitudes.

I had a wonderful time, and things did change, and went on changing after I'd left – until Mrs. Thatcher came in, and Mrs. Thatcher – I'd already had some battles with her before when she was Education Minister, she wanted to abolish the Census. 'Who cares about a census?' She didn't think there was such a thing as society. But she was defeated. So we'd had our rows. (p 20)

Social Science Research Council and UK Data Archive

While he was working for the Labour Party *Michael Young* had published a pamphlet proposing a Social Science Research Council. He says:

Yes, it did help to get a precursor of things set up… I was keen on it, partly because I was still keen on social sciences. I mean I'm still keen, not in the way I was… I hoped to make social sciences – what I'd hoped for really when I started the Institute: the agitator and handmaiden of policy. Generator, agitator and – handmaiden is a bit too mild. Handman. (Laughs). Hangman of the government. (C 408, p 94)

It was eventually set up in 1965 and he became its first chair. It had already been decided it should be organised around subject committees covering Economic and Social History, Economics, Education, Human Geography, Management and Industrial Relations, Political Science, Psychology, Social Anthropology, Sociology and Social Administration and Statistics. Michael was also presented with a long list of potential board members.

I thought the structure they had was probably unavoidable. Which was basing it, at any rate to begin with, on disciplines. But I thought I'd have to do all this, because it would have to carry people in the universities with it. And the only way to influence people in universities was through people in the universities who were reasonably well respected in their different disciplines. But also I hoped to get really good lively people as well. And I took a great deal of trouble over picking of the people. I interviewed I suppose about sixty or more leading people in the social sciences, or not leading as well, and I asked all of them who they thought would be the best people to be on it. (C 408, p 96)

From this list he created a 'great grid', 'sociometry', and started interviewing for the board. 'And then I did a sort of great grid rather like Peter Townsend's. And – I mean got the people out of it.' He chose some who were thought 'the key people were in their own subjects' and rejected others whom he thought 'too hopeless'. He also had

> quite a few people who weren't from any subject at all. And that was one saving grace of it. But I didn't have enough of those. One chap became the secretary of the TUC... And a very good man from industry who is now the Chairman of the Abbey National Building Society. Campbell Adamson. And a few others. Some people from education. But I chose badly for education. Very badly. Lord James, God help me, was then the headmaster of Manchester Grammar school. He turned out to be my chief enemy on the Council. (C 408, pp 95–96)

As part of his plans for social research, Michael had also proposed a national Data Bank, which was set up with a grant from the SSRC in 1967. The idea was that surveys were very expensive but that the future of the social sciences lay in the analysis of data of this kind.

The subsequent changes of institutional name were to reflect not only changing attitudes among researchers but also the thinking of politicians. Thus in 1983 the SSRC was renamed as the Economic and Social Research Council (ESRC) as a compromise with the views of Conservative leaders such as Sir Keith Joseph or Mrs Thatcher who did not regard social research as a science or even in the existence of society. It enabled the Council's survival. More positively, in 1994, with the setting up of Qualidata, ESRC recognised that that qualitative data is also worth saving and sharing. And most recently the Archive's primary name has been changed to Service to emphasise its prime function.

However, in 1967 the plan was to establish an archive which would hold and distribute survey data in a computer-readable form, and that would not lend the data, but distribute the data in a computer-readable form to other social scientists who wanted to use it. However, it got off to a very slow start: too few depositors and too few users. *Ivor Crewe* became director in 1974 and soon realised there was a crisis brewing:

> When I arrived at the Data Archive in 1974, I remember, after a few days I saw a card file box, long card file box in the main office, and I asked Marcia Taylor, who was one of the Assistant Directors, what it was, and she said, 'It contains the names of

those who have been given data from the Data Archive'. So I opened it, expecting the drawer of this card file, which must have been about, I don't know, eighteen inches long, quite a long card file, to be crammed full of cards, and what I found was this thin pack of about 25 cards held together with an elastic band, and the rest of the drawer was empty. In fact, the Data Archive had had very very few users. It was due for a renewal of its SSRC funding, I think in 1976 – so another two years to go – and I knew that if the Data Archive couldn't demonstrate that it was of use to a very much larger number of social scientists than – none had used it so far, but the likelihood was its funding would be stopped. (p 26)

So he set about drumming for support and eventually, with senior colleagues in the Data Archive, trying to win more support and use for the Archive. 'We did get the number of users up by 1976', but the key turning point came soon after when they realised that what most prospective depositors wanted were

the very big government surveys or statistical databases, and they were interested in those studies that were repeated – longitudinal studies or panel studies – so the Labour Force Survey, the Government Social Survey, the Census, the National Expenditure Survey, National Food Survey, National Crime Survey, British Election Study. These were the kind of surveys that were in demand, and what the Archive had to do was to get the government to agree to deposit these surveys in the Archive... And that's what we tried to do in the late seventies and, I think, largely succeeded. The turning point was getting the government to deposit the Census data in the Data Archive, and the Labour Force Survey. After that, others followed. But once we'd broken that – once we'd persuaded the government to do that, then it was that much easier to get other Departments in Whitehall to submit their surveys. (pp 26–27)

There was a separate battle, successfully led by *Sara Arber* from Surrey, to get this survey material also available for teaching.

Academic centres

Within the universities, in parallel with the independent Institute of Community Studies, innovative social research could be organised both by individual departments or as special units. Particularly notably, social policy research was spearheaded at the LSE Department of Social Administration founded by Richard Titmuss. He became its first professor in 1950. *Townsend* says he left the Institute to work with Titmuss as an 'apprentice'. He in turn went on to give social policy initially a central place in the new department which he set up at Essex from 1964.

Medical sociology at Aberdeen and methods at Surrey

Similarly, Raymond Illsley ran a very strong Medical Sociology Unit in Aberdeen. *Mildred Blaxter*, who in the 1970s researched on the meaning of disability on an SSRC programme grant at the Unit, conveys some of the creative atmosphere that could develop in a specialised centre:

> [We were] a whole group of, at that time, and all – except for me, young – like-minded people who were interested in these new methodologies. And we talked and talked and talked… We had a Common Room, and the Common Room was the scene of where most of this went on. We all took different subjects, it resulted in books… A whole series of books. We were all inventing our own methods as we went along. I think this is terribly important. It was before qualitative methods had solidified…
>
> So we were all doing qualitative research, which was very much based on symbolic interactionism, ethnomethodology, it was more or less theoretical, depending upon taste. But it wasn't just pure sociology theory, because it was paid for by, at that time, SSRC, and it was under Raymond [Illsley]'s guidance, so it had practical purpose. It was about health and welfare services, and it had to have practical implications, to say something about these systems, or these professional relationships. So it was an amalgam of very practical Health Service stuff, with a fairly high level of theory. (pp 25–26)

Other institutions focussed especially on aspects of learning how to do research. Thus, from the 1960s Surrey University led the way as a nationally influential centre for methods training. This was broad-based in both scope and practice. *Sara Arber* recalls the approach of their founding professor:

Asher Tropp's view was that all researchers, all staff, should be doing empirical research. All students should learn how to do empirical research, it doesn't matter if it's qualitative or quantitative, but they should be collecting data, and analysing data about real-life issues, not just sitting and doing armchair theorising. So we all did that. So that's why I think we were very vibrant...

I think this is what has been fundamentally important about the Department of Sociology at Surrey, is that we are a Department which equally respects that there's a place for all these methods. I've taught qualitative methods – not very well – but on undergraduate courses, and if you're going to do good quantitative research, and I've run some surveys, you've got to start that good quantitative research with qualitative research. How do you know how to ask people things? What to ask people? So that good qualitative research underpins a good survey...

But we were teaching it years ago – to make sure those questions actually mean what you want them to mean. Rather than abstracted empiricism. (pp 33–34)

Centre for Contemporary Cultural Studies

The Centre for Contemporary Cultural Studies in Birmingham, founded in 1964 by Richard Hoggart, was intrinsically innovative in both its focus and internal workings. *Stuart Hall* was there from the start, and from 1968 its director. They had to set about creating a new field in which literary and qualitative social approaches were intertwined, and especially a critical analysis of the rising influence of the media. Stuart recalls how initially they 'didn't know what cultural studies was... I was making it up, and Richard was making it up! And the students were engaged in making it up! There's no cultural studies to teach. We were making it up out of elements, bringing all the elements together' (p 78). The involvement of the students in the process was particularly remarkable. It developed into an unusual model of co-operative research which was based on its student reading groups. Thus, there were reading groups on media, literature, Marx, Freud, race, feminism and so on. But not just reading:

They not only started to publish things, but they started to do some work of their own together. So, for instance, a section of people in the Centre started to work on popular magazines, and they worked on analysing an issue of *Woman* magazine, in which there was a story, and the story was called, 'Cure for Marriage'. 'Cure for Marriage' was about a woman, locked into the domestic role, always in the kitchen, etc., not really part of her husband's wider social life, who develops a fantasy relationship with Cary Grant, and has a dream about him. And this dream, as you can imagine, in a woman's magazine story, reconciles herself to her marriage, so everything's all right in the end. But we did an analysis of this.

Well, what was it? It wasn't anybody's thesis. The Centre had no publications of its own. It consisted of papers that every member of the Group contributed. You can't publish that in a journal, you can only publish it for other people in the Centre and slightly wider than that, by using the Roneo machine! So everybody used the Roneo machine, and produced what were called 'working papers'. And these working papers were the results of individual and collective research in the fields where the groups were working. (pp 102–104)

In practice, this semi-published collective working could rarely be sustained beyond the initial student phase. But it was an appealing alternative approach which reinforced the growth of small-scale qualitative studies in sociology as well as cultural studies.

One-off projects and community studies

Up until the 1970s, there were also a series of major collective social research ventures which attracted special attention. These ranged from David Glass's first national social mobility study to social policy projects such as *Peter Townsend*'s vast study of old people's homes. Here we focus on the two Banbury Studies and the Affluent Worker project which were seen as offering principal ways forward for social research.

The two Banbury Studies

The crucial importance of the first Banbury Study is that it was a community study of an ordinary middle-English town. There had been no British equivalent to the American *Middletown* series. Community studies had long been a typical form with anthropologists, but their studies in Britain were at the margins, in the rural west and Scotland. With *Tradition and Change: a Study of Banbury* (1960),

Margaret Stacey highlighted the potential of the community study as a key sociological method.

Margaret (later *Meg*) *Stacey* was a Londoner, was the daughter of feminist parents, and her father an independent small printer. She studied sociology and social work at the LSE, and then worked in a Clydeside war factory. She came to Banbury in 1944 as an Oxford extramural-teacher. It was then a small market town and her key role was teaching workers in its new wartime aluminium factory. The idea for a community project arose while she was teaching a three-year class with these factory workers. She got the class researching on how Banbury was changing. She wanted to do more with this material. 'I took *Middletown* and *Middletown in Transition* as models of a kind' (p 18). With a small grant from Nuffield, two assistants (one a volunteer) and the continuing help of her extramural students, the Banbury Study was launched. It was based on an interview survey and some participant observation. The book from the project eventually came out in 1960. It proved highly successful.

> So the first Banbury Study was very well received, to my amazement! It was thought to be important, and it was on everybody's syllabus, and everybody who was young, at that time, had to read it in their undergraduate courses and stuff. So that made it relatively easy to, I suppose, say, 'Let's have another study like this'. So I got the money for it. (p 39)

The second Banbury Study was again funded by Nuffield, this time much more generously with sufficient resources for three professional research workers as well as volunteer helpers from an extramural class of 35. But fieldwork nevertheless proved much less easy. The story becomes a joint one with *Colin Bell*, who was to become the best known of her researchers. Colin had read history and geography at Keele where he was inspired to take up community studies by *W. M. Williams*. He went on to Swansea, writing his thesis and first book, *Middle Class Families* (1968) – and there meeting *Margaret Stacey*.

From early on, there were troubles between the three fieldworkers. Margaret had chosen Anne Murcott to 'interact with the women', Eric Batstone to explore the more traditional local Conservatives, and *Colin Bell* to work with Banbury's trade unionists and 'labour people'. It seems that none of the three researchers were enthusiastic about living in Banbury, which Margaret herself had 'loved'. For Margaret now had a job in Swansea and a young family, so she could not supervise easily. She put Colin, as the most experienced fieldworker, in charge.

But there were 'manifold problems' which he failed to sort out. 'He was a good, brilliant fieldworker, as I say, but he wasn't a good team leader' (pp 39–40). Thus, the two men complained that Anne was too often out of the office socialising with other women – which precisely what she was supposed to be doing!

Meanwhile, Colin was becoming increasingly critical of the whole research design, and these doubts pervaded the writing-up of the project. He doubted whether a community study was possible in a town as large as 20,000, rather than in a small town or village. He complained that the interview guide confused class and status, and that despite Margaret's feminism they were classifying households by the work of men. He thought that the questions were not focussed enough on change. But then he no longer believed in her concept of 'tradition and change'. A replication or follow-up was not possible without belief in the concepts of the first study. He foresaw that a book written by a disagreeing committee was not likely to be a big hit. And, indeed, when *Power, Persistence and Change* was published in 1975 it had none of the impact of the first Banbury Study.

The Affluent Worker

Meanwhile, in between the two Banbury Studies, the three volumes of the *Affluent Worker* study had come out in 1963–69 and secured their long-standing place in sociology teaching. It was undoubtedly a prestigious project, financed by the government Department of Scientific and Industrial Research and based at Cambridge, where its two leaders, *John Goldthorpe* and *David Lockwood*, were both very early sociology appointments. Both were also from working-class Yorkshire backgrounds. John's family were miners, while David's father was a shoemaker who died early, so that David had to leave school and work in a textile factory. They had also both been to the LSE and were now at Cambridge. There were two others in the research team, *Frank Bechhofer* and Jennifer Platt, both with distinguished later careers. The project had a double social class credibility from its leadership: a sniff of what the new sociology could offer.

The study focussed on Luton car workers and how far the impact of higher pay with the skilled workers might be affecting their attitudes to their work, social class, and political allegiances. Luton was chosen as a critical case study because it had a concentration of well-paid workers, so that any impact should show up clearly. The answer was largely negative: attitudes to class were not changing very much.

Looking back, for *Frank Bechhofer* the project's lasting legacy is its brilliant research design. But the long-term influence of the Affluent Worker is less easy to evaluate. This is partly because neither of its two leaders have been at ease to speak a full story. *David Lockwood* says little. *John Goldthorpe* now describes it as only significant in terms of industrial sociology. He says, 'I don't think there's anything remarkably new in the *Affluent Worker* studies' and they 'should have been consigned to history 20 or 30 years ago' (pp. 36–37). *Colin Bell* has raised the interesting suggestion that the project was originally intended to be a wider community study and the interview questionnaires asked for much information on family relationships, which it seems was collected but never analysed. A volume on family relationships was promised but never appeared. Why was the opportunity for a full community study missed?

The high moment of community studies and beyond

The late 1960s were the high moment of community studies in sociology. For example, another crucial project was *Race, Community and Conflict* (1967), a study of Sparkbrook, an immigrant area in Birmingham, by *Robert Moore* and John Rex. *Colin Bell* describes this as 'the most important book written on institutional racism ever, probably, and it was done in a community'. Nevertheless, it was Colin himself, with *Howard Newby*, who dealt a hammer blow when in 1971 they published *Community Studies: an Introduction to the Sociology of the Local Community*. Their critique exposed the underlying confusions in the theories of community and change then used in the genre. It should be said that they could have launched similar attacks at many other forms of sociology. And it was a paradox that it came from Colin. As he puts it, he became 'famous for writing this book that killed the field that you're meant to be in love with… And I feel guilty' (p 91). But the critique was powerful, and hard to answer. It destroyed the confidence of sociologists in community studies as a research form for the future.

The most promising signs of later revival came in the 1980s. In Kent *Ray Pahl* had begun his Isle of Sheppey study of family and work in 1978. He was generating new interpretations about the informal economy and the contrasts between work-rich and work-poor households. A much wider opportunity then came with the Social Change and Economic Life Initiative (SCELI), which was launched by the SSRC in 1983 in defence against Thatcherite attacks on the value of social research, and was intended to show in a broad way the relevance of social research. It was led by *Duncan Gallie*, who designed it with a subtle combination of a core set of issues about employment and families researched in six localities, contrasted in terms of unemployment or prosperity. It was intended that the local teams could develop additional themes and would produce their own community study. 'So the community contrasts drove very intensely the original conception of it.' But very surprisingly, the local teams failed to find inspiration in the particularities of their localities, and chose to relate more to the national core issues. 'Each team was supposed to produce a separate monograph on its locality, and they notably failed to do this' (pp 41–42). Had they lost the knack of finding meaning through community studies? Or was this a failure of nerve? Either way, it looks to have been a big loss, even seemingly ending what had once been an influential and popular type of sociological research.

National surveys and evolving quantitative analysis

Meanwhile, very different new types of social research were developing with national quantitative surveys. There were already many existing sources. The government had long supported the Census, and a whole range of economic, health, educational and other surveys were supported by Departments. There were also three independently run longitudinal studies: the 1946, 1958 and 1970 birth cohorts. The first was supported by the Medical Research Council, and run by James Douglas, a left-wing doctor. The two others were less secure in their backing. They were run by Neville Butler, a visionary Professor of Child Health at Bristol, whose fund-raising efforts involved big parties, and rallying large numbers of volunteer teachers as survey workers. These cohorts were joined in the 1980s by the new British Household Panel Study at Essex.

However, these large surveys had been very little used for research. The first reason was that they had not been usually accessible. This began to change in the mid-1970s, when *Sara Arber* won access to the official General Household Survey data for teaching. Before long official surveys began to be deposited in the Data Archive for public use. And very gradually, detailed documentation was introduced to help users. Even the Census became partly available for social and medical researchers through a special longitudinal sample.

The second reason was that before computerisation large data sets were very hard to analyse. *John Bynner* recalls that even Neville Butler didn't believe that you could do longitudinal analysis, because he couldn't see how you could link the data. 'It was just too big, too vast' (p 45). This began to change from the 1960s with the rapid development of computer technology and the new mathematical forms of analysis which then became possible. The computer itself was still a rarity in the mid-1960s, an excitement in itself. As *Harvey Goldstein* remembers: 'About 1964, there was one computer for the whole of the University of London! You had to queue up to use it… I thought it was wonderful, because the things you had to do before with hand-calculating machines, little mechanical machines… It was a great liberation… We thought this was wonderful, this was the future – and it was. We learnt how to programme' (pp 48–49).

The lead in the early pioneering was American. Thus, the first national British study of social mobility had been carried out in 1949–54 by David Glass in an elementary quantitative style. In the late 1960s *John Goldthorpe* had become interested in social mobility and as he recalls:

> I became aware that I did need to improve my statistical knowledge. Because by that time you had people like Otis Dudley Duncan in the States using regression approaches to social mobility, and then developing these into causal path analysis. So I began to be more aware of how relatively advanced statistical techniques could have major sociological potential. (p 25)

So, when John and his Nuffield colleagues Jean Floud and Chelly Halsey launched their re-study in the late 1960s, they brought over Otis Dudley Duncan to show them how to design and analyse a new national study. Others learnt the new skills in America. *Elizabeth Thomas-Hope* learnt computerised spatial analysis through her time at Penn State in the late 60s, while in the early 70s *Sara Arber* began postgraduate work at Ann Arbor, Michigan, where she was fired with enthusiasm both for gender perspectives and for secondary data analysis. Typically, by then they were using Statistical Package for the Social Sciences (SPSS). She calls the student assignments 'cutting edge stuff at the time':

> we were using punch-cards, we were analysing real data, general social survey data and other US [surveys]. So the US was way way ahead of us in terms of methodology. They had what they called 'Public Use Samples' from the American Census, from 1950, 1960, 1970, so a lot of my colleagues, both the lecturers and the academics, and the students, were using real data. (pp 19–20)

In a similar spirit as late as 1979–80 *John Bynner* spent a year in 1979–80 at the Institute of Social Research at Ann Arbor, 'where I really learnt how computing, how the use of statistics, everything was really done' (p 34).

There can be no doubt that the growing interpretative power of computerisation brought deep changes to British social research. Essentially, it widened the divisions between different types of researchers. On the one hand it brought new opportunities for advanced teaching as well as research. A few could become creative in further methodological developments, such as *Harvey Goldstein*, who was already trained in mathematics and statistics, and played a key role from the 1980s in developing and testing new statistical modelling techniques, most notably in multilevel modelling technology. Some researchers, among them *Peter Townsend*, switched much of their focus from ethnographic to quantitative evidence, testing its new potential as 'the really creative stage' in analysis (p 110). But there were also large numbers of researchers both then and subsequently who – no doubt often due to inadequate earlier teaching as well as the climate of innumeracy in British culture – lacked the confidence to take on computerised numeracy and turned away altogether from numbers towards purely qualitative research. And towards the split which is discussed in our Chapter 5.

The growing contrasts in scale and time-space as the older pattern of stand-alone projects gave way to repeating large-scale surveys meant that there were more research work opportunities of an administrative kind. They certainly have had key problems which needed inventive solutions. For example, while many social researchers are glad to have their data available for re-use, medical scientists more often see the material which they collect as private. As *John Bynner* comments, 'it's been a battle, and it's a matter – I think a very interesting one – of two different cultures about this... That's been a major tension for years. It's not fully resolved even now, though there's been a move more and more in the social science direction' (pp 39–40). There is a parallel conflict between openness of access and the confidentiality offered to interviewees.

A third recurrent problem is response rates. With birth cohorts this has always been so. Many devices – such as sending out birthday cards – are used to attach interviewees from childhood, hopefully for life. Yet, nearly every cohort gradually becomes a group of social survivors. Response rates have also become a problem with one-off surveys. And with factory case studies *Duncan Gallie* remarks that with declining union power and tighter management control 'time has been squeezed out in work situations' so it is no longer possible to fit interviews in (p 35).

There are also hints in these interviews of a widening gap between administrators whose professional pride is in producing 'clean' data and the experience of research at fieldwork level. This risks cutting them off from other signs of changing social realities. Some administrators have little experience of interviewing, show little interest in the process or in what people are saying, and do not use verbatim quotes in their reports. But as *Sara Arber* remarks, for them this may be the essence of the job: 'I like numbers, yes. That's why I'm a quantitative sociologist I suppose. But I like numbers because of what they're trying to tell me about class inequalities in health, or gender and inequalities, or whatever it is. You're analysing somebody else's data, yes. You don't need – you just need a data set. You don't need to talk to people' (p 23).

Another continuing issue is how far social research should have directly expressed policy recommendations. There is a long Civil Service tradition of political neutrality which has been closely guarded. *Claus Moser* recalled his anger when Harold Wilson tried to interfere with his reporting on the economy. Although there was also an openly political tradition in social policy, large-scale surveys implied more dependence on funding bodies, whether public or private. As public political culture gradually moved to the right, shocking disclosures and radical recommendations such as those which *Peter Townsend* published in *The Last Refuge* (1962) became much rarer. Some still spoke out, but for others it seemed wiser to be more discreet, or silent. *Sara Arber* comments: 'You do research because you find it interesting and important, but then it's up to somebody else to do the policy' (p 44). For *Karen Dunnell*, who earlier worked in independent social policy research, once she was within the Civil Service, 'well, you did refer to the policy implications, but that really wasn't the job' (p 25).

Lastly, there was a key institutional influence in the reshaping of research careers. Inevitably, the change brought a fiercer thirst for money, between one-off projects, surveys and between institutions. It was this which led *John Bynner*, after fruitful years researching on youth in the social policy field, to become a shrewd and successful entrepreneurial builder of research institutions.

The rise of longitudinal studies

One of the most striking instances of this changing research world is the rise of longitudinal studies, as recorded by *John Bynner*. A London insurance clerk's son, John studied psychology at Bristol University where he became active in the Student Union. He ran a brief survey on student meals which proved a crucial moment. To his surprise 'the University responded very well to the report, and immediately set in an action plan for doing what I recommended! So I was absolutely amazed!' But from then onwards, 'collecting data, and then seeing action arising from it, became a very important theme of my career... You've actually made a contribution, as well as just improving understanding, you improve action' (p 11).

In this social reforming spirit John worked on a variety of survey projects: first the Sexual Behaviour of Young People run by Michael Schofield; next, in 1963–70 with the Government Social Survey – where he learnt much more about surveys, although he was then still without a computer – while focussing himself on young people's smoking; and after that to work at the Open University. From that base he took part in the follow-up from the Plowden Committee's 1963 Report on English Primary School Education at the time of the same children's transition to secondary education. This is what alerted him to the potential of longitudinal studies and the crucial importance of the time dimension in research.

Nevertheless, the key turning point came only in the early 1980s. The 1958 cohort was struggling for a renewal of its funding, and criticised because so few researchers were using the survey which had been deposited in the Data Archive. John was asked by the ESRC to evaluate the situation. He wrote a positive report published in 1983, which recommended advertising the data, making it more easily accessible, setting up a User Support Unit, and moving the whole enterprise from the National Children's Bureau to City University, where it was run by John Fox. But when Fox left in 1988 Bynner took over control of the cohort. Then in turn the 1970 cohort ran into serious financial trouble. Neville Butler came to beg John to take it over. It was an enormous risk, a huge task, and he was advised against it. But John could see the potential of having two cohort studies which could be compared. 'I thought I would move heaven and earth to do it'.[3] He succeeded in managing both projects effectively. John had also gained some experience of difficult conflicts. When Neville Butler retired from Bristol in the late 1980s 'there was a battle royal about who owned it... It went into court and all the rest of it, as to who owned the Study' (p 23). But then, in the early 1990s, when the British Household Panel Study had just begun its fieldwork, he faced perhaps his biggest challenge, his 'battles' with the ESRC and Essex.

That was decided in a national strategy developed by ESRC, that the future of these longitudinal studies lay in one place. We, at one time, were kind of in partnership, then we were bidding against each other for who would run the UK Centre for Longitudinal Studies. Now, the ESRC had always been very keen to get the best return it could from the Essex centre, which was a real gold-plated enterprise... That was the jewel in the crown for ESRC, and they thought it made sense to co-ordinate all this. They had various consultants and people who recommended it. (pp 72–73)

John smartly set up a Joint Centre for Longitudinal Research at City University as a battlefront. 'We managed to fight that off – the takeover – partly because the nature of the [cohort] studies that we were doing was so different from the Panel Study' (pp 72–73). And he went on to set up a Centre for Longitudinal Studies at the Institute of Education, now at UCL, where the two cohorts became based. In John's career, in short, we see yet another type of researcher. His principal contribution, as he sees it, was his role in 'the institutionalisation of the life course' (p 44). He had the imagination to see what could be done, a vision for longitudinal studies, and how the cohorts and institutions could be handled and remodelled; but he also became a tough fighter for his corner.

VOICES 4

Old and new trends

Research projects are rarely straightforward. However logically first planned, their success depends on negotiating misfortunes such as ill-health or interpersonal competition, and also rivalry between different groups in the wider research world. Here are some accounts of conflict and also of building up research groupings.

Difficulties in community studies

Colin Bell and Margaret Stacey on the Banbury Studies

Much was expected of Margaret Stacey's second Banbury Study. It proved a disappointment, and a turning point, the start of the decline of community studies. *Colin Bell*, lead fieldwork researcher, reflects on the tangle of intellectual doubts and personal difficulties which led to this crucial disappointment:

> *So, to Banbury. Your Tikopia. You once wrote, 'Banbury will forever be the social system with which I compare all else. It is my Nuer land and my Tikopia.'*
>
> You see, that's there. You see, it was there, I really wanted to be a proper anthropologist! I think that's no longer true. And I went through Banbury fairly recently, and was quite sort of taken aback with the changes. But it was, it was expansive fieldwork. It was a full community. It was a full range, there were poor people, there were titled people. It had a working economy, an aluminium factory. While we were there General Foods moved Maxwell House Coffee and Birds Custard out of the centre of Birmingham to Banbury...
>
> I think, this is almost metaphysical, and I don't really think I understood – I do now – the constraints that anyone who does a replication, is going to be under, if the person who wrote the first study, which is a bloody good book – a bloody good book – the constraints I was actually under, and I don't think, deep down, I didn't own those constraints, I hadn't internalised those constraints. Loads of the trouble there really was, was me

not really, really understanding that you didn't have the kind of freedom to do anything you liked. It wasn't your Tikopia, it was Margaret's Tikopia. That's the mistake. Banbury was Margaret's Banbury, and I ought to have understood that...

It could have been done easily, superficially. And I think the book (*Power, Persistence and Change*, 1975) is astonishingly superficial – our book, not Margaret's. Our book is astonishingly superficial. And in part it was because – well, because I left the project, I suppose – but also I no longer had any faith, belief, in Margaret's *Tradition and Change* model, that there was tradition and then there was the non-tradition. She does – I mean, the terms that we just started to use at those times, and we used to talk about all things 'reified', is it a social system? With people, the social system? Is he a traditionalist? Is he a non-traditionalist? We got ourselves in a massive confusion over those sorts of things. (pp 59, 60, 61)

There was another thing about the design, that you mentioned, that you felt the survey was not deep enough to really be meaningful.

I think it was too sociographic. There's very few attitudinal questions in it, very little about culture. We were counting, in a rather narrow sort of way...

We hadn't theorised the difference between class, status and other dimensions. It was all terribly occupational against the Registrar General. Anne has said to me since, and she's right, that notwithstanding the fact that Margaret was a kind of proto-feminist, you couldn't handle female occupations at all well, or female activity. Households were classed, as they are in social mobility studies, by the occupation of the man. I think I found none of that stuff terribly interesting, in the end.

We weren't even thinking about changes. I've thought about it a lot since, so I know we weren't thinking about it then, changes in the British class structure between the period of reconstruction, say '45–'50, and the period of the beginning of affluence. If only words like that had been used in the second Banbury Study, the book would be a lot more interesting. You see, *The Affluent Worker* wasn't out. The first *Affluent Worker* article is in the first volume of *Sociology*, which didn't come out until 1967. We didn't know how to conceptualise affluence, and affluence and the class structure. (pp 73–74)

Why do you think it's a failure? In what sense do you mean that?

102

I don't think it adds much to the first study. I think the first study is a gigantically important book in British social science. I think you have to read *Tradition and Change* if you're interested in modern British society. I don't think you have to read the follow-up study at all, I think it's a great disappointment. (pp 76–77)

Margaret Stacey reflected:

There was this big difference between the first and the second studies, that the first one, you can properly say it was fairly amateur, but it was also amateur in the sense that it was being done for the love of it, and that has a good deal of its own merit over against the very professional approach...

And by the time we came to do the second study, which wasn't all that much later, there really had been a sort of great bursting forth of sociology, a certain amount of it on the American model still... But it's difficult to really talk about it too much, because there was a very public squabble about it, and you've no doubt read what Colin had to say. (pp 37, 39)

Anyway, I was in Swansea and had young children, and there was no way I could be in Banbury very much. So I put Colin in charge of it, who was senior, because he was older and had done more research, and he was a brilliant fieldworker...

The problems? Well an important lot of problems came around Anne, because the blokes complained to me that she wasn't working and so on, and she complained that they weren't being nice to her. And she wasn't in the office... But she wasn't being paid to be in the office, she was being paid to interact with the women...

Colin was a good, brilliant fieldworker, but he wasn't a good team leader... So that turned out, that study, to be far less – although it was richly endowed – far less satisfactory than the other one. And when Colin finally walked out... I found it very difficult, and I've never really – I've never made a reply to any of that stuff that he came up with...

It's very strange, and it made me conclude that, really, replication isn't possible... In any tidy sort of way. I'd always resisted the idea, which I read in various places, that you couldn't do these things because personalities were so much involved, or individuality if not personality. But I really began to feel that that might be so. (pp 39–41)

Duncan Gallie: The Social Change and Economic Life Initiative

SCELI was a last chance in the 1980s that also failed to show the potential of community studies. It did not work out like that. It was led by Duncan Gallie. The focus on the local and particular was being edged out by the growing confidence in survey-based research:

> What I recommended was a sequence, a series of inter-connected surveys, so you would have work attitudes, work experiences, work history survey, and attached to that, floating off it, you would have an employers' survey, and you would have a household survey where we interviewed both partners, so it was quite an interconnected data set. (p 38)
>
> The community contrasts drove very intensely the original conception of it. They diminished as the analysis went on. People became more concerned with the themes and what the overall pattern of the data showed about those themes. And the community studies never, never really materialised. (p 42)
>
> We all started off from the assumption we were going to find really major differences, there would be differences which would be related to level of unemployment, so the experience of unemployment would be very different in high unemployment communities than in low, and that the past historical experiences within each of these sub-groups would lead to very different [patterns]. This didn't turn out to be the case.
>
> I think one of the things that puzzled us as we went through was that, actually, experiences were remarkably similar for people who were either in employment, or in unemployment, across these communities, so people who experienced unemployment in one of the more prosperous areas, actually experienced it just as severely as people who were in a high unemployment area. So we found relatively few differences at the level of community comparisons, and I think, in the book, one of the striking things is that, actually, although the different areas are in there as sort of control variables, there's not a great deal of direct comparison of [localities] because people were not finding anything that was very interesting. Each team was supposed to produce a separate monograph on its locality, and they notably failed to do this. (pp 41–42)

Computers come to social research

Meanwhile, the whole world of social research was being transformed by the introduction of computing and its growing power. The result was an exciting but often confusing scene of rapid step-by-step change:

Harvey Goldstein: London University's first computer – the young and the old react

> About 1964, there was one computer for the whole of the University of London! And you had to queue up to use it. Called an 'input queue', and the 'output queue' was at the other end of the computer... There was, literally, one computer, just down the road – at Mortimer Market. But soon that changed.
>
> *When the computer came, were you glad, or were you concerned?*
>
> I thought it was wonderful, because the things you had to do before with hand-calculating machines, little mechanical machines – when I came to University College, there were Ph.D. students who did nothing for three years but turn the handles – well, these were electric calculating machines – but do calculations. That's what they did. They were exploited, of course. And they usually came from Greece. But (Laughs) can you imagine it!... It was a great liberation...
>
> *Do you think, did some of your older colleagues find it hard to adapt?*
>
> Yes. I mean, there was one, one member of staff who ran a course on computing. And who went? It was all the younger lecturers, and the graduate students. We were really, we thought this was wonderful, this was the future – and it was. But the professors didn't go. We learnt how to programme.
>
> *So did you overtake them quite quickly because they couldn't do it?*
>
> I guess they used their research assistants to do it. Yes. No, that [older] generation never learnt. (pp 48–49)

Elizabeth Thomas-Hope: computing at Penn State, US, late 1960s

> In those days we had to develop our own computer programme... Because you had to develop, you had to insert your algorithm into a computer framework, in a framework for it being read

by the computer. And, of course, in those days you went to a computer room or place, in Penn State it was quite a big building and they had this huge computer somewhere, which you didn't see, but you were sat at a desk with cards that you had to then type into, and leave for them to put into the computer, and so, if it didn't work, if your algorithm had a blip in it, you had to then go back and bring it out again and put it in again. Yes, we learned, it was certainly difficult having to work your way through what we now just do automatically – we use a programme, and we have no idea how the programme really works, from a computer point of view. It was a good training in logic, a good exercise in logic, trying to work out how a computer thought. So that's what we had to do. (pp 21–22)

Sara Arber: SPSS at Ann Arbor[1]

Basically it was just a computer programme which – to analyse data files. You do a survey of a thousand people, and they're all asked lots of questions, and that data file has got rows of variables, answers to each of those questions, probably columns, and then the other way round would be the [answers] of each person, so you've got, like, a big matrix there, of a thousand people, lines of their data for each of those questions. So it's just relating the different things together, so you could look at, 'What is the level of class inequalities in health?' You know, 'These are the health of people who are middle-class', 'These are the health of the people who are working-class. Are they different?' 'Why are they different?' And then putting in other variables to try to understand why.

The data would have been on magnetic tape, at the time, so the data would have been put on punch cards, and then the punch cards would have been read on to a magnetic tape as a big file. Read by a computer – big main frame computers then. And then the programme was SPSS programme. We would write, so I learnt how to write SPSS syntax – that's the only way you do it – so you could re-code age as a linear variable into age groups, or education or what have you, and then do a cross tab of health by class, by age, so you're looking at class difference in health, and does that differ by gender, or differ by age and so on.

So what I learnt there was to do SPSS runs, to do the statistical analysis. So I did the statistical analysis courses, which wasn't just cross tabs, but it was kind of multiple regression and other sorts of function analysis and this, that, and the other. But we would do the exercises using SPSS to do that statistical analysis. Then we'd have to interpret the statistical analysis which came out of the SPSS – the print-out. So we would do the cards on a punch card machine, you'd sit at a machine here, and you'd punch like typing, and it types patterns of holes, basically, and those patterns of holes are read by the computer to mean, you know, whatever the instructions are, and it's sent away to the computer, and you get your results the next day, or an hour later, and that comes out, it's printed out on this great computer paper. (pp 20–21)

Harvey Goldstein: multi-level modelling

In the 1960s and 1970s, people engaged in educational research – not me, because I hadn't really gone into it by then – were very concerned about what was often called the 'Unit of Analysis Problem'. And that is, briefly, you've got children, you've got schools, and you want to look at relationships, for example between attainment and social background, whatever. Do you do it at the level of the school – in other words, do you relate average attainment of school to the average social background of the children, or do you do it at the child level? And there's a literature about this, because they were actually, if you can, do them both – because both are important...

Around about 1980, in this country mainly – someone called Murray Aitken... I and he, and another group in the United States, more or less independently worked out how to do this statistically. We're all doing it different ways, but coming to the same conclusions. So we began to realise that we were actually doing the same things, but using different computing techniques to get to the answers. And that became known as 'multi-level modelling'...

So – being a bit technical – it's a generalisation of something called 'regression analysis', which has been a standard technique for donkeys' years, but this enables you to use that technique and similar techniques when you have data that has a complicated structure. In this case, you've got children who are grouped within schools, so the performance of any given child is affected by the fact they're in this school rather than some other school. It may be the quality of the teaching in the school, it may be that one school is more selective than another, so

107

knowing which school a child is in tells you already something about the child's likely attainment. And that's information that is informative. So how do you incorporate that information, when you're studying relationships at the child level? So do children with high attainment come from socially advantaged backgrounds? How do you take into account the effect of the school when you know that schools matter in terms of children differ between schools. So that's what it's about. It's how to deal with structures that have that hierarchical structure...

Then the really nice thing is that once you've worked out how you deal with that, and that involves some fancy computing, then it turns out that those techniques apply to all sorts of other structures, in the world... You can apply it to hospitals, you can apply it to all sorts of disciplines. You can apply it commercially, you can apply it to firms who have outlets, different outlets for different places. (pp 45–47)

The rise of longitudinal studies

John Bynner: the time dimension in research

It was at this point, from [the Plowden follow-up] you realised the importance of time?

Absolutely. And the beginnings of a life course perspective that, really, people's lives are shaped by these experiences happening through the normal developmental process of just the environments in which people grow in, but also the influence of policy on that – policy frameworks, external events – and in other words, a historical dimension to the understanding of human development, which is bringing that secular change into the picture as well. And the more I got into this, the more I realised the limitation, say, of psychology, that had no interest, whatsoever, in social change! ...

Well, it's time in a variety of ways. It's historical time, developmental time – yes, absolutely! And the time at which you do things, the time at which you collect data, the period effect. I've written a number of things about this. Time is really vital and quite complex, because it has these three effects on data at any point in time – the period, the cohort and the development. (pp 31–32)

John Bynner: the transformation of analysis

That you, on a memory stick, that big, you can capture 30 gigabytes of storage, and that means you can have the whole of the British Household Study just there in front of you, you know! So this is a massive change. It's a massive change in terms of what you can do, statistically, in terms of analysis, but also what you can do in terms of storage and secondary analysis. This whole resource becomes feasible in a massive way. The institutionalisation of the life course [paper] will be published later this year... But there I say there are three things that have happened. One was the technological transformation of this field through the access to manipulation and storage of data. The second is that that released analytic potential on a scale that was unbelievable, because the mathematics became reality in terms of actual procedures and processes that could be used with ease, of which structural equation modelling is one of the classic examples. And the third was theory. Theory, itself, could take off, because it could become holistic, interdisciplinary, anything you like, because you could encompass such a wider range of evidence and information... You can test, yes, you can utilise data on a very wide scale across time, particularly the time dimension becomes incredibly important. (p 44)

CHAPTER 5

Fighting or mixing: quantitative and qualitative research

This chapter focuses on the age-old debate in the social sciences about the primacy of methods and the relationship of our Pioneers to one of the main ideological battles blighting disciplines such as sociology. There are a variety of methods that are used in the social sciences to uncover different questions. They can be grouped into two main strands – qualitative methods (involving participant observation, structured in-depth interviews, unstructured interviews, and focus groups) and quantitative methods (such as secondary survey data analysis, and experimental methods) with a backbone of usually inferential statistical techniques. Every researcher makes a conscious decision to adopt a method in their social enquiry and it would have been extremely unusual for the Pioneers not to engage with a sometimes oppressive responsibility to pick a 'side', and the dogmatic prescription to stick with it.

For some of the Pioneers, the primacy of one of the methods over the other is undoubted. As we have seen, *John Goldthorpe* led two of the key projects in post-war British sociology, first on the Affluent Worker and then on social mobility. He became one of the strongest supporters of quantitative methods; and homage to survey techniques underlies the active current of his interview, and indeed of his career. He argues clearly for the importance of quantification in sociology to bring the discipline to scientific rigour. John sees British sociology as weakened by the debate and the rejection of positivism. In his own words:

> This so-called 'reaction against positivism', and then the attacks on quantitative methods, and I thought – and I still think – that was the big disaster in British sociology. I really didn't have much sympathy, or very much patience, to be honest, with the various alternatives that were floated around, ranging from phenomenology and ethnomethodology at one extreme to weird forms of structuralist Marxism, Althusser, et al – at the other. I thought that was going nowhere. (p. 25)

Importantly, John was highly aware of how his academic standpoint brought him into an ideological war with his colleagues who were less interested in quantification, and ultimately brought about isolation from British sociology. By contrast he felt a natural affinity with European traditions, especially with French sociology:

> The same year, or around that same period, I remember going to one or two BSA Conferences, and one on race relations in particular, when nobody seemed to be reporting very much research on race relations. It was all going around sniffing each others' position, whether they were racist or not. There was all this ideological argument. And that was my last BSA Conference. I stopped subscribing to BSA, and I've never been a member since then. It's sad, in a way, but I just didn't find what was happening in British sociology very appealing, and not intellectually interesting. So I was very fortunate that, you know, I had these European contacts. (p 46)

Thus, his insistence on identifying empirical regularities and trying to explain them transcended for John the study of any particular society and became a universal language with which he engaged in debates across the Atlantic and in Europe. He felt that this eventually made his professional involvement in British bodies untenable. It certainly created a number of acute frictions with colleagues. Isolation loomed large, either self-imposed or actively inflicted we might never know (we cannot judge on the extent of hostility towards him as it does not appear as a theme in the interviews):

> Since the mid-seventies, I've had very little connection with British sociology. I was editor of *Sociology* when I first came here [to Oxford] – '69-'72 – and I found it increasingly difficult to deal with the BSA Committee, because I followed Michael Banton, who was first editor, and we both put together a Board we thought comprised the people who were doing the most important work in British sociology at the time. There were some very good people there. People at Liverpool still doing industrial sociology, Raymond Illsley in Scotland, doing very good medical sociology, and I think, if you look at the people who were on the Board at that time, they all did have very well-deserved and well-established reputations. But I was under constant pressure from the BSA Executive to change. We had to have so many Marxists, and so many phenomenologists, and so many women, and so

many people from Polytechnics. I thought, 'No, that is not the way to go'. So relations became more and more strained, and I didn't want to do a second term as editor, and I don't suppose I would have been allowed to do so anyway! (p 46).

The less connected John became with British sociology, the greater his personal and professional involvement in European research. This affinity with European researchers stemmed from methodological camaraderie, an understanding that 'other people in other European countries were having the same difficulty as I felt here' (p 45). John's work builds up almost a geographical divide that positions European and American sociology – and especially the major American journals – on one hand; and British sociology on the other:

[Looking back now] I feel pleased that I could do something to push sociology on in the way in which I think it should go. No, I just enjoyed it. It was a very exciting time. And what I – to be honest, what I feel – if it's a case of feeling proud – what I feel more proud about is the part that I've been able to play from a more, if you like, organisational standpoint in European sociology. I was one of the founder editors of the *European Sociological Review*, which we had to found because other people in other European countries were having the same difficulty as I felt here, that there weren't journals that would want our work, or where we would want it to appear. And that's now going very well indeed...

And then I was one of the people who helped found the European Consortium for Sociological Research, which is going strong still, and bringing together institutions in Europe with similar ideas of where sociology should be going, and what it should be like. We've now, I think, over 40 institutions affiliated to the Consortium. Then more recently, I wasn't involved in an organising role, but I was an active participant in two EU networks of Centres of Social Excellence... So I was very fortunate that, you know, I had these European contacts. (pp 45–46).

Prompted by his disappointments in the British profession, John appears very cognisant in his interview of the position of isolation in which he finds himself in Britain. This alienation has reached almost an extreme in which he has stopped identifying with the subject area or finding any common ground with British sociologists that do not espouse the same methodological leanings. Could he have tried harder, should he have tried harder given his position of authority? A resounding 'No'

113

comes through the interview and leads more credence to the idea of self-imposed boundaries.

> I've not been able to do the same things that I've done in a European sociological context, in a British context. Since the mid-seventies, I've just felt a complete outsider as far as British sociology is concerned, and I've not seen any way of doing that, because I think the prevailing conception of sociology in Britain since the mid-seventies has been so different to what I would have in mind. So that it's been very difficult to do anything. If I look at a journal like *Sociology*, or the *Sociological Review*, it's as if it's a different subject, a different discipline to the one that I work in. I can't see any common ground at all. Well, BJS [*British Journal of Sociology*] is a bit more mixed. But that's been I think the major disappointment. And some time towards the end of the seventies, when I had this very good group of graduate students, or people who were just starting their academic careers, we talked about this, and I said, 'Do you think there would be any point in getting more involved in the BSA and trying to change it?' And we talked about this, and their view, in the end, was 'Well, no'. They'd rather just get on with doing their own work more in a European context, and not bother with British sociology. (pp 63–64)

On the other side of the debate, the opposite end of the spectrum, we have *Judith Okely*, who as an anthropologist has worked on many themes, ranging from Roma families to girls' boarding schools and the professional practices of anthropologists themselves. Unlike John Goldthorpe, Judith embraces the importance of following one's insights as an anthropologist. She argues against hypothesis testing (the foundation of John's methodological universe) but in favour of a 'wandering' approach that brings about knowledge and understanding of life's puzzle through raising research questions and also being ready to modify and update them. Change is an essential quality of research according to Judith, because researchers are likely to modify and change their focus in the field – an essential part of their experience. This is an initial approach precisely picked out as 'a worry' by John:

> It was an early version of what's become known as 'grounded theory', where you constantly adapt your theoretical, or at any rate, your conceptual position, to new data. And as somebody influenced by Popper, I felt that was a bit of a cop-out. I mean,

at some point I think you have to come forward with a clear testable proposition and see whether it stands up against the empirical data. And, okay, you may want to refine it a bit, and modify it, but you've always to keep in mind that, at some point, you may have to say, 'No. That's wrong!' And start again – not this endless adjustment and adaptation. (pp 21–23).

Judith insists that the brain is only good if it is accompanied by constant curiosity and scepticism. She had an early baptism of fire while a survey interviewer in Cowley, Oxford. She felt that the survey she administered did not allow her freedom to listen to the experiences of interviewees. It felt unnatural and stifling. More importantly, it seemed thoroughly at odds with her research aims – trivial, banal and devoid of any external validity. A method that served to mask more rather than illuminate:

It was terribly informative to me, because (a) I didn't know Cowley – it was white working-class, Morris Motors and Cowley Motors then, it was full employment. You had to go to every third house, and you had this questionnaire of about three or four pages. It was all about shopping habits, and you had 'Yes', 'No', 'Don't know' – they were pre-ordained answers. And then there was, right at the end, there was two inches, 'Any other comments'. That was one of the most important lessons for me later – to learn about the limitations of questionnaires. Because you would knock on the door and there would be an elderly woman who was desperate for company, and 'Come in and have a cup of tea'. And then you'd say, 'Do you buy your Sunday joint on a Friday or a Saturday?' And she'd say, 'Look at me. I live alone. Do you think I'm going to have a Sunday joint? Do you think I can even afford it? I go to the butchers when it's closing, and I might get a chop at a discount'. There wasn't room for those answers. And then I would keep filling up the later paragraph, you see. So that was the most useful practical lesson in scepticism, with pre-ordained questions. (pp 53–54)

These early experiences led Judith towards a deep scepticism of the value of quantitative methods in general. In her view, relying on survey data brings real dangers of misinterpretation and misinformation:

There was another book called *The Official Statistics* – I've got upstairs – showing (that came out the time [in the 1980s] when

I was at Essex) how you could have 80% answer 'Yes', but it's actually 80% inaccurate. So just because it's the majority said 'X', it doesn't mean it's true. And I remember this wonderful guy – I made notes – he was talking on the radio years ago, and he said, 'The more you generalise, the more you lose the detail, and in the end you're left with banalities'. And that's what I felt. (pp 79–80)

Crucially, in Judith's view quantitative research did not allow for the expression of people's voices. For her it felt more like a form of suppression, an antithesis to the guiding principles in her personal and professional life to understand the cultural underpinnings of social phenomena. Her interview gives many examples of how she believes misinformation comes about, for example in terms of studying Roma and their villages. This issue came up early on in her work for Barbara Adams on the Cowley survey:

But, of course, I'm more sympathetic to Barbara now, retrospectively. But she kept saying, 'This is a policy-oriented (the dreaded word!) policy-oriented project', and 'the government will only respond to numbers'. She actually said, 'The ideal for this report' – which is what we thought we were going to produce – was to have tables on every page, of figures. You know, totally bogus! I began to look at that government Census, and in the Census it talked about real Romanies and reproduced the stuff [figures]. And she had a photograph of a gypsy marriage in that Census – I've got it upstairs in my attic – and it said, 'A gypsy marries for life'...

Of course, my wonderful – what would I say? 'weapon' – is a brilliant article by Edmund Leach... The point, the crux of that article is that Leach had done over a year's fieldwork in one village... And Leach showed [how] the one intensive study shows the system, *the system*. Numbers don't show the system: they concluded that the majority of people in these 52 villages were landless peasants. Leach said, 'I know, from studying the one village, I know the inheritance system, and the majority of those so-called landless peasants are going to inherit'. So they're not landless peasants. Just simple things like that. (pp 79–80)

In Judith's words, it is following her instincts that allows her to get better results than other researchers and to access difficult to reach groups. She cites Malinowski as a major source of inspiration – 'the anthropologist pitches his or her tent in a village' (pp 79–80). Thus, immediacy, interaction and understanding, and the ability to change focus depending on what comes about in the field, are fundamental principles in Judith's work and they can be compromised by the mechanical process of quantitative exploration which means testing specific hypotheses – to the constraint of what Judith views to be research freedom. She goes on to describe the 'funnel method' which she adopted:

> The 'funnel method' was that you're open to everything, and then you refine it. So I've made lots of jokes in lectures saying, the 'funnel method'... and it shut them up! I said, 'It's phallic, it's hard. It also appeals! It's a tool!' I was lecturing in Nottingham about four years ago, and they said, 'Thank God, Judith, we're now going to introduce the funnel method'. It means being open. There's a wonderful passage which I used to quote in lectures, 'When you go into the field, you arrive with part of your life history, the latest novels, everything, you go with yourself. You go with everything. And then that is a resource'. (p 117)

She also recounts how she challenged a professional body to accommodate the methodological flexibility which she believes should take primacy:

> It's no good a grant body saying, 'What hypothesis are you testing?'... When I was helping to fill in ESRC forms, the students would come to me – in Edinburgh – and it would say, 'What hypothesis are you testing?' They were bewildered. And I wrote to the ESRC, and I said, 'This is not how anthropology works'. Now they've changed it. I haven't looked at one recently, but it says, 'What research questions?' That's good, 'research questions', you can have these puzzlements and you may change. (p 118)

However, while the contrasts between the views of John Goldthorpe and Judith Okely help to bring out the issues, it is important to remember that they both represent the extremes of the debate. In the post-war decades most social researchers took much more of a middle position. This includes anthropologists. In Voices 5 *W. M. Williams* describes how in the 1950s producing statistics through carrying out a community household survey was taught as standard practice. This was equally true of those working abroad. *Raymond Firth* not only used similar methods but also developed as a 'systematic method', a daily diary divided into thematc sections recording his own work. He included his own 'frustrations' and 'moral dilemmas', but briefly: 'In those days, I think we didn't engage quite as much in the navel gazing as anthropologists are apt to do now!' (p 78).

Jack Goody describes how in Ghana he combined participant observation and a survey with historical research. 'I've always been very eclectic as to methods. As I say, but when I went to Africa, I obviously did as other anthropologists. I spent two years in a village, working on that. I also worked on the records quite a lot in Ghana, Ghana National Archives, and in the PRO [Public Record Office in London]' (p 63). Later, when he was carrying out much wider comparative demographic research on family size and on 'stopping systems' – on when people stopped having children – he mapped populations using a variety of statistics, and came to think that many British anthropologists had too much of a 'crazy emphasis' on direct fieldwork (p 65). More broadly he argued for the unity of the social sciences and attacked 'the heavy curtains of institutionalised boundaries between the disciplines' (p 70).

In sociology many of the Pioneers had been first trained as anthropologists. And all of them, as we have seen in Chapter 4, were living though a period of rapid development in statistical methods bringing major new research potential. They needed to respond. And as *Duncan Gallie* recalls, as late as 1983 when he launched the SCELI, a lot of basic new learning was going on in a cheerful spirit:

> It was a very, very stimulating collaboration, and my sense is that most people enjoyed – not everybody – but most people enjoyed it, and felt that they learnt a lot, and they learnt a lot both substantively, or theoretically, but also in terms of methodology. Because not many people had done survey work at that time, and we were all learning, we were running very fast to keep up with the thing, especially longitudinal data analysis. Even at its best it was pretty primitive in those days. We [were shown] these spaghetti diagrams, which made your mind just whirl with how you could interpret the stuff! (p 39)

Peter Townsend had been interested at least by the early 1970s in computer-assisted analysis, and his perceptiveness of the need to combine both qualitative and quantitative methods in his research is certainly prescient. This comes with a heightened awareness of the faults of both approaches. For example, he is fully aware that surveys can be unrepresentative not only of the whole population, but also of particular segments of it: for example, surveys of family expenditure that do not cover the top of the income distribution, or that completely disregard the experiences of the most deprived in a society:

> It's a familiar story which comes from the Family Expenditure Survey... Namely that, at the top of the income distribution, the Family Expenditure Survey is singularly fluffy about the rich, and it's quite clear that they don't get a sufficient representation. Nor are questions asked enough about the appropriateness of the questionnaire for some of the rich because, of course, a lot of the questions are almost beside the point, in terms of the way in which large pots of gold are managed...
>
> But among the poor, it's been quite clear to me for many years, and this has been glossed over, frankly, by those administering the Survey, that the sick and disabled are greatly under-estimated, and the extreme elderly are under-estimated, generally speaking... And one could make the same point about what we know to be the case, a lot of younger people who sleep at different flats, and at their friends, and homes of their friends in order to get by, but are not considered homeless because they're not actually on the streets or trying to get into a hostel. We know this goes on among teenagers, and this is probably under-estimated... Another group that occurs to me, of course, are ethnic minorities... There are more unemployed people, therefore a little bit more of a mobile population, of family break-ups, and, therefore, not always quite certain about who is in the household and who isn't... So these are new features of the population, new elements in the population, that are not quite covered. (pp 114–116).

Peter aptly captures the inherent fallacy in any method and is highly aware of their deficiencies. His vibrant observations use his wider knowledge. For him, this constitutes the realm of good research practice, rather than making a choice of one of the methods over the others. A good research practice also means that the researcher must be highly aware of the process of selection that he or she engages in – including how bias is possible in choosing illustrative quotations to present interpretations:

> I was struck by the fact that when people gave quotations in books, from interviews, much turns on how you weigh

the importance of that, in terms of who said it, and in what circumstances, and what kind of person they were... That is sometimes left, in effect, to the author to convey, and the reader takes time to decide how reliable it is. I often had criticisms, subsequently, of this method, because people said, 'Oh well, he just picked out those things he wanted to illustrate, and, therefore, he got very biased'. But then, frankly, that's true of almost every method that you adopt, because you still have to select. It's true of statistical stuff, and we all know that even collecting quantitative answers about behaviour, rather than even opinion, the way the question is framed, the way it's pre-classified, the way it's coded, what you do about 'don't knows', what you've done about people who haven't answered the questions in the first place, these are all highly significant questions, in terms of how you interpret the statistical results that you're presented with. (pp 40–41)

He sums up with an almost poetic outline of the three stages of the research process. This shows acute understanding of the importance of triangulation to further the social enquiry – that you need to know the population that you are supposed to survey, to ask potential interviewees questions to see whether the survey will work, to look for new statistical patterns.

And, quite frankly, it's worth saying that, sometimes, if you think of a survey, of carrying out a set of interviews, and you want to calculate what per cent of people did this, and what per cent did that, I think you have to think of doing it in three stages.

Don't, for God's sake, develop a list of requests as long as your arm, when people will produce, you know, four feet deep of print-out. To wade through all that is almost an impossible job. Your best plan is to devise a short set of requests, to open up the subject, as it were, get the rough outline of the scope of a structure that you're investigating. Whether you're talking about different people in the population, for instance, if you're asking them about their occupation and their class, yes, everybody can think of the various ranks into which people will fit, and you need questions about the rank that people feel they occupy, as well as what that in their view means. And you can compare that with some sort of 'objective' designations of what that means.

But, in the first instance, you need to kind of get your information about what the shape of the sample, the people you've interviewed, what it looks like, where the majority of people put themselves. That's an obvious point, but sometimes you will find that 70 per cent of people put themselves in a particular category, and you've got to break that down into the second stage, and try and discover to what extent it's composed of certain sub-groups. That's an obvious point about going to a second stage.

What I'm trying to say is that not only should you proceed like that in dynamic interchange with the programmer, if you don't do the programming yourself, but that you need to remember that you've got a third stage of being really creative with statistics. And by that I mean that in the process of carrying out a survey, you discover certain things about housing, or you discover certain things about political opinion, or things about disability, if you're any good, which hadn't occurred to you beforehand. Part of the point about doing any research is to discover things you weren't quite aware of beforehand. And that will mean, sometimes, devising, putting groups together that you hadn't anticipated, to explore the results of doing that – looking at gender, for example, in a new way.

If suddenly you become aware that gender differences are not, perhaps, as covered as you'd like, and that you want to try and check a particular thesis or conclusion, it's almost like saying, if I dare put this, the first stage is the initial outline, the second stage is the follow-up into sub-categories, if you like, which is easy to understand. The third stage is the really creative stage where you are checking your conclusions, and that is a very important way of using statistics creatively, and sometimes changing what you thought about methodology in the first place, but also using your statistics to the hilt. (pp 109–110)

Observation also has primacy in how *Glen Elder*, founder of the 'life course' school of longitudinal research, approaches his investigations. He too has always drawn on data created by multiple methods. Significantly, in contrast to other British survey researchers, he regularly combines qualitative and quantitative material in his longitudinal cohort data. He especially emphasises the need to look at interviews within a wider context and a long time frame:

> Lives are lived in a changing world, and if you study those lives longitudinally, over time, and ignore the context, the situations they're living through, you're going to miss most of the story.

And I think that's the big point, for all of these longitudinal studies that are going on throughout the world. We really do live in an age of longitudinal studies, and it's so easy for people to ignore context, and just do the study and forget about where they've been.

So I think this is the major contribution that we can make to the study of lives and human development: it's to get the people who are doing the studies, to realise that it's not just simply a cohort sequential design that they need. They need to pay attention to the changes that are taking place in the lives of these people, in a macro sense as well as a micro sense, and [to bring them] together. (pp 50–51)

In developing the life course approach he was originally influenced by interactionist thinking in American sociology, 'for example, in the study of socialisation'. And the Californian longitudinal study on which he based *Children of the Great Depression* included health data and much rich psychological evidence from observation as well as interviews, and it already covered several decades, so it was effectively partly historical. He brought all these elements together in a 'more structural' perspective:

So I always had a cross-level view. One can think of linking social structure and personality, as a multi-level way of looking at this. You'd have institutional arrangements at the macro level, and then you would have these influences being processed and being expressed through families, interactions of families, family members, through peer groups, through all kinds of interpersonal processes. And they became a way of thinking about why, how people developed the way they do. That's kind of similar to what *Children of the Great Depression* represents, because it's the family that represents the connection, the link, between the economic changes that were taking place and the children, this cohort. (pp 58–59)

Another Pioneer who in his work on depression among women has experimented with a new combination of approaches is *George Brown*. In his projects he combines observation with recording in-depth interviews to generate hypotheses, but at the same time he insists on imposing new kinds of measurement to assess what interviewees are trying to say and how strongly they feel. This has included measuring the emotional impact conveyed by the power and tone of the voice itself. He clearly puts a high value on fieldwork observation:

> There's one kind of research where what you're interested in what you can see happening. You can see how a nurse responds to somebody [who is] handicapped, or you can see how a mother is responding to a patient... I think a lot of qualitative work in the social sciences is [often] very, extraordinarily good work, done on this kind of level. (pp 54–56)

But he also underlines the importance of studying a research question at several points in time in order to adopt a proper causal perspective. Without denigrating the importance of other methods, instead he argues for them to be operating side by side:

> I think there are many other key things that we're concerned with, that have much longer causal trajectories, and you can't get any confidence [about what might be going on] from just being present at one point in time. You see the end point, but it's very difficult to get any sense of what the hell's going on. So you have to turn to a rather different kind of comparative approach, that can take account of time, of things occurring over time. (pp 54–56)

Thus, the researcher should acknowledge that gathering information should come first whatever the method. This may seem counter-intuitive initially even in relation to a complex subject matter such as depression, especially as there is a group of interviewees whose situations need to be improved. At the time of his interview in 2000, George was reflecting on the possibility of developing yet another new form of methodology, through experimentation:

> As I see it, in broad terms, all our work has been moving towards the issue of experimentation. And we have, in fact, recently put in three grants, in order, in fact, to have controlled trials [based on ideas] coming out of our research. We've run into difficulty here... The basic problem has been that we felt that where depression is concerned, it's not like treating cancer or something like that, where you can have one treatment and, quite rightly, find out whether that's having an effect or not. Depression is far too, it seems to me, complex a condition, when seen in the

community, to just offer one thing. And what we wanted is to offer a range of things, according to the circumstances and the wishes of the woman and so on. And this ran counter to the idea of the Medical Research Committees, that you wouldn't then be able to know what really was important...

Tirril [Harris] and I, after 30 years, really feel, very much, that most of our future work should be in terms of some kind of intervention and experimentation, not only because, ultimately... that some of the issues are so complex that, even in scientific terms, we can't at all be sure about certain things without this kind of experimentation. (pp 74–75)

Glen Elder is equally open in thinking of crossing methodological lines:

Well, you could think of working with archival data and building in that way, and I think saturation of interviewing to a point where you've known, you've basically covered the ground, you've interviewed enough people. I think, in some ways, you can think of archival data doing that too. You read and read and read until you think you really understand this process, and then you call it quits, and you move from there. (pp 68–69)

It is important to note that there are a number of our Pioneers who clearly relate to a lesser extent to the possible primacy of a particular method. For *Janet Finch*, the method is just a tool. The main focus should lie with the research matter itself, be it social welfare, school choice or poverty. In Janet's interview, a discussion of the relationship of the researcher to the methods is present, but it is the openness to debates around the ethics of social enquiry, to the depth of rapport achieved that is of importance to her. Furthermore, she makes it clear that she wants her words on the method not to be taken out of context, to be reduced to simple binary positions when her position is in actuality a complex one:

It's been wildly misquoted to say that Janet Finch says that men can't interview women. And I don't think I quite said that! But that is not the point, actually. The point is something rather deeper than that, about [how] in a society which is quite divided on gender lines, in terms of people's experiences and their assumptions about who you can trust and that kind of thing, that it is a different sort of dynamic when you get a woman interviewing a woman, than when you get a man interviewing a woman. (pp 60–61)

Her characteristic skill in finding complex solutions to subtle social distinctions is illustrated by the sample she developed in her study of clergy wives:

I took the Anglican Diocese of Bradford, and interviewed people in four denominations, within the geographical boundaries encompassed by the Anglican Diocese. And so that was Anglican, Methodist, Baptist, and Congregationalist...Those [second] two, I think, subsequently merged, but they were separate at that stage. And so I defined it by geographical area. I then got the complete list of clergy, and sampled different fractions, according to the size of the churches, so that I ended up with not equal numbers, but numbers which would enable me to make comparisons. So that meant I sampled proportionately a lot more of the Anglicans than I did of the Nonconformist denominations... And then I went off and interviewed them wherever they were. And, I mean, it was far too ambitious... Subsequently, when I started supervising research students myself, I was horrified at the scale that I'd been allowed to... It was something like 150, which I conducted, transcribed them all myself, analysed them. Probably not terribly – you know, not as thoroughly as one would do now, but... I did everything myself. (pp 28–32)

There are other Pioneers who are very comfortable with acknowledging the primacy of mixed methods. Some like *Elizabeth Thomas-Hope* do not reflect in detail on the mixture of methods although it is clear they adopt them in their work. Others such as *W. M. Williams* describe in detail the process of triangulation, the sequencing of methods: starting with quantitative analysis of patterns, following with interviews with stakeholders and relevant interviewees, and then engaging in an elaborate process of matching information.

Other Pioneers like *Peter Hall* discuss methods more in terms of the training they have undertaken and the process of establishing their research agenda:

Berkeley taught me the value and also the know-how of very high level close empirical research, on which I think the top American research universities are absolutely unbeatable. I learned a lot in those years... Well, two kinds of empirical research, which are combined in those books. One is number crunching – again, just finding out where stuff was happening. And number two, critically, tracing the historical sequence – again, this deep belief that the way you go is by what I call 'the economic history approach'. So if you take both of those books, they're essentially telling economic history stories about how things happened in places, sequences, and involving people taking actions. And I remained firmly convinced that that's the way to understand deep – what I think is a bit pretentious – deep economic processes you can only understand by unpicking it in terms of economic history. (pp 42–45)

Jonathan Gershuny captures a different type of methods experience, the excitement of trying a new methodological tool and thereby expanding the research agenda.

On the Millennium Cohort, we actually got all the children to keep a diary either on a laptop or on their telephones. We did that last year, and we're just starting to work on this. And most recently, and most excitingly, we have a validation study that I'm writing up today and tomorrow, which is comparing three sources – a written diary of the traditional paper sort; an accelerometer, a wrist-worn accelerometer; and a wearable camera. The wearable camera takes a photograph every 45 seconds or so, and producing about two and a half thousand images a day. And basically my colleagues go through and produce a diary interpreting these pictures. Very intensive. It's hugely expensive. It's a wonderful research tool for all sorts of purposes, so if you're looking, for example, at eating, you get much better pictures of eating using that, but it's not a practical research tool for most purposes. (pp 108–110)

Similarly, for *Karen Dunnell* the key memory is the excitement of working as a government civil servant and dramatically expanding the General Household Survey to give a longer and fuller view of women's sexual and pregnancy histories, which she published as *Famiy Formation* (1979). In other words, developing the use of a particular method, applying it to new themes for the first time and thus facilitating groundbreaking new research:

We began to document all that in this longitudinal history method that we'd come up with. So it was very very exciting from that point of view. And the thing was nobody had ever ever asked women before whether they'd had abortions. We knew they were under-reported, but nevertheless – and we'd never asked women when they'd first had sexual intercourse. It had never been asked in Britain before. So it was very very exciting from that point of view. Lots of people were interested in it. And I think it's another aspect of – I've spent a lot of time in my life thinking about health inequalities, but actually a lot of it stems from what happens to women early in their life, if they have – and we asked them whether their pregnancy was wanted or not, and stuff like that. It was amazing. Very very interesting. (p 40)

However, Karen was much less happy when new technologies brought redundancies to the survey world. New policies of savings included using fewer open questions:

I've never been at work when there haven't been terrible budget pressures, but we must have had budget pressures because I can remember being quite active in the movement to get rid of these armies of people we had doing coding, because actually the computer did probably 95% of it. Then people started questioning, 'Well, why do we want all this other stuff anyway?' I mean, it was radical. It was terrible, because people got made redundant, or didn't get replaced when they left. So it dwindled, but it dwindled rather after – I never fell in love with it! (p 39)

Many of our Pioneers did not necessarily reflect on the methods they used. This is not to say that they did not adopt systematic explorations in their studies. But for many of the Pioneers, mainly because methodology had been as yet so weakly developed in Britain (see Chapter 6), their approach of social investigation was sometimes almost journalistic. For them the excitement of going out in the world and trying to understand it took precedence over methods and research stages. *Dennis Marsden* remarks on his fieldwork for his 1960s research at the Institute of Communities Studies:

We hadn't got a method, you see. I think the thing about the Institute that was attractive but also, I think, an Achilles heel, was that they were, I think they were determinedly amateurish – in a best sense, rather than the worst sense – in that they almost prided themselves in not being specialists. Which was probably a good thing, since what they were doing was not really an English mode, was it? It would be seen, in England, as journalism. Whereas in America it was perfectly acceptable methodology – not ethnomethodology, but qualitative methodology had been practised ever since the Chicago School and before. (p 73)

What mattered above all in his view is that these early classics did bring new understanding. They were not mired in statistical details and for him that meant that they could speak more clearly. He said of his classic *Education and the Working Class*:

Well, you couldn't possibly base any kind of scientific conclusions on that sample of [88] from one Grammar School. But it's never been repeated, and it was enormously successful, it sold hundreds of thousands – although we never made any money out of it. So, at some level, it must be emotionally convincing, it must be coherent. It has a coherent argument, and it performs, I think, one of the ideal functions of qualitative research, which is to explain what's going on. When you've got large data sets with fairly striking messages but you don't understand what it is, or, at least, you've got the wrong idea of what it is, it gives you a different explanation of what's going on. But it also works at the level of novel, I think, it communicates people, through people. It gets pictures of people. (p 70)

In short, the juxtaposition between quantitative and qualitative methods which is central to the interviews and the respective research views of *John Goldthorpe* and *Judith Okely* almost never flares up to the same extent in the other interviews. If anything, there is a sense, for example in the interview with *Michael Young* (Voices 7), that there is a space for everybody, for a variety of approaches to be recognised. As Chapter 6 will show, the spirit of amateurism and gleeful diving into the field that marked the research beginnings of many of our Pioneers were seriously challenged by advances in technology and the stringent requirements of Ethics Boards. Many of the Pioneers acknowledged these developments as positive and necessary for the discipline of sociology; although it is unclear whether this has resulted in less methodological infighting at the present-day research scene.

VOICES 5

Into the field

Let us listen to how two of our earliest Pioneers set about their fieldwork – neither with much formal guidance.

Raymond Firth's voyage to Tikopia

In 1928, the anthropologist Raymond Firth – the oldest of our Pioneers, whom we have already encountered earlier – set out to spend a year on the Pacific island of Tikopia, which was to be the prime focus of his life's research. He was to be a lone researcher there, out of even radio contact with the wider world. It would be virtually impossible to organise a journey to such a destination in today's interconnected globalised world: a measure of how the experience of anthropology has changed.

> Having studied the Maori, I thought it would be interesting to see a Polynesian community at a much earlier phase of development... Tikopia was a second choice, because Durrard, the missionary, had done a little on its language... I went to see him, actually, in New Zealand, and got from him some photographs and so on... I gathered information about it from the Mission vessel, which used to call there about once a year, or every two years, and I discovered that it was obviously a very simple community, technologically, with very little, very isolated, very little contact with the outside world, and so I thought, 'This is an opportunity to see what, really, Polynesian life was like', away from contact. (p 57)

So with no more than this scanty information, he packed his food stores, clothing and some equipment and presents, and launched himself into the unknown:

> I set out for Tikopia from Sydney. I first of all took the *Matalum*, which is an ordinary passenger vessel, going once a month to the Solomons, and to Tulaghi, which was then the headquarters of the Solomons. And from there, I took the Mission vessel. And it carried me right the way round through the Solomons, the whole

Eastern Solomons, on their regular tours which they did once or twice a year. Tikopia was very rarely visited. It's about five or six hundred miles from Tulagi. In the end, after quite some weeks, seven weeks, or something of the kind, we got to Tikopia...

So they put me down, with my stores, which I'd had to accumulate in large quantity. I mean, I'd bought jam, for instance, twelve dozen tins of jam! Crates of this, and crates of that, and biscuits and so on, tobacco, sticks of tobacco in large quantity. I knew that that, at least, would be welcome. Clay pipes, I received a hint that clay pipes would be welcome, and they were indeed. And steel tools. (p 58)

Once landed, he was to spend a whole year on Tikopia, the only white man in the island community:

My father had given me an adze, thinking it would come in useful if I were doing any building for a house, or anything of that kind. And this was an object of immense interest to the Tikopia, because they were canoe builders, in hard wood, and seeing this, I thought I'd better capitalise it. So I wrote to my father, and asked him for another half a dozen adzes. And the ship, the *Southern Cross*, came at the end of three months with further supplies, including these adzes. And then it didn't come for another nine months. It was supposed to come after seven months, but she broke her rudder... somewhere else, had to put back to Auckland for repairs, and so she was two months late. Nobody knew, of course, on Tikopia, what had happened. They said, 'You don't need to worry. You're all right, you're on land. They may have gone to the bottom, but you're on land'. Anyway, they did come, and so I was there just the twelve months...

I was completely out of touch. I used to go out and sit under a tree and look out, and there was the horizon all around, you see, and that was that. Nothing broke the horizon for months on end. (p 59)

He reflected on his situation:

I wasn't lonely... That is, there were always people around me, and I don't think that I missed the company of people like myself, because I was so absorbed in the Tikopia... So, in a sense, it is true, I think, I was not lonely. On the other hand, what I came to realise was that I must be completely self-reliant. That if some kind of emergency occurred, there was nobody of my general background, to whom I could turn. The Tikopia would help if it were a physical emergency, but otherwise...

For instance, to begin with, I was trying to obtain information about their religious rites, and they, not unnaturally, were not keen that I should do this. And I remember, on one occasion, I was going to a ceremony around the lake, and before I set out on the path, I wondered, 'Is it possible that they might club me?' because they used clubs. And I thought, 'No. This is very unlikely'. But I remember thinking then that this was a decision for me, there was nobody else to whom I can appeal. And I think that, in a way, this kind of feeling of, 'I must rely upon myself alone', was one of the aspects of the study. (p 60)

He was more concerned about his health:

Yes. Quite definitely, I was... After a long period of religious ceremony, about a month, there was all kinds of late night dancing and so on, I was sitting out in the night, just with a shirt and trousers, in a deck-chair, and I got a chill. And I suppose I realise it now, it may have been a form of pneumonia. But I was certainly very ill for quite some time, two or three weeks. And the Tikopia, very cheerfully, said, 'Well, friend, you're very ill. Don't die here. Go and die in your own land, because if you die here, the Europeans will think that we have killed you'. So I promised them, to my best, I would not die there! And I didn't! (pp 60–61)

Without being asked, Firth recounted how living with the Tikopia changed his own way of thinking about sexuality. He had been brought up with strict puritanical views. He explained how he quickly got used to seeing the women in very scanty clothing. He then went on to say:

I did not take a Tikopia mistress, but as a bachelor... I was assigned to, as it were, the group of bachelors and the unmarried girls. And as such, we could indulge in very free conversation, and did. So I learnt a great deal about the sex behaviour of the Tikopia, in evening discussions, laughing, songs and so on, gossip and the like, you see. And, in fact, it was one of the things which I think helped, as you might say, to broaden my mind! Coming from a Methodist background, one had been rather stiff about sexual matters. But I came to look on them with much greater freedom than before...

[To take a mistress] would not have been dangerous, but it would have been inexpedient. Because I would have had to have a relationship with a particular family, which would have put me at a disadvantage vis-à-vis other families. I would have been very much at their beck and call. So no... I regard that as – not on, from a scientific point of view. (pp 77–78)

W. M. Williams comes to his English village, Gosforth

W. M. Williams was born in 1926 into a mining family in South Wales, and from there went to the University of Wales at Aberystwyth, learning the skills of studying local Welsh communities from the inspiring teacher Alwyn Rees. His community study of Gosforth in Cumbria led to his first book, *The Sociology of an English Village* (1956), which he then saw as a traditional community – but a different social world from Wales. Here he describes his first visit, and how he set about his studying the village:

I grew up being accustomed to friendship networks, work networks, kinship networks and so on. When I then went to Gosforth, I regarded myself as going to a foreign country, and when I got off the bus in Gosforth, there was absolutely a beautiful example of this, which made me convinced I'd come to the right place. Because I got off the bus, and there was a woman coming down the road, on a white horse, and she stopped outside the shop – Barnes's shop – and Mr. Barnes came out and actually touched his forehead, and said, 'Good Morning, Miss Keene', and she said, 'Good Morning, Barnes', like (Laughs) – you wouldn't do that in Merthyr! And she then gave him her order, and he wrote it down and said, 'Yes, I'll bring it up this afternoon, Miss Keene', and off she went. I discovered that Miss Keene was actually the Rector's daughter, and the Rector's daughter clearly belonged to a different social class from Mr. Barnes. And I thought, 'Here is the English class system in action!' And it couldn't be more different from industrial South Wales, where there was a strong egalitarian ethos. (pp 5–6)

Well, I'd three methods. First of all, Alwyn said, 'You have to collect statistics'. He said, 'You have to collect statistics', so I had to collect statistics! So I drew up a questionnaire with his help, which asked basic questions of every family that I interviewed, genealogical questions, but also age, occupation, owner-occupiers/tenants, things like that. So I had this basic data that I collected for every household in the village. Only in one case did I actually have to have it done at second hand – this was a family called 'The Hermits', who lived up on a remote farm – and I met the postman, I was going up, and he said, 'Don't waste your time, because I've been delivering the post there for 20 years, and I've never seen them!' So that was the basic data, which allowed me to say things about the demography of the village, and quite a lot about the economy, the farm economy. I'd ask how many cows they had, how many sheep, how much land and so on. I drew maps of the farm holdings. And then I did interviews, so I interviewed someone in every household, except The Hermits.

I took notes. And what I did, actually, was – this was before the days of tape-recorders, and if you'd had a tape-recorder, it would have been the size of a small suitcase! There was a bridge over a stream, just outside the village, and I used to take my lunch with me, sandwiches. When I'd finished in the morning, I would rush and go underneath the bridge, where I couldn't be seen, and I'd eat my lunch, and I'd write up as much of the verbatim comments that I could remember, against the skeleton that I had of the notes as I went along. So if someone said something that was particularly striking, I'd tried to memorise it and write it down. I got very good at this, actually, with practice...

I would try to record everyone who attended anything, and who the office holders were, so I discovered that a small group of people were actually the office holders in most voluntary organisations, the secretary of one thing would be the secretary or chairman of another. They drove the social life of the village. I would then try to match up the material with the interviews. And I also discovered the 'good informant' – these were the days when anthropologists made much of the 'good informant' – and I found half a dozen people who were willing to talk, endlessly, about life in the village, and didn't mind...

They all had their own perspectives. But I could call in to see them at any time, and they'd give me a cup of tea, and they'd say, in so many words, 'What do you want to talk about now?' So I would say, 'Well, I've been looking at sheep farming, and it doesn't quite make sense, you know, can you' – and they would tell me about sheep farming, and things like that. (pp 19–20).

CHAPTER 6

Fieldwork: making methods

We have just heard the voices of *Raymond Firth* and *W. M. Williams*, two of our oldest Pioneers. Firth is setting out in 1928 on a lonely voyage into a new culture. He makes his solitary way to a remote island to study the way of life of its people. Ultimately published eight years later, his book, *We, the Tikopia*, became a classic of anthropology. Williams is describing how he studied a village in England. His book *The Sociology of an English Village: Gosforth* (1956) was one of the most notable British community studies. Through their voices we can sense the development of a new approach to research: an ethnographic approach less concerned with measuring, counting and science and more sensitive to feelings, understanding, imaginations. Firth was on his own and in a sense had to invent how to do his research as he went along. Helped a little by the earlier comments of missionaries, seamen and travellers, and the few cultural anthropologists before him, his work was full of risk. In his time there was scarcely any fieldwork training and not yet any manuals on how to do it. Researchers just had to get on with it. Williams came two decades later and he did have the benefit of some training and advice from his supervisor. This difference shows how things were already changing – and hints at how much they were to change!

So in this chapter we look a little at the early days of a 'soft' human methodology in the making in Britain. Some of our researchers went out into the field, and into the natural world, in order to understand different lives and human worlds through living very close to people in other cultures, trying to see and sense their world from their point of view. Like poets and writers, philosophers and dreamers, they wanted to understand human meaning, to capture the fragility of human inter-subjectivity, to become intimately familiar with human stories, and to document this for others. All this set profound challenges for good research: both practically and theoretically. This chapter will explore how this humanistic research style began to evolve. It will listen to what some of our Pioneer practitioners had to say as they struggled with these early first challenges to create a human social science.

Perpetual change: a very brief history of fieldwork

It will help us to have in mind the evolution of this research style over a longer time span. It has moved forward under many names, including fieldwork, ethnography, participant observation, life stories, oral history, intensive interviewing, diaries, letters, photos, film and most recently digital research.[1] Today, and at its most general, it is called qualitative (to contrast with quantitative) research: highlighting *qualitas*, the qualities of what is being studied. There have been a number of attempts to grasp this evolving history, but here we will just briefly glimpse five major overlapping waves, each with its own contested history.

To begin at *the beginning*, we could go right back to Herodotus and the ancient Greeks; to the descriptive writings of the Renaissance; and to a motley crew of travellers with their notebooks in the eighteenth and nineteenth centuries, lone pioneers in exotic lands. James George Frazer's *Golden Bough* (1890) is the most celebrated, documenting an encyclopaedic treatment of religious and magical practices. There were also, in parallel, literary authors like Charles Dickens and George Eliot. We also sense the earliest days of the lone scholar, the start of colonial anthropology, and the beginnings of sociological research notably in the early works on poverty of Charles Booth and Seebohm Rowntree. Here is a long and diverse *early era*.

Out of this came a *development era* when fieldwork started to become recognised and somewhat institutionalised. The early twentieth century was British anthropology's founding fieldwork moment. Led from the new and rival departments at Oxford and the LSE, it was a time of tension and disagreement about the nature of anthropology.[2] Fieldwork was most clearly developed in the work of Bronislaw Malinowski, who took up the chair in Social Anthropology at the LSE in 1927, the first chair of its discipline. His appointment heralded a *Golden Era* of over 30 years of outstanding new scholars, including Firth himself, and others such as Edward Evans-Pritchard, Audrey Richards, Meyer Fortes and Edmund Leach: leaders of a whole founding generation of ethnography. The charismatic but controversial character of Malinowski was the central figure, busy advocating that all his students should go out into the field. *Raymond Firth* was one of those students.

Sociology lagged behind. In this period, it was largely dominated by the theorists based at the LSE – Hobhouse, Ginsberg, Marshall – and empirical research was left in the hands of just a few mavericks. This underdevelopment is very odd because in this same period ethnographic methods were flourishing in the US. Celebrated in such classic texts as W. I. Thomas and Florian Znaniecki's five volume study of *The Polish Peasant in Europe and America* (1918–20), Clifford Shaw's life story *The Jack Roller* (1930), and the exemplary earlier case studies of W. E. B Du Bois in *The Philadelphia Negro* (1899), the research methods of ethnography, fieldwork and life stories were being shaped as distinctive sociological tools. But these advances in North American methodology were not, it seems, being replicated in Britain. What did happen in these early years can be seen as a few 'oddball advances': notably, the Mass Observation studies of Tom Harrison and Charles Madge; Humphrey Jennings and the rise of the documentary film; and the earliest British textbooks on methods.[3]

It was not really until after the end of the Second World War in 1945 that we start to see empirical research being taken seriously within British sociology. This was the time of *rapid expansion of social research and teaching*. Most of our Pioneers carried out their significant work in this phase or the next. Initially, it was identified with the growth of community studies.[4] Usually conducted within an anthropological fieldwork frame (the boundaries between sociology and anthropology were far from clear at this time), the researcher would typically go to live for a year or more in a community to try to understand its ways of life, most often investigating how 'traditional' local ties and bonds were changing. Observation and informal interviewing became prime tools. At least nine of our Pioneer researchers engaged with some version of this: *Williams, Frankenberg, Young, Townsend, Stacey, Bell, Pahl, Moore* and *Newby*. They wrote at a time which Charles Madge called 'the Golden Age of Community Studies'. Inspired in part by American studies, and notably Robert and Helen Lynd's *Middletown* series (1929 etc), they echo an early preoccupation of sociology with community and its meanings. Prominent studies – all published within the span of five years – included not only W. M. Williams' book on Gosforth (1956), but also Ronald Frankenberg's Welsh study *Village on the Border* (1957), Michael Young and Peter Willmott's *Family and Kinship in East London* (1957), and Margaret Stacey's *Tradition and Change: A Study of Banbury* (1960).

In the US, this period is depicted as a modernist phase: from roughly the end of the Second World War to the 1970s. Certainly, the newly emerging British ethnographic fieldwork drew heavily on the now established American ideas, and most notably on the neo-Chicagoan works of Howard Becker, and the experience-moulded 'grounded theory' approach of Barney Glaser and Anselm Strauss. Discussion began of ideas about the nature of the qualitative data, its links to theory, how it can be analysed. Earlier work had largely taken data as given, adopting a kind of crude realist stance; but now a new sophistication begins to be brought to analysis and textbooks appear to provide a canon of recommended work. In Britain there had been very little of this, so that the new approaches of the 1960s–70s started from reading American texts to see what the debates were. But most of our early Pioneers were not following textbooks or taking training courses; they were still creating their methods as they went along. Nevertheless, looking back we can observe a flurry of sociological fieldwork which included ethnographic work. We can find new studies of youth, work, education, deviancy, medicine and culture along with the arrival of the first modern fieldwork ethnographies – like *David Hargreaves'* study of a school community in Salford, *Social Relations in a Secondary School* (1967), or Paul Willis's Birmingham-based *Learning to Labour* (1977). Alongside these first major sociological ethnographies, in anthropology fieldwork continued to flourish, by the 1980s often through local studies of communities in England rather than overseas, such as *Judith Okely's* major work on *The Traveller Gypsies* (1983) and *Ruth Finnegan's* exploration of a New Town's culture in *The Hidden Musicians* (1989). It was also in the 1970s that oral history and life stories came to be developed as methods.

Gradually, over the same decades we can sense a move towards a phase of *paradigm challenge*. Change is in the air, with widespread talk of an epistemological crisis and paradigm change, first stimulated in part by Kuhn's *Structure of Scientific Revolutions* (1962). The enthusiasm of the 1960s and 1970s starts to fade with the beginnings of postmodernism and the rise of new right-wing politics in Thatcherism. By the 1970s, anthropology starts to become notably more self-critical of its findings and research modes, again led from America with the influence of Clifford Geertz' *The Interpretation of Cultures* (1973) and *Local Cultures* (1983). A concern with thick description and blurred genres brought a crisis of representation, of how best to convey the findings of ethnographic fieldwork. This was linked to the spread of postmodern and post-structural ideas which challenged both the authority of conventional methodological truth and questioned the very act of writing texts. There is a growing rejection of orthodox theory – especially through the rise of cultural studies and these anthropological critiques. Much of this was also tacitly shaped by the growth of new social movements including feminism, which came to play a key role in developing ideas around new research standpoints.

And so we reach *the contemporary moment*. More than a hundred years on, the kind of research conducted in social science now looks very different. If our original Pioneers were to meet with the new twenty-first-century Pioneers, they would probably be a little shocked as they had to confront the growing transformations of research to handle:

- The importance of digital transmission and the media, and the rise of digital methodologies of all kinds: digital ethnography.
- The widespread importance of film and photography: once rare and specialist, it has now become easy and ubiquitous.
- The significance of taking seriously the body: an embodied ethnography which highlights the growing significance given to the senses, and the worlds of affect and emotion.
- The importance of performativity, self-awareness and self-reflexivity.
- And ultimately a much extended discussion about the ethical and political nature of research.

We can see glimpses of this in the earlier work. Today fieldwork confronts a wide and challenging eclectic diversity of approaches (including digital, sensory, visual, or multi-sited ethnography) and methods (for example, Skype interviews, internet ethnographies, or new participatory methods) in response to the rise of a global, digital and transforming socio-economic order. The research world of the current moment looks very different from the world of our earlier Pioneers. Every problem of the field – technical, practical, personal, epistemological, theoretical, rhetorical, ethical and political – now gets its own analysis and treatment in multiple handbooks, conferences, training courses, textbooks, journals. Nowadays, there is a deluge of methodological writings about both how field research is done and should be done.

But it was not always so. So in this chapter we look at just a few of the observations our emerging fieldworkers made about these earlier days. What we start to see in these interviews is a stumbling move towards a greater degree of self-awareness, reflexivity and self-consciousness about the skills of social research. We see methodology slowly starting to become its own subject and concern.[5]

Starting out: messy beginnings

Thus, most of our Pioneers learnt their skills and pioneered their methods on the job. Few had any training in methodology at all. As *Bruce Kapferer* bluntly says: 'In those days, the idea was that you were dropped in the middle of it. I think that happened to everyone, certainly the older generation, and in the next generation – that which was me – we just went and walked in. That was it. And that's what we did basically' (Part 2, p 4). *Colin Bell* declares clearly, 'I was never taught how to interview… I had no research training. Well, up to the [arrival of the] SSRC, we never had any of that' (p 47). Anthropologists, in particular, seem to have been told to just go and find themselves a tribe and study it. Here is an intriguing piece of interview extract between the highly regarded anthropologist *Mary Douglas* and Paul Thompson. Mary did not even have an effective supervisor, so she relied on the advice of the experience of another Oxford anthropologist, Godfrey Leinhart:

> *So you were just told that you should choose a tribe?*
>
> Yes. I wanted to do a matrilineal people… [Godfrey] didn't believe in fieldwork methods as a formal thing, he believed much more in interest and personal initiative…
>
> *Was he there at the same time?*
>
> Yes, the second part, yes. Yes. He came after I'd started. And – 'I haven't got any idea what to do with fieldwork, nobody's ever spoken to me about taking notes or anything'. So he said, 'Well, what do you want to know?' So I said, 'Well, how does one take notes?' So he looked at me, quizzical. So he put his head on one side and looked at me, and thought, 'Well, you don't smoke, do you?' 'No'. He said, 'Ah, that's a pity. I always wrote my notes on the back of cigarette cases!' (LAUGHS)
>
> So we had no formal training whatsoever…
>
> *Were you not taught how to interview at all?*
>
> No. No. Even the idea of interview is slightly suspect, compared with just being there. Yes. Participation.
>
> *You weren't taught to observe either?*
>
> No! Not really! (LAUGHS) I frankly, say, no. No.
>
> *And would that be normal in anthropology departments at that time?*
>
> Yes…
>
> *But why do you think that was so? Was it meant to be inspiration which made you understand?*
>
> Empathy. And common sense. You had problems, you wanted to know how they lived, what sort of things they minded about. How did they reconcile the contradictions in their lives? It all followed from itself. And we had these marvellous models of Evans-Pritchard's and Meyer Fortes's books, and Audrey Richards. (pp 26–30)

The situation was little different in sociology, as *Frank Bechhofer* describes when he joined the team for the celebrated study *The Affluent Worker*:

> If I was being modest, [in terms of methods] I would say we were innocents abroad! ... Because, in fact, everybody was an innocent abroad. Although, you see, there'd been quite a lot of work done by people who had anthropological backgrounds and had done studies and so on, there was very little written and talked about this stuff in those days... Nonetheless, it seems to have been my fate! I taught myself to do surveys – then, all of a sudden, we were teaching ourselves to do these things, you know! ... We actually did develop a technique with a lot of these people, who were confident, articulate, perfectly happy to talk about what they were doing. (p 67)

Or consider *Dennis Marsden*'s account of how the research was planned for Jackson and Marsden's *Education and the Working Class*, generally seen as one of the most celebrated, influential and important works of British sociological works of the 1960s. Dennis shows here how the culture he worked in was more or less oblivious to issues of methodology. He describes how the book was designed:

> It was terribly easy. We bought a tea of halibut and chips, and then after tea, we kind of got down on the mat and sketched out what the sample would look like, who we'd talk to. They would be people like ourselves, who'd been to grammar school – from a working-class background – been to grammar school and been successful, and then what happened to them? ...
>
> The design was that we'd follow up the ones we could get via the parents. And fortunately, because Huddersfield was very stable at that time, although not since, we could trace quite a large proportion. I don't know whether we've got the exact details, but what's really weird as well is that, without any credentials, we bowled up to the school and got the samples, you know, even without an introductory letter. (p 60)

The project was backed by *Michael Young* at the Institute of Community Studies, where Dennis had been working. The Institute was a major research centre; but it cannot be said to have engaged with methodology at all deeply. Indeed, Jennifer Platt's book on the Institute, *Social Research in Bethnal Green* (1971), largely concentrates on showing its many flaws.

In retrospect, Dennis Marsden willingly accepts this: 'We hadn't got a method... I think the thing about the Institute that was attractive but also, I think, an Achilles heel, was that they were, I think they were determinedly amateurish – in a best sense, rather than the worst sense ... They'd almost prided themselves in not being specialists' (p 73).

Many other Pioneers made comments that might shock modern funders (or readers). That said, they certainly produced lively, interesting and influential books. Certainly, there was no systematic qualitative methodology in Britain before at least the 1960s. Before then people just went out and did it. Nevertheless, through their self-critical recollections we are also witnessing how a recognition of the need for more thinking about methods was beginning to emerge.

Diverse fieldwork styles: getting started

So how did our Pioneers get going? There were indeed some who throughout their research lives continued to favour initial spontaneity, in a zestful almost amateur spirit. Thus *Ray Pahl* would advise would-be researchers:

> I would just go round talking to people. I really enjoy doing that. Basically, I think research is fun... I just love the sort of mooching around and getting the feel of a place, and just looking a lot. So, in each case, you know, I'd drive around and just explore the place to begin with, and stop and talk to people... Just very vague questions. And they just chat. And I get a feel, from talking to different people, about what it all is... I was just, really, being curious. I have this great curiosity. I really find it very interesting to find what other people's lives are like, and how they see it from their point of view. So it's their perspectives, really. And I've got a curious capacity – I just seem to have it – that I can slip into... the mode of the person I'm talking to. (p 58)

David Hargreaves was in a more specific situation. He had to choose a single school to study because he was working within a much wider project on school ethnographies. He already had a definite sense of purpose and he set about it in a rough and ready but rational way. He came from a working-class family in industrial Lancashire, where he attended Bolton Grammar School, 'a very good school. It was in beautiful buildings. It was a very traditional boys' school, now independent, with teachers wearing gowns' (p 5). He went on to Cambridge and then to teach for three years at Hull Grammar School, before moving in 1964 to Manchester to work with Max Gluckman on the Secondary School Research Project. The choice of school in Salford for his ethnography was left to him. He determined on a deliberate contrast in social class terms with those schools already under study by his colleagues.

> They'd started the project. I was the third person to be added, working on schools. Two had already started – Colin Lacey... and Audrey Lambert. Colin had chosen to work in a grammar school, boys' grammar school in Salford; Audrey went to the girls' grammar school; so the question was, where would I go? ... So I thought, 'Well, there's only one thing to do, is to go to the absolute opposite end of the scale'. (pp 21–22)

So he decided to look for a tough working-class secondary modern school. The way he found it and secured access highlights the informality of the research context in the 1960s:

> I got on a bike and began cycling around Salford till I found the worst looking school I could find, which was a worn out sec. mod. opposite the docks in Salford, and I went back and said, 'I think I should go there'. So the Department [of Anthropology] then arranged a meeting with the Director of Education. In those days they were rather grand men who Headteachers called 'Sir', (LAUGHS) and I went to see him, and he called the Head of this secondary modern school, Ordsall Secondary Modern School for Boys.
>
> The Head was there, the Head was called Haggerston, some name like that, and [the Director of Education] said, 'You'll have this man, Haggerston, in your school, won't you, Haggerston, have this man in your school to study the students?' And then the Head said, 'Oh yes. Yes, of course'.
>
> So this must have been in the summer term, so I duly turned up on the next day, not having a clue what I was going to do. And the Head said, 'Well, what do you want to do? I mean, you're here till the end of term'. And I said, 'I'm sorry, you've got this wrong. I'm here for possibly a couple of years'. 'Here for a couple of years?' I said, 'Yes'. Well, he couldn't go back to the Director and say, 'I've been misled', so I was kind of there! (LAUGHS) And that's when I began my ethnography of the school!
>
> I just was dumped in, and went along there every morning, and tried to worm my way into a school where everybody was

> suspicious of this kind of Cambridge guy, who was from the
> university, and they don't really know what anthropology is,
> and, 'What's he doing in our school, except spying?' (pp 20–22)

By contrast, there were others who recall much more meticulous planning. As we have seen, *Janet Finch* described in some detail how her sociology project on clergy wives was 'a quite well-planned project, carefully thought through selection procedures and that kind of thing'. She explained how her sample was based on clergy lists within both geographical and denominational boundaries (pp 28–32). And among our Pioneer anthropologists we can also spot how their research approaches could develop through their lifetimes.

We can find a good example in the work of *Ruth Finnegan*. Born in Londonderry, daughter of a storytelling mother, she grew up in wartime rural Donegal. For her doctoral thesis at Oxford she chose the Limba people in Sierra Leone, where she developed her focus on local storytelling, its variety of techniques, and also its creativity – which anthropologists looking for transgenerational myths had overlooked. This led to her classic *Oral Literature in Africa* (1970). A year earlier she had moved to Milton Keynes to teach at the Open University. She was provoked by colleagues who disparaged the new town as a cultural desert. But she could hear the Salvation Army band, see children with violins or guitars, go to amateur opera, sing in the local choir, and she soon discovered that many schools had an orchestra and a choir and many pubs hosted live music. Inspired by Howard Becker, she decided to compare the different musical cultures within the city. And she found even more rich musical culture than she had expected. She reflects on the diversity of methods which she used:

> a huge mix of methods. Participant observation was at the heart
> of it... I also used documentary sources. Newspapers are a
> wonderful source which are really very much underestimated...
> It wasn't just that they gave accounts of performances, but there
> are all the little advertisements, 'We want an 18-year-old to join
> our reggae group', or 'The Cock and Bull pub is putting on its
> usual folk performance this evening', or 'We're auditioning for a
> part in the opera': all the little things like that – a huge amount,
> every week! And the list of forthcoming music events in various
> different places. Or the church advertisements, of their choirs
> and their organs and so on, or advertisements for school teachers
> and so on. So newspapers are great.

I also, as I hadn't done before, had a research assistant... who did a number of interviews for me with local bands, pubs, churches, clubs. I think that's the main lot. I did a postal questionnaire with schools...

[I did] fairly short interviews, yes. Not recorded. No. They were structured, but not too structured. Some were more structured than others. There wasn't a huge amount I needed to know from the pubs, so they were questions like – what they put on, how many people came, and things like that. With the bands, it was more open-ended. And she [the research assistant] was great. Some were face-to-face, and some were telephone. (pp 69–72)

Ruth calls participant observation 'the heart' of her methods. But there were new complications in working that way within her own community in England:

Of course, there were big problems about that. There are problems about participant observation anywhere, but they're somehow played down when it's overseas with faraway people.

But with these different musical worlds, I participated in them in different ways. For in the classical world – as I call it – that is simplifying it, I had long been a member of a local choir, and, in fact, I took my local choir as one of the case studies. My children were learning music in the classical way, going through the graded exams. I was a part-organiser in local classical music – putting on various events, a member of the committee there. I had played the cello, but very, very badly, at school, so I at least could talk to people reasonably about that.

So that was very much my home terrain, and I could participate both as audience and performer and parent in that. With some of the others, I could very much appreciate their music, like the brass bands, the folk music, and very much be again, a perfectly acceptable role of audience member and admirer, and talking with people on a fairly equal terms with a certain amount of knowledge, so those were all acceptable roles.

What I wasn't going to do, was to learn how to be a jazz drummer, or a country and western firer of guns – a really extreme rock performer. But I could go along in the sense of being a fan, or with some of the local bands that performed at people's weddings, not pretending to be a potential client, but they could see me, they could talk to me in the sort of way that they would to somebody who might be going to engage them. And I could always go along and be sometimes an anonymous audience member, and sometimes that was quite acceptable in pubs. Or in some large event I could be a member of the audience. So I could participate in a number of different roles, but they were different in different musical worlds. (pp 69–72)

Some emerging challenges

After their initial planning and choices of methods, what more specific problems did our Pioneers confront in the field? Let us illustrate some of the issues which many of them faced. Probably the commonest were the choices in style of *interviewing and recording*. David Silverman, a major pioneer of qualitative research in the UK, suggests that today we now live in the 'Interview Society'.[6] In the 1950s/60s interviewing or being interviewed were relatively much rarer practices: there were fewer surveys, and ordinary people's voices were much less commonly heard through the media. So our Pioneers were contributing to shaping the arts of interviewing and listening. Within qualitative tools, the interview takes pride of place. But already it came in many forms. Some studies used lengthy and highly structured interview guides, which were often circulated between researchers and carefully adapted as new themes were raised. Others went out to interview with little more than a few headline openers in their minds. There were also linked issues about how best to record interview proceedings. Some used transcriptions, while others took notes, often leaving this to memory until after the interview. At first only a few used tape recorders.

Dennis Marsden used interviews in all his five major studies. Favouring flexible and open-ended questions, he believed that as an interviewer you should be 'prepared to let your respondent dictate what is the topic of interest, and let it run if you find something interesting. You don't know why it's interesting, but you think, "That's a good quote". You can't imagine how it can possibly go in the final version, but somehow it will. So you run with the quote and let the interview go to its full length.' He describes interviewing for his first major study, *Education and the Working Class*:

> I did have a full list of questions worked out, with possible probes, as if it was a questionnaire, so that it was in my head. But, of course, people didn't answer in the right way. Their lives didn't fit my preconceptions, so we never used that stuff. But what I did use it for – and it's amazing how it comes back – sometimes

I had notes with me about main topics, and the big danger with being a flexible interview is, you miss out a whole area of life like money, or sex, or marriage. You get out and you suddenly find you've lost it! So I had a check-list at the end. You know, 'Can I just look through this and check that I haven't missed any anything out?'... [Afterwards] I went down my list of questions and tried to restructure the interview, and order them. I didn't stick rigidly to that, either because quotes, actually, can make either four or five things, so you run with the quote, but try and keep it [within] the structure of the questions that you're interested in. (pp 102–103)

Dennis also raised a problem common for our interviewers: how to take records of what was spoken? Some kept notes; a few wrote diaries; and a good few depended on memory. Systematic data collection, as we may now like to call it, was rare. Nevertheless, from the outset *Raymond Firth* certainly saw the importance of keeping a record through a thematic diary.

Well, I tried to develop very systematic methods. First of all, my diary. A daily diary. And I divided it into sections – weather; myself; people; and very soon I added food. And that meant that, day by day, I could look back and see what sort of changes had been taking place. And as I've just given you a few examples, I recorded my own... frustrations and feelings, moral dilemmas and the like in this, not very fully. In those days, I think we didn't engage quite as much in the navel gazing as anthropologists are apt to do now! (p 78)

When *Ruth Finnegan* was asked how she kept notes, she laughed and said:

It wasn't really very organised at all... I had lots of different – I had notebooks that I wrote down things when I talked to people, or had been to see some event, and they were kind of running by date. Yes, this was a very good bit of advice I got from John Blacking [a musicologist-anthropologist friend]... He said, 'If you're participating in something, *make* yourself write notes about it'. And so every time when I came back from my evening with the Sherwood Choir, which was my choir, I really, really tried either then or the next day, to write notes. And it's hard to make yourself do that, and really hard to make yourself notice things that you'd just taken for granted. But that was such good advice. So I had all that written down. (p 74)

Meanwhile, the technology had been changing. While various forms of recording machine had been in use, most often for music, since the end of the nineteenth century, before the 1960s their quality was too poor and they were too cumbersome for fieldwork. *Jack Goody* describes how he began to use recording machines:

> I had no recording machine. I did it by hand. Well, they didn't exist at that time, the transistor had not been invented, or adapted. The first time I did recordings was some years later, in Gonja, in a different area, where I got flown a machine from the BBC. It was an old German machine, which was used to play things in the trenches, or record things in the trenches – it worked on a battery, and had valves – that was flown out to me, and I took it, with great difficulty, to an African village, and actually used it to broadcast. I did a broadcast of it when I returned. But that was so heavy that you needed somebody to carry it around if you haven't got a car. It was only later on that the portable tape-recorder turned up, and I then went with my friend, Kumbano, back to the first place I'd been to, and made some recordings at that time, and we've recorded ever since. (pp 40–41)

However, it seems that even when more practical recording machines became available, unlike Goody many leading researchers were very slow to take up their use. *Michael Young* discouraged their use at the Institute of Community Studies. *Judith Okely* felt them inappropriate in her work with the marginal and persecuted Roma families. 'I never recorded them speaking. I dictated the notes on to the tape, but to come with a tape-recorder, no, except right at the end when... I said, "It's always good to tape people after you've known them for a while".' And *Pat Caplan* remembers that her supervisor explicitly advised her against their use for her fieldwork in Tanzania:

> He was all for being very sensible, and so you had your notebook and pencil, and when I told him I was going to take a tape-recorder, 'Oh, I don't know about that, Pat', he said, 'just encumbering yourself, and an extra thing to worry about'. He was not at all interested in technology and stuff like that. But I did take a tape-recorder into the field, and I had this massive

UHER, which weighed a ton. I think it weighed something like 12 lbs, that I used to walk around with it on my shoulder... So I made quite a lot of recordings...

They would have been higher quality, had I not done a foolish thing, which was that I got the longest – there were extra-long play tapes, which, I didn't realise at the time – they lasted for a very long, about two, three hours, each tape, because you could turn them over. But they were very thin. And so some of them deteriorated. When they were digitised, there were some parts, because they were so thin, they would stretch very easily, and then they would get spoilt. (p 20)

Peter Townsend describes similar initial problems with reel-to-reel tapes:

At that stage, tape-recorders were pretty novel. They weren't all that good in the way they worked... It was a great trial to me even... In the 1970s I tried to get them re-recorded on to modern cassettes, for example, and I found that two or three of them were on tapes which couldn't be [copied] without an enormous difficulty, and I still have two or three which, I was told, it would be enormously difficult to reproduce in cassette form. (p 39)

Both Peter and Pat remark particularly on the new difficulty brought by recording and transcription of interpreting such large bodies of material. *Pat* remarks:

Doing a transcription and then doing a translation is a huge amount of work... It's very, very slow, very time-consuming work. I mean, it's wonderful to have them, but it is a lot of work, especially if you're operating through another language where you've got to do the transcription in that language... Well, you should, technically you should. And then you should do the translation afterwards. (pp 21–22)

Peter describes how he tried to get round with this problem of initial interpretation:

Of course, it's very difficult to [use transcriptions]. I mean, it's an easy thing to do, in a sense, you think you've got it all on tape, and you have. But, my God, if you get back home, and you've done a hundred interviews, and you've got 500 hours of tape, or 300 hours of tape, the problem of selection is fantastic, without taking up the same amount of time looking for the things that you wanted, and then having to re-repeat them. I think, still, the best plan, even if you record, and I've tried to do this myself a few times, if you record an interview, to be absolutely punctilious about what was said, so that you could, with your hand on your heart, say, 'This isn't recollected afterwards, but this is actually what they said'. Then the ideal is to, even when you've heard a recording, to go back home and then take another half hour, in your own way, repeating what you think were the key points that were expressed during that interview. And then I think there's more possibility of getting back to those interviews which were particularly revealing, and important for you to illustrate. (p 40)

Peter's comments here lead us towards the broader challenges of *the interpretation of fieldwork data*. On this our Pioneers offer a multiplicity of examples. We can contrast two very different approaches. Thus, on the one hand *Mary Douglas* seeks to understand the strangely different mental world and metaphysical imaginations of the Lele people in the Congo, who had become Christianised but still believed in their forest spirits. Her method was essentially through empathetic conversation and intense listening.

I'd go out with a notebook, and a little stool on my arm, that I can sit down on, and asked them to help learn some grammar, or give me a few words, and then I hear there's a meeting, and I go to it, and I found it very hard, at the beginning, to hear at all what was said, but gradually I got to understand – particularly the women helped me a lot. And I got reproached for talking like a woman! They talk quite differently... Well, you start sitting out with people who are sitting out. It's a little bit like being in a doctor's surgery, as it was, because in the daytime, all the men went hunting.

They wouldn't let me into the forest, in the first village, because they said that the spirits in the forest wouldn't like me going there, and they, themselves, were terribly careful of taboos in a forest, so if I went, a log would fall on me, or I'd fall on a log and I'd break a leg, and then the government would be on them like a ton of bricks. They couldn't really risk having me around, unless I stayed in the village – which bored me stiff! I got no exercise, and I couldn't see what was happening. [But in the second village] I was able to go into the forest whenever anybody went, and I had a number of women friends who would say, 'Come on, we're off. We're going to get some water', and so I'd go with them. And that was delightful. I did lots of things with them.

But any time I wanted to go and talk to somebody, I could go and sit on – they had these lovely benches that they made out of split bamboo fronds, which they sat on all the time, so I could sit on one. And they were so polite, you see. They're charming, polite people, so they'd ask me, small talk, you know, and try me out on my language. 'Why do we hear that the white people, you have wars, do you?'... So I said, 'It's mostly about money. We fight for everything, but perhaps mostly money'. 'Why money? We fight, but we fight for women, always'. And you got delightful little sidelines from those conversations which meant nothing. But you had to edit it all up. (pp 35–36)

She would make rough notes during the day and then edit her notes in the evenings. And gradually she felt her way into their mental world. She found a path especially though talking with them about the forest animals:

I wanted to know – what I did find, these metaphysics of foreign people, those wonderful romantic ideas they had. So when I got to the place where they were all talking about animals, I would say, 'Why can't women eat this animal?' Or, 'Why doesn't anybody eat it?' or, 'Why can only warriors, who have killed a man, eat it?' They'd always start answering me, first of all, 'Well, that's what the old people told us', and when I still insisted that wasn't good enough an answer, they said, 'Well, have you ever seen it?' So I said, 'No'. And then they would describe its life habits, the habits and the look of the animal, the appearance of it.

And I realised eventually, not too soon, but within a few months, that they were answering my questions. And if I put all the answers together about all the animals, I could do something systematic about their view of their universe. And that then became a very exciting pursuit. So I really focussed on animals for a long time. I had to get the names of the animals translated, because there weren't many left in the forest, they didn't get them very often...

I was the first person to do a systematic account of all the animals that they classified, and a classification of the animals. But that was what we had been trained to do, you see. So that would be a system... You soon found that there were ground animals – under the ground – and that these were considered very influenced by the ancestors who were buried under the ground. And then there were animals on the land, and they were forest animals, or bush animals. They'd be carnivorous or herbivorous, or nocturnal or diurnal, or water animals, and by that classification, you found that there was a whole picture of the social system. There were sky animals – that was squirrels and birds – and sky animals had no implications for people, but all the land animals, and the burrowing animals, were so classified that you had a projection of the social system on the menu, who could eat what, you see. Pregnant women this, and women wanting to be pregnant that. And it was fascinating, it became a marvellous passion for me to watch it and go on asking, and then to get to know the answers myself as I came across new animals. (pp 28–29)

The interpretative approach of *George Brown* in his lifetime of studies of depression in women is again based initially on listening, but his techniques are totally different, both softer and harder, qualitative and quantitative. On the one hand he is more psychological, recognising *the power of emotion*. He sees that finding significant meanings cannot be simply a cognitive process through a rational analysis of words spoken in the interview. Emotion, whether anger, stress or affect, needs to be recognised as playing a major role in the process. But more surprisingly, he also believed that a serious social scientist should *measure* emotion. Today, researchers are likely to take emotionality very seriously; and this is a path in which George Brown was an early explorer.

George was not trying to document a new cultural world. He wanted to understand what triggered depression, why individual cases differed. Like most of the women he interviewed, he too was born into a London working-class family, and he first saw mental illness within his own family. Lacking any educational support at home, he accidentally came across social psychology at an IQ testing unit in the army, and only later as a mature student took a degree in anthropology. This led on to joining a research team who were observing activity in mental hospitals. George chose to live in two or more of these hospitals, sitting around the wards and observing. It was a time of great change, when the high walls round mental hospitals were being demolished and patients given much more freedom. George not only watched, but also he already measured. Some of these measurements were very simple, such as whether a patient had a comb or toothbrush, and what they owned, but he also introduced attitudinal measures, and time budgets. He carried this dual approach into his own interview-based projects, becoming increasingly interested in the role of emotions:

> I sensed, in a few seconds of going into a home, you could sense [either] a tremendous tension, or more relaxedness. It was something that was almost palpable in the air. And this is what I became interested in. My interest in emotion, which I see is central. And where I think so much sociology has gone wrong, or not done enough, is to leave out emotion, and to see human beings in terms of [only] the spoken word. I think this is a tremendous shortcoming, both of psychology and sociology, and psychiatry, for that matter. (pp 36–37)

And he committed himself to developing a growing set of measures of emotion:

> We started proper measurement. It was based on the idea that when you [spent time with] a family, you could sense what was going on, by talking. And it was then I got involved, if you like, in paralinguistic elements of speech. I sensed that what, in general, social scientists were missing, was the fact that emotion was the key system of meaning. Also, I might be reconstructing a bit, but that it's now clear, in terms of evolutionary evidence, that the larynx is tightly tied into the emotional system, in terms of development of speech and so on. But there's a direct link. It's extremely difficult to not convey emotion in speech, because of the construction of the system – without going into details. And this partly holds for facial expression...
>
> I think there's a lot of redundancy in emotional display, but you've probably got more control of facial expression than you have of paralinguistic [aspects of speech]. Often you can pick up clues about, shall we say, criticism, hostility, by facial expression and also by speech. So you've got content [in terms of what is said], you've got the vocal aspect of speech, and you've got facial expression. (p 50)

Alongside the paucity of explicit methodological practices to guide researchers, it is equally remarkable how little attention was given to *ethical issues*. There was rarely any consideration of the implications for the subjects of research. When *Raymond Firth* went to Tikopia he did not seem to be bothered about the potential impact on the local economy when he brought in adzes and types of steel tools and fish hooks which had been previously unknown in the island community. There were certainly not yet any professional guides to ethics. Such issues were only informally discussed. When Firth went to study the Tikopia, the main ethical issues he mentions were to do with his own feelings. For example, he was directly confronted with infanticide among the Tikopia, and remarks: 'I think I had to revise my views about the taking of human life. Infanticide was practised to some extent, and I could see the expediency of that. New-born infants having their faces turned down… against… a shortage in food supply. I had to think that one out a bit' (pp 70–71).

But these are scattered odd remarks. There was no general concern with research ethics even into the 1970s, when Ann Oakley comments:

> In those days you could get names of people to interview without going to Ethics Committees. So I got the names from two general practices in West London – I was just let loose in the files. I looked up names, and turned up on people's doorsteps, [with my tape recorder] in a shopping basket. (pp 12–13)

Since the 1970s, all this has started to change dramatically. Most professional associations like the Association of Anthropologists in the UK (ASA) and the BSA have developed their own ethical codes (usually in several editions). All universities will now have ethics committees. Discussions of ethics have become commonplace in research texts. All this was a big change, and our Pioneers played their part in shaping the new practices from the past. Here we find *Pat Caplan* worrying about its significance and much of her interview shows an acute awareness of these moral qualms:

> I was Chair of the ASA, and we decided that the ethical guidelines that we had at that time were not really – they needed updating, and so the committee – well, one guy in particular, who's now left the UK, Richard Wilson, he did a lot of work on that. And the Committee discussed it, and so we revised the guidelines. I see from the ASA website that they're now being revised again. So that raises an interesting question as to what extent ethics are universal and timeless, and to what extent they need to move with the times. And there are very obvious things that are changing, not least technology, which makes things possible that weren't possible before, and, therefore, raise different

kinds of ethical questions that were not addressed. Like the internet. (p 84)

Probably the most widespread issue was over problems of respondent confidentiality and publishing. Most British survey researchers believed that confidentiality was crucial to the response rates of their surveys, and therefore were particularly hesitant to allow research access to outsiders, or to introduce in-depth questions which made it easier to identify particular interviewees. *Dennis Marsden* recalls how his funders for *Mothers Alone*, the National Assistance Board, restrained him in his choices of who to highlight:

> You'd walk in the morning, perfectly ordinary house, just another name, and stagger out nine hours later! Well, you'd be there all day, kind of thing, with odd interruptions from neighbours calling round, and you'd think, 'Christ! People's lives. How amazing!' So there were certain people like that who kind of stood out...
>
> I mean, I learnt a lot of things. I had another woman who was very frightened, because she was a victim of a sado-masochistic man, and she described, quite chillingly, how she sat by the fire and he was asleep, the man was asleep – her husband – on the other side of the fireplace, and she was, of course, divorced by then, but she said she used to plan whether she could murder him and get away with it, because he was such a bastard to her. She once tried to have a bath, he used to come and sit on the end of the bath, he was kind of lusting after her. And she tried to have a bath by herself once, and she said, 'He banged and he brayed that door', he says, 'You'll never have a bath without me being there again', he kind of bashed the door in...
>
> There were certain key characters that I wanted to, to write in more prominently. But the NAB objected that they would recognise them, which was true, in a way. (pp 93–94)

It is noticeable that for Dennis the issue here was whether or not to publish, not of whether there might be an ethical obligation to report such a case to the police. *David Hargreaves* also reflects on dealing with confidentiality and publishing:

> I'd very carefully tried to mask [the respondents and participants] and the school, and most of the staff material I'd discarded on ethical grounds. I particularly could say very little about the

Headteacher because it would be obvious it was him, and the same applied to the Deputy Head, so I said much less than people would say nowadays. But there was a sense that I was portraying the school in a bad way and that was wrong – that was the negative half. The positive half said, 'This is great, you're telling it like it is, and people don't tell stories about schools like they are, and you should absolutely go ahead'. So in the end, I said, 'Look, any errors of fact, or anything that you think would betray a trust, tell me, and I'll remove them'. And I removed a few things.

But I found, interestingly, that then most people were guessing some of the quotations. And I'd say, 'Where are you quoted in it?' They'd get it wrong! They'd attribute to themselves things they'd never said, and attribute things they'd said to other people! So that was interesting! It shows I'd covered it up pretty well actually. Of course, the boys, I couldn't consult. But that was that. (p 30)

Peter Loizos was researching in a Greek-speaking hill village in Cyprus, but he was well aware that 'there were several people from the village who'd got excellent English, and then there were lots of people who'd got a bit of English, and then there's the rumour mill. So what you actually said, and how it got replayed and so on, all sorts of problems.' Hence there was certainly 'stuff I haven't published' (p 83). He was also clear about how to decide when silence was wise. 'I think the things people care about are things where their family honour is directly identified and impugned. So I avoid writing things that would upset them in the sexual honour sense. [And when] I am aware of semi-criminal or criminal acts, I tend to avoid identifying the perpetrators' (p 99).

On the other hand, thinking about these boundaries led him to challenge the theories of John Campbell, whose *Honour, Family and Patronage: A Study of Institutions and Moral Values in a Greek Mountain Village* (Clarendon Press, 1964) is one of the best-known works in Mediterranean anthropology. Loizos goes on to say, 'I picked stuff up by osmosis and by overhearing stuff. A lot of things are said and done in joke'.

I'll give you one example. All right? My cousin Tomas is going to go off on a Communist Party agricultural delegation to somewhere... So he's getting ready to go to the airport, and he's standing around with his wife, and they're about to separate, and she makes a joke! Somebody says, 'Maybe, who knows what foreign women he'll meet when he's abroad', and she says, 'If I had my way, I'd cut it off and keep it here!' All right?

Well, you hear a thing like that, everybody laughs, and you think to yourself, 'Honour and shame? Come on, guys!' There's another level in which these people interact and talk about these things, which isn't in Campbell. There's an earthiness and a directness there. And probably, if I were an outsider anthropologist, they wouldn't have said it in front of me. So you do get privileged access. (pp 56–57)

In the same spirit, Loizos told a story about prostitution in the village:

There was a man in the village who was a pimp, right? Everybody would tell you, behind his back, 'He's a pimp. And his prostitute is Egog'. They knew the name of the prostitute he pimped off – she wasn't a daughter of the village – and they knew he was a pimp, right? Now, in Campbell's honour world, you would have expected a certain social distance that, so when he went to the coffee shop, people avoided him. Did they hell! They flocked around him! He was a figure of interest, and a certain sort of terrible glamour, I suppose. So when I realised that they didn't stigmatise this man – I never wrote about this because there are things you don't write about – I saw there was a problem with honour, or I thought I could see a problem. (p 37)

Thus, our Pioneers were certainly aware of some ethical issues. But they worked and wrote without any formal guidance, making their own rules. Some helped to push forward change. And certainly since then social research has become increasingly a self-consciously aware and a deeply ethical and moral practice. It always involves a relation between researcher and researched. And it is always lodged in issues which earlier were rarely expressed: issues of trust, respect and exploitation; care, harm and damage to subjects; justice and equality; dignity; informed consent between subjects and researchers; privacy and confidentiality; deception, honesty, confidentiality; truth telling, accuracy; and ownership. Thinking about such issues was also part of methodology in the making. Nowadays all this is part of conventional methodology.

One final issue stands out: *how to take writing seriously.* Our pioneers researched in a time when many sociology and anthropology books became best sellers. Nevertheless, not many spent much time talking about the importance of writing in social science. We will see how

Michael Young thought writing was a crucial skill for would-be researchers (Voices 7). Here are two others who thought similarly. *Stan Cohen* speaks of how he came to take pleasure in writing and literary skills.

> I was then, I think, even more self-conscious about pretences to literary skills, in the sense that I'd always seen myself not as a scientist, but somebody in a kind of liberal – creative writing, humanist, I don't know – secular humanism, whatever, in that tradition. I mean, when I read Hoggart, even though I didn't feel anything about the English working-class (always totally alien and foreign to me), but Hoggart's idea of using words to communicate, or being clear, that part became interesting...
>
> But I was also aware of the literary and communicative aspects of it, that I should write in a clear way, and that I should use concepts which are dramatic, and I should use metaphors. I then was more conscious of the writing, and I think it was in that writing part that I truly felt most at home. The methodological part was – well, it was the material that had been worked, and reworked and reworked. This was when I discovered that I *loved* writing, and that it came very easily, and I could just go over and over something, and know, automatically, what was wrong with it. (pp 43)

Finally, *Dennis Marsden* captures what he felt mattered most about the outcome – a genuinely readable book. What made *Education and Social Class* such a success?

> At some level, it must be emotionally convincing, it must be coherent. It has a coherent argument, and it performs, I think, one of the ideal functions of qualitative research, which is to explain what's going on. When you've got large data sets with fairly striking messages but you don't understand what it is, or, at least, you've got the wrong idea of what it is, it gives you a different explanation of what's going on. But it also works at the level of a novel, I think. It communicates people, through people. It gets pictures of people. (pp 66)

Back in the 1950s, C. Wright Mills's *The Sociological Imagination* sensed an emerging fetishisation of method taking place in the US: research methods were starting to become ends in themselves. As we have seen, this was certainly not the problem in Britain. There is a certain freshness – maybe even naivety – in the approach to methods we find among our Pioneers. But even here methodology was in the making. Jump to the twenty-first century, and the world has become methods obsessed. By no means all our Pioneers welcomed this change. Indeed, *Pat Caplan* spoke for many when she said, 'I took early retirement because I must say I was increasingly fed up with what was happening in academia, and the stress on the whole audit culture thing was one issue' (p 85). Today's students are required to spend much time studying research methodologies they may never use; many degrees are now awarded entirely based on training in research skills. And there are many journals, books, conferences and professional associations devoted to the vast new discipline of methodology. Professional methods has now become the hallmark of the professional researcher. There were also already some signs of resistance to this change. Was Wright Mills right to protest, 'Let every man be his own methodologist, let every man be his own theorist'?[7]

VOICES 6

On the margins

Researching on the margins heightens the possibilities of new insights, but it can also bring special dangers of both physical and emotional dangers, as these two voices tell.

Maxine Molyneux: fear in Afghanistan

Well, there were some dangerous bits, yes. There were some dangerous places. I think when you're young, you don't think of risk so much, do you, you head off into it, and it's quite exciting. But looking back, I was a risk-taker, and I didn't mind that, it didn't affect me at first. I think the time I was most aware of my own mortality was in Afghanistan, when Fred [Halliday] and I went in 1980. It was just after the Russians invaded, and it was a very unpleasant, frightening trip, because we were targets – I mean, we looked Russian apparently. We both had leather jackets on, and that's what Russians wore, and we stood out. And we were taken around in armoured personnel vehicles. It was terrible.

We were told that So and So had been blown up yesterday, and a German TV crew in Herat had been killed in exactly the same spot. I was trying to do work on women's organisations, and they were doing such fantastic things, it was heartbreaking, trying to train young women, and give them an education and so on. So I went to all these projects, but under armed guard, with a platoon of soldiers behind me. But we got stuck in a market – I'll never forget – and the driver was absolutely terrified. You could see that. He said, 'We've got to get out of here. We've got to get out of here'. It was that, I think both of us came out of there, we went to Delhi after that, just feeling pretty rocked by that experience, to the core! But yes, you don't think about it. That was the trip I really did think about it. (p 30)

Avtar Brah: the struggle in academia

Avtar Brah grew up on the edge of the colonial British Empire. Her family fled to Britain to escape racist persecution in Uganda. She not only became a successful academic, but also fought on the front line for the welfare and rights of other Asians in Britain. She chose at the very end of her interview to voice how, nevertheless, she still feels marginalised in British academic life.

> If you're a person of colour, it's quite a struggle in academia. It's not something we've talked about actually, but it's difficult always to pinpoint. It's not that people are overtly racist or anything like that – Heaven forbid in academia you won't! But there are all kinds of barriers that you face. I mean, you have to be almost twice as good at something before you can be listened to, so to speak. So I've had a lot of struggles within the academy, although I have done very well as well. I can't say that I haven't. But it's been a struggle throughout – the work relationships.
>
> I don't mean the work relationships in the sense of close friends and colleagues that I got on with. So I think that I find that racialisation in all its complexity leaves a deep seated imprint on one's psyche and one's body. But I've been very lucky. I've been very lucky with friends…
>
> So yes, life, on the whole, has been good to me, but there have been difficulties.
>
> *Do you see that in terms of people being explicitly racist, or is it more that their networks are already with white people, and the subjects they think of are to do with white people, so they can't really understand the way that you're thinking?*
>
> They're not explicitly racist, no. But I think people, some of the people are beginning to realise that people used to think of race as something that was separate from white people. But now we have studies of whiteness, which is a racialised category, and so you then begin to say, 'But actually these are not separate things. It's a different way of thinking about these issues'. (pp 35–36)
>
> Obviously, questions of structure are important, but so are questions of emotion, so the emotional turn, the emotional turn in theorisation has been important, the cultural turn has been important. Yes, I think it's a particular take on research, it's a particular way of thinking about research questions which needs to be addressed. And I think my struggles in academia haven't been just intellectual, haven't been just about *me*, what obstacles put in my way, but actually it's a way of thinking about things that one had to kind of struggle, you had to cross. (pp 36–37)

CHAPTER 7

Social divisions: class, gender, ethnicity – and more

We have seen how research grows out of historical social conditions. As times change, so the problems, strategies and, indeed, the very methods of research are transformed. Even the histories of disciplines and research can come to look out of date very quickly. Reading A. H. Halsey's *A History of Sociology* (2004) is salutary: it shows how few women were involved before the 1970s, how there was a major neglect of race, and demonstrates the lack of interest in anything remotely postcolonial or 'queer'. Halsey's important history, published only 17 years ago, already documents a very different bygone world: a much more gentlemanly and privileged world. The worlds of research methods and its subjects keep being constructed and reconstructed, moving on through time and space.

In this chapter, we take issues of class, race and gender as major examples. Ill-defined and often absent in research of earlier periods, these become key issues strategically developed through research fields and methodologies. We show briefly how by the mid-1980s a major multiple/intersectional research field of social divisions was being carved out – one that did not exist before.[1]

Researching social class

As *Frank Bechhofer* recalled of the 1950s:

> We thought, everybody had been studying the working-class, it is a miracle that the working-class of Britain did not rise as a man and slaughter the sociologists, even if they didn't overthrow the government, because every sociologist in Britain seemed to be studying the luckless working-class! I mean, I think every miner had their own sociologist! It was really strange! (p 15)

As Bechhofer's observation suggests, the 1950s were a prime time for interest in social class. It was not always so. A cumulative inventory of post-1945 researching on social class suggests four major emerging concerns that helped construct it: the long-standing evolving history of research on poverty; the popular interest in community studies and change; the growing awareness of just how education and culture was shaping society – possibly creating new possibilities for less privileged groups to advance in social life; and, finally, the growing concern with finding how to measure both class and mobility.

First then, the growth of *poverty and inequality studies.* One thing is clear: social research has had a long-time interest in the lives of the poor. From the early-Victorian writings of Engels on poverty in Manchester and Mayhew's portraits of the London poor to Booth's documentation and geographical measurement of early twentieth-century London slums and poverty, this has been a well carved out field yielding a series of striking insights. In the post-war decades through at least until the 1970s this challenge was sustained through a cluster of major researchers including Richard Titmuss, Brian Abel Smith, David Donnison and *Peter Townsend.* We have seen how Townsend in particular brought a sharper focus into research on the lives of those with low incomes, the aged, the disabled. Thus, for example, looking back later *Mildred Blaxter* recalled how she was inspired by *The Last Refuge* (1962) – Peter Townsend's study of old people's homes – and the 'whole tradition' of 'brilliant' descriptive and openly progressive sociology. When asked how she came into sociology, she said:

> I think I have to say Peter Townsend. I have to say it was another book [*The Family Life of Old People*]. I have to say that I started out with Peter Townsend. I don't know how I came across these, but I got fascinated by that whole school of writing and went on from there... to *People of Ship Street*, *Coal is our Life*, *Family Life in East London*, *Education and the Working Class*, that whole tradition of brilliant, old-fashioned, British welfare/Socialist, descriptive sociology. And I thought, 'Yes. That's what I want to do'. And 'that's sociology, so I'll go off to university, and I'll do sociology, if that's what sociology is'. I mean, I wasn't quite right in that, but that's what I thought. (pp 20–22)

Blaxter herself took up this tradition in her own *Mothers and Daughters* (1982) on health and family life in Scotland. And, indeed, Townsend's books were certainly impressive, professionally innovative but also powerfully written. His research deployed multiple methods, thick with descriptions of the poor alongside statistical analysis. More: he developed key ideas, initially around absolute and relative poverty and later inequality and human rights. And his work was marked not just by analytical thinking and data, it encouraged activism. From his work grew the Child Poverty Action Group and the Disability Alliance. In his later work this question is drawn even more widely: to a global understanding of human rights and inequality. Social divisions had now become a global phenomenon. Big trees from little acorns grow.

Second, we see the developing discussion of *class in community studies*. We have observed (in Chapter 4) the rising importance in this period, and then fall, of community studies as a prime research model. It is symbolised by the development of *Michael Young*'s Institute of Community Studies, with its deep interest in working–class culture, exemplified in Young and Willmott's *Family and Kinship in East London*, as well as Peter Townsend's *Family Life of Old People*. It was also the launching point of *Dennis Marsden* and Brian Jackson's highly influential *Education and the Working Class* (1962). In most of the community studies, we are given an image of social class grounded in human actions and lifestyles. It was in this spirit that *W. M. Williams* summed up his first visit to his chosen village, Gosforth in Cumbria: 'I regarded myself as going to a foreign country'. As soon as he got off the local bus, he spotted the shopkeeper taking an order from the rector's daughter, who remained sitting above him on her horse. 'And I thought, "Here is the English class system in action!" And it couldn't be more different from industrial South Wales' (p 5).

The third focus was on the role of *social class in education and culture*. Three works shaped much thinking about class in this time: Michael Young's *The Rise of Meritocracy* (1958), Richard Hoggart's *The Uses of Literacy* (1957), and Jackson and Marsden's *Education and the Working Class*. All were grappling with the expansion of education and its links to mobility and class. *Young*'s fictional forecast was of a dark, satirical dystopian coming world where hierarchy was based on merit. *Dennis Marsden* remarked that: 'everybody was doing their best to stop him [publishing it], and saying, "It's boring", and "nobody would read it", and they kind of disparaged it, and pulled his leg about it. Little did they know that he'd invent a word that would become common!' (p 51). In fact it was an academic bestseller and very influential – in ways that Michael Young strongly disapproved of.[2]

Hoggart's book was a literary study that became a 'watershed' for cultural studies, demonstrating the power of radio and television, the emerging media, in changing traditional working-class cultures, while Jackson and Marsden's study was an empirical one that examined how working-class boys fared in grammar schools. Very influential, it is still being discussed: one recent study 'argues for a reinvigoration of the elusive search for the kinds of understandings of working class pioneered by Marsden, as the basis for a just and equitable schooling for working class children'.[3] In each case the emphasis was on how culture was shaping class. While class had long been incorporated into literature and novels, classic and new, the publication of these works were landmarks for a whole generation (and more). It brought a new focus on the links between class and culture.[4] Here was a vision of the problem ahead. As *Stuart Hall* says:

> Hoggart, though he doesn't discuss this directly, knew perfectly well that the sketch that he offered of an older working-class culture in which he'd been born and brought up as a child, and what was happening now, was a key contribution to this debate [on class consciousness in the post-war period], though people were conducting the debate in political terms, and economic terms, but not in cultural terms. But actually, if there was no social milieu in which these ideas could take root and become institutionalised, they weren't going to survive.
>
> So that's what we fastened on in [the 1950s New Left movement in] Oxford, why we took *The Uses of Literacy* as so important, because it was our discussion about how is capitalist society changing in the post-war period? What is the meaning of affluence? What is the meaning of the coming of television? What is the meaning of the coming of mass advertising to Britain? What's the meaning of the rise of an independent youth culture? What's the meaning of music? What's the meaning of Elvis Presley? What does it tell you about the mind-set of another generation, altogether different from Hoggart in his teens, in Hunslet in the thirties? (p 76)
>
> I meant there was a growing sense that people were being loosened from their class position and origin, and that in any case the content, social and cultural content of economic classes was being very different in the new period, and we had to come to terms with it, and to find a language to define that difference. (p 40)

Finally, we can turn to the theme of *social class in mobility studies*, which were then relatively new, but soon to become a major British sociological tradition. This originated with the pioneering work of David Glass (1911–78). Son of a London tailor, he was married to the urban community sociologist Ruth Glass. He had worked as a researcher on the Beveridge Report on post-war welfare and was to become a professor of sociology at the LSE. His *Social Mobility in Britain*

(1954) was a landmark project, providing the first major data set of the mobility across the social classes, and it became a benchmark study.[5] Its influence was substantial. For example, *David Lockwood* spoke of how he decided to write his thesis, which became

> this book on *The Black-Coated Worker* [1958], write the thesis, switch the thesis, and I was allocated to David Glass. Well, he was doing this big project on mobility, and there were people writing on the professions – Kelsall – and higher Civil Service – and Asher Tropp was doing the teachers, and I thought, well... I thought I'd do the lower middle-class. I mean, I had to narrow it down. So that was that. (pp 25–26)

At the same time, there was a growing suggestion that an increase in affluence would assimilate workers into the middle class, in turn embracing middle-class values and social life: the so-called 'embourgeoisement' thesis. These ideas became a precursor to the landmark studies of the Affluent Worker. As we have seen (Chapter 4), this was a major SSRC-funded project on the working class and the concept of class identity within Western industrial society. In retrospect, it is clear that the research team pitched themselves into the project with surprisingly little preparation. *Frank Bechhofer's* first degree was at Cambridge in mechanical sciences and the theory of engineering at Cambridge, and he subsequently took a course in industrial management. He tried and failed to get permission to research in an industrial plant in Yorkshire. *John Goldthorpe* then suddenly appeared in his life, like a devil 'with horns on his head', but they got on very well, enjoying playing squash together. So he started a PhD with John as supervisor on how engineering graduates adapted to work in industry. But he still had no training in how to interview. Nor had his co-researcher Jennifer Platt, although she had started reading books on survey methods while in Chicago. Frank recalls:

> All of a sudden I find myself plunged into this full-size, genuine sociological project. I mean, with one bound, I was a sociologist! This is ludicrous, looking back, today. But there it was, and I found myself in this office... with Jennifer Platt, who, of course, was not a sociologist either, although, at least, for Heaven's sake, she had done a Master's in Chicago, having started as doing English literature at Cambridge. And she had at least come back with a Master's from Chicago! ... Then we were at the point, therefore, of actually doing it. And we were at the point

of negotiating access with these firms, something on which you will recall, I had a wonderful track record! (pp 25, 29)

Frank nevertheless designed an interview questionnaire which he feels still stands up well against more recent practice. 'We piloted the whole thing, and it was all pretty kosher stuff, really, insofar as there was a Talmud at the time!' (p 34). And he also recalls how well the research team worked together:

> But the dynamics – well, David and John were obviously the senior figures, and they were the prime drivers, if you like. But certainly considering how little I knew, they were amazingly tolerant of me, and with the whole study, there was an enormous amount of collaborative debate. And, incidentally, I think that's the other thing that's had a permanent effect on me, was that... and it was quite unfashionable in some parts of British academia, we did work as a team, although, you know, if very very rarely, the chips were down, and somebody had to make a decision, it would be David and John who made it. Obviously, if the chips were down, it was their project. But most of the time the decisions were collegiate. Sometimes, after furious debate, I mean really furious, and the fur used to fly. (p 29)

The investigation focussed on the attitudes and behaviour of high-wage earners in three Luton-based companies, and how these attitudes were shaped. Luton was a relatively prosperous town with a rising standard of living. The project looked at these local firms (Vauxhall Cars, Skefco Engineering and La Porte Chemicals), making comparisons between workers in different types of production systems and exploring workers' class identity. It also examined the wider imagery of social class. The interviews with the workers showed little sign of a move towards middle-class cultural values – instead, affluent workers seemed to hold on to their working-class identity and attitudes. The researchers concluded that growing affluence does not entail the end of class, or of class politics; on the contrary, class remains an important part even of a prosperous, affluent society. It was published in three volumes. A follow-up study was made 30 years later.[6] Although in retrospect its lead researcher *John Goldthorpe* complained that it had been wrongly 'enshrined in British sociology' (p 37), the Affluent Worker project certainly raised issues of methodological design and logic that had been largely missing from British researchers, and Mike Savage has ranked it among British studies as 'the most influential ever conducted'.[7]

For *John*, however, the Affluent Worker remains a stumbling stepping stone towards the much more significant Oxford-based social mobility study, which originally hoped to replicate the Glass social mobility study. This was the real turning point:

> I think we were able, for the first time, in a national survey, to really get to grips with some fundamental, conceptual issues in studying mobility, and to translate these into appropriate statistical techniques. What we planned to do originally – and this was really Chelly Halsey and Jean Floud's idea – was to do a study that would, on the one hand, replicate Glass, and so bring Glass up to date, and allow for comparisons over time with Glass, and secondly, would replicate Blau and Duncan with their more advanced regression methods, and allow a comparison between Britain and the United States. What we discovered, in the early years of the project – and I think I was quite heavily involved in this – that neither of these two things was, in fact, possible. We couldn't replicate Glass because the basic coding in Glass, of occupations, was to the Hall-Jones Scale, which was defective in many ways, and there was no clear guidance, no clear manual for doing this coding. The two documents that were available were contradictory in regard to many occupations. And we couldn't get the original schedules to re-code the data. (p 37)

From this point onwards he continued to explore the issues of social class in mobility, using important new comparative measures, such as odds ratios. His later work also focussed almost exclusively on mobility among men, whose mobility paths were much easier to measure than those of women. This tactic in itself stimulated further debate, including among our Pioneers.[8]

Researching gender

In the 1970s, as a direct result of the social explosion generated by the second wave of the women's movements, a whole new field of 'gender research' was opened up.[9] Women had sometimes been subjects of social research, especially in community studies and social policy, but 'gender research' now brought a powerful new perspective, highlighting social inequalities in a different way from class, and raising issues about methods: in particular, the nature of the interview relationship, and how far it was acceptable for men to be researching on women as subjects. Through raising both personal and political issues, and their intertwining, it injected a new and explicit political stance into sociology. It also brought a new terminology. *Ann Oakley* recalls how she first made the distinction between sex and gender, on which so much subsequent work depended:

> A publisher called Maurice Temple Smith commissioned me to write my first book, while I was doing my Ph.D., because I'd started to write stuff about sex and gender, essentially. So they commissioned, *Sex, Gender and Society* [1972], which is in a series called 'Towards a New Society'. That book is still in print, with a new introduction. I wrote it in six weeks, and I delivered it on time, and I learnt that you're not supposed to deliver books on time. The publisher was deeply shocked when it arrived! But the Oxford English Dictionary credits that book with the introduction of the modern sense – definition of gender. Now, I had absolutely no idea –
>
> *Were you aware that you were introducing a new term?*
>
> No, no. Robert Stoller was a doctor working with people with gender problems, and so the original separation of sex and gender came actually from the medical psychiatric literature, but it hadn't moved into common parlance, and certainly not into the language of social science until I did this book. (Part 1, p 14)

From the 1970s onwards growing numbers of women came to play increasingly important roles in social research. Most of our women Pioneers were influenced by or directly involved in this major shift. They had to respond to the rise of second-wave feminism, and most, but not all, fully embraced it. They became actively involved and rebuilt both their lives and professional disciplines through it. Some were more sceptical. And like the movement itself there were different positions from liberal through socialist to radical. And the early 1970s was their key moment.

Our Pioneers recalled especially four issues. The first was the obstacles which they confronted. The second was the importance of building networks of support and solidarity. Third, some of them spoke of how eventually they became role models for the next generation. And lastly they spoke of how new agendas were set; and generated not only new solidarities, but also tensions and conflicts.

First then, *obstacles*. Many of our women Pioneers recounted restrictions which as women they had faced through their education and professional careers. Thus, *Judith Okely* spoke of her experiences at Oxford, and of having to sign a contract at St Hilda's College to say she would not marry while a student. 'One girl, she was found in bed with her boyfriend during visiting hours, and she was expelled. And Miss Major, the Principal, wrote to every university she applied to, and to her grant authority, saying she was unfit for education' (p 48). Likewise, *Diana Leonard* found the relationship between the male majority and female minority of students at Cambridge very unsettling:

> What can one say about Cambridge? There were ten men to every woman. It was bad for the men, and it was absolutely worse for the women. You were never allowed to forget that you were a woman, and they were constantly hitting on you, but you didn't know whether they were hitting on you, or they were just hitting because they felt they had to have girlfriends... So, all told, my time at Cambridge, I was quite lonely. I felt harassed. I felt that I should be having a good time, and I was having a perfectly horrible time. (pp 13, 15)

Leonore Davidoff, who had come to Britain as an American graduate and completed an MA at the LSE, describes her extraordinary humiliating treatment in her first job interview:

> That was the unforgettable interview I had which, looking [back], years and years later, I realised had pushed me more into feminism. I was interviewed in London, by Charles Madge [the founder of Mass Observation], because the job was in Birmingham, and he used to come to London regularly. He was a member of the Athenaeum Club, and so he arranged to meet me at the Athenaeum Club for the interview. So I arrived, and he proceeded to interview me on the steps of the Athenaeum Club, because women weren't allowed into the Club! I was a bit taken aback, and fortunately, it wasn't raining, it wasn't foggy. And I got the job. But it's things like that that stick in your subconscious. At the time, I thought nothing – I wanted the job, and I got it. (p 39)

Most commonly, there were the day-to-day practical problems of a woman trying to combine pursuing research work with being a mother in a society in which most fathers played slight roles in childrearing. *Diana Leonard* recalls:

> I seemed to spend years dressing children up, strapping them into cars, driving them to school, unstrapping them from cars, walking them, taking their clothes off – because, of course, the primary schools didn't approve of children staying at school all day long, so you had to go and pick them up and bring them home for lunch, and that just occupied all my time! All my time. (p 24)

Many of our women researchers spoke of the ways in which they found new *networks of support* by creating, or finding and belonging to a women's group of some kind, and just how important this was for them. Most often, as we have seen (Chapter 3), these were informal local community activities, often also providing services for women. But other networks were professional. Thus, in the early 1970s women's caucuses were established in both anthropology and sociology. Here are some extracts where women speak about joining these groups. *Janet Finch* recalls how such group activities provided 'intellectual anchor points' for her:

> The BSA Sexual Divisions Study Group, BSA Women's Caucus, BSA Family Study Group, to some extent, but a slightly less extent, [are] all enormously important intellectual anchor points for me. These were the places at which I met, on a regular basis, people from round the country who were in a similar position to me, with similar interests to me. And, you know, we did meet much more regularly than, I think, the equivalents meet now – entirely at our own expense, and very cheaply. We would meet, for example, in Bradford, because Sheila [Allen] was often involved in this. We would just meet entirely at our own expense, for a Saturday afternoon, and go off for a curry, and it was great! ... So it was often a mixture of intellectual work and plotting women's careers, and how to take over the BSA, and things like that! ...
> I ended up chairing the BSA Executive at a very early stage in my career. Oh, '83-'84. I was on the Executive from 1980. It was Margaret Stacey that did that. She persuaded me to stand for the Executive. (pp 47–48)

Similarly, *Pat Caplan* speaks as an anthropologist joining women's groups:

So I got involved in feminism, into feminism in two ways. One was through local groups – consciousness raising groups, book-reading groups – with women who were in kind of the same boat as me, they weren't anthropologists, but they'd all got degrees, and they'd got children the same age as mine, and so that was one thing.

But on the other side several of us formed the London Women's Anthropology Group, which met for a number of years, and produced a collection at one stage, and ran a few conferences. That was very, very important, because we talked about anthropology, and we began to realise some of the kind of biases that it had built in – although, I suppose if I'd thought about it, which I didn't very much, anthropology was attractive as a career, because there were some women who'd clearly made it. When you actually looked at what kind of recognition they'd had, we began to realise that for example, Margaret Mead never had a tenured post. Audrey Richards, who was also a pioneer anthropologist, never got a professorship, and so on and so forth. So that there were limitations, and it was much harder to do whatever you wanted to do.

So that was very, very important for me, being involved in that group, and really re-thinking who I was, what I was, what it meant being a woman anthropologist. So when I started to think about what I would do on the next research project, I wanted to do something connected with gender, or 'women' I suppose we would have called it, in those days. And we had the very strong feeling that women were under-represented, not only in the profession, but also as subjects for study in both sociology and anthropology. And the people who were in our group included people like Diana Leonard Barker, Annie Whitehead, Olivia Harris, quite a few who went on to make names. (pp. 51–52)

Pat also worked as a volunteer at a London feminist resources centre:

Then the third sort of feminist contingent I was involved with were at an organisation called 'The Women's Research and Resources Centre', which was set up in the early 1970s... and I volunteered my services there two days a week, and there was already Zoe Fairbairns, who's a novelist, she was there part-time, as the only paid worker, and then I joined her as an unpaid volunteer worker. But that was a fantastic experience, because

> I learnt a lot of things, it boosted my confidence a lot, it was a very interesting place to work. So I met a lot of fascinating people – Lee Davidoff, for example, in another group. (pp 51–52)

The movement also became strengthened over time as more women rose to senior academic positions and were therefore able to give support to younger social researchers through *becoming role models. Janet Finch* was well aware of this:

> Oh, I think I feel a huge responsibility to [be a role model for younger women], yes. Not particularly self-consciously, I think. I've always enjoyed encouraging younger people's careers, and it comes very naturally. And I'm happy to play that role directly, wherever I can. It is, of course it's a very common experience for women, in any leadership position, that you have very high expectations when you're appointed, other women have high expectations, that you will be able to change things. Of course, that almost always ends up in disappointment, because you never can change things as quickly as they would like, and that you might like yourself. (p 100)

As an older researcher, brought up as a feminist, *Meg Stacey* had an outstanding professional career, publishing 14 books, and culminating in becoming Professor of Sociology at Warwick and President of the BSA in 1982. She recognises herself as a role model, albeit with a touch of reluctance:

> They have told me, in hordes, since, that I was an important role model, and I'm still left with my mouth slightly falling open about this. I mean, it has to be true, because so many people have said this. I suppose I saw myself as pioneering in quite a lot of areas, not only gender, but other things like in the methods of social research, and doing the kind of research I did, that we were talking about. But basically, I was just doing what seemed, to me, to be right, and however people saw it was, really, really their business. It's rather a piece, I suppose, of one saying, 'I never set out to have a career', because that, you know, that wasn't something that I thought might be possible, really, or it certainly wasn't a high priority, it was something that would be nice to do, if one could. But I hadn't thought of a sort of career path. And in the same way, I, therefore, don't think I thought of myself, particularly, as a role model, although I knew that it

was part of what I had to do, to support other women. And this I did whenever I could.

Some feminists, I noticed, really only used it for their own self-advancement, to my great shame. I always felt very ashamed about that. But I just determined I wasn't going to do that, so when I got a share, I just said that I would keep the faith. So I've always supported any younger women who wanted help or were in trouble. But I wasn't thinking of myself as being a role model, I was thinking that I was a very lucky woman. Here I was, I had great doubts about whether I should ever have taken a Chair at all, in terms of what it meant in working in a hierarchy and things like that, so it bumped into one of my personal conflicts. But, no, I don't think I thought of myself as a role model, but I think I was one. [Laughs] (pp 56–57)

Central to the whole movement was the *opening of new agendas*, socially, politically and intellectually. Women's interests come to the fore in their own right. At the same time fundamental issues of the life cycle – like childbirth, childrearing, housework, the stresses of marital life, lesbianism, sexual violence, health and ageing – are now seen from new perspectives and start to be re-problematised.

Thus, through *Ann Oakley*'s innovative and prolific researches on the stresses of becoming a mother these are transformed from individualised mental issues to problems with the unequal basic division of labour in parenthood. Much of her work, she says, 'has interrogated this whole notion of post-natal depression, which most of the time is actually a label for women who are chronically exhausted and sleep-deprived, and just have too much to do' (Part 1, p 11). *Sara Arber* has opened up whole new fields on the gender inequalities of ageing, and also on the surprising gender differences revealed by the sociology of sleep. *Diana Leonard* had completed her fieldwork on courtship rituals in South Wales, but could not find a convincing interpretation of her material before she found fresh thinking through the women's movement. She recalls:

I didn't manage to write up my thesis for years – in fact, it wasn't until I finally landed an academic job that I finished my thesis. I couldn't work out a theoretical framework for writing up my thesis until I encountered the Women's Movement and particularly the work of Christine Delphy, which said that marriage was women's employment. Then I realised that I could take various people's approaches to the entry into the labour market, and use those in terms of women's entry into marriage. But that they were in a different situation, in that when you go into the labour market, you both have your teachers and you have your family who are all helping you to get your first job. But the extent to which they are able to help you into marriage is actually severely restricted, and you have to not even appear as a woman, to look as if you are interested in getting married, because that's unduly forward. And I couldn't work out how to analyse the material I'd collected from young couples – men and women – in the process of getting married, and choosing their wedding, and establishing themselves as a new household, until I hit the Women's Movement. (p 24)

The intellectual impact of feminism came remarkably swiftly and has made a lasting impact. Diana herself played a key role in this. For sociology, a galvanising moment came with the BSA Annual Conference on sexual divisions in society held in Aberdeen in 1974, leading to the highly influential publication – with the same challenging title as the conference – of the two-volume book *Sexual Divisions and Society* (Tavistock, 1976). It was co-edited by Sheila Allen, professor at Bradford, and *Diana Leonard*, enthusiastic feminist, at that point a little-known researcher. Sheila and Diana ran the conference together. Diana's account of how it happened highlights the speed with which gender arrived as a major topic, and also the informal non-hierarchical approach to organisation which was typical of the new movement:

I was working with Joan [Busfield, at Essex], as a Research Officer, and as well I was in the British Sociological Association, and organising one of its Study Groups along with David Morgan. He was keen to revitalise the one on family, the Family Research Study Group, and we did a few meetings together. And I met Sheila [Allen], who was newly appointed to a Chair in Sociology at Bradford. We met in the kitchen of some student residences and got talking to each other in the middle of the night. This was at a BSA Conference that I'd gone to, and she was not one to stand on status, unlike many other people in the BSA at the time.

Let me clarify. There was a big problem for the BSA, because they had planned to hold the next conference, which was to be called, 'Into Europe', because Britain had just joined the Common Market, or was in the process of doing it. They couldn't get anyone to organise it, and the other conference topic didn't happen either. So the executive of the BSA, which included Sheila, and Mary McIntosh, were approached with the possibility of, 'Why don't we do something on the family? – you know, in default, do something on the family! Mary McIntosh had recently organised a BSA Conference, the topic was something around crime. And they also asked Sheila if she'd be willing to do it, and Sheila said, 'It's not my field. I do stuff on race'. 'But you're a woman, so you must be able to' – Anyway, the two of them both decided that maybe I, because I was becoming better known for being active within the Women's Movement, might be a possible person to work with one or both of them, and it ended up being Sheila.

So I was working with David Morgan on organising the special interest group, and with Sheila Allen on a possible future conference – which had to be done very rapidly, because it was all left to the last possible moment. And Sheila and I sat down, and we thought there was not a lot of good sociological work on the family, but there is a lot of activism around, and the family is one of the topics, so why don't we really go for something about what's happening in the Women's Movement at the moment? And Sheila managed to push that through the Exec...

So because they were really pushed for it... we were allowed to go ahead and organise something. Which we then said, 'It's not going to be on the family, and it's not going to be on women, it's going to be on sexual divisions in society'. (pp 42–43)

It was also very much in keeping with the new mood that the conference platform was opened up to participants in a more informal way, rather than just through delivering academic papers:

We also broke the BSA Code, which used to be that people were invited to give papers, and we opened it up to people who were interested. And we invited quite a lot of folks to reflect upon their past work in the light of current emerging interests on gender, and some, bless their hearts, like Ronnie Frankenberg, and Colin Bell and Howard Newby, took it up and actually did do that. But we did have some hostility. Curiously, Ann Oakley was opposed to it, because she thought we should have made it on women and not on gender. We actually made it on sexual divisions rather than on women or on gender – *Sexual Divisions in Society*. (p 43)

Innovation, of course, is rarely good news to all. Hence, part of the impact of the women's movement, feminism and studying gender was *experiencing new tensions*. One of the most striking features of all social movements is that they develop schisms, disagreements, tensions and hostilities. Sometimes these are extremely marked – and the women's movement was no exception. There were researchers who preferred to focus entirely on women, rather than comparing gender differences between women and men. There were hot arguments in the 1980s between radical feminists and socialist feminists. There was also the never-concluded domestic labour debate. Although both sides represented forms of neo-Marxism, *Diana Leonard* recalls the 'huge rows' and 'fierce political battles' which this provoked:

> The major opposition that Christine Delphy got was from Mary McIntosh and Michelle Barrett. I don't know if you recall that? Those famous articles in *Feminist Review*, that they edited. And then Christine came back and attacked them... – they had criticised for failures, which, if they'd actually kept up to date with her publications, they would have known [that] was not, in fact, what she was arguing. There were awful personal rows... They were horrible and painful [fights], and personally difficult. (pp 49–50)

There were in the meantime 'big fights and slaggings off' at the BSA over, for example, the control of agendas years ahead (p 51).

There is also an issue which was much less spoken about. The grounds on which our women Pioneers were fighting were the issues which seemed most relevant to white women in Britain, and especially to white middle-class women. *Maxine Molyneux*, born in Pakistan, and working in Latin America, felt little connection with this scene:

> I was an offshore feminist. I wasn't, in any way, connected with the BSA feminists, the British school feminists, they were doing something totally different, and they weren't interested. The people who really I had the most intellectual interaction with were people working in gender and development, which was an area we pioneered, in fact. I mean, that group, we called ourselves 'The Subordination of Women Group', I think established some very different ways of doing and thinking about research in the global South, from a gender perspective, and that's where my most immediate interaction, intellectual engagement, was

with. And it was a very new area of development... that has now become very mainstream.

It was that world that was where the intellectual nourishment was, where you got some feedback, you got some recognition. It wasn't within British sociology as such... Of course, the Yemen, that didn't really – except within a small group of Middle-Eastern studies people. So again, I think the theme I'm becoming aware of as I talk, is that this sense of being an outsider continued, actually, for pretty much throughout my career – which is an odd thing to say, isn't it! It's certainly how I felt. Probably something very deep and primal! (Part 1, pp 28–29)

As we have seen (Voices 6) from *Avtar Brah*, this feeling of marginality could be still more painful for a non-white feminist woman researcher working within Britain.

Researching ethnicity

There is a long genealogy of conflict and tension in writings on 'race', 'ethnicity' and 'race relations' in Britain. Practised within the context of Empire, the social research of the late nineteenth and early twentieth centuries highlighted biological, evolutionary and eugenic themes, which are now largely seen as racist and colonialist. Despite earlier interest in minority seaport communities, typically focussing on 'picturesque' aspects such as Chinese opium dens, it was not until after 1945 that serious social research into race relations in the 'homeland' really took off. Earlier migrant flows had been primarily of white British migrating outwards to work or settle in the Empire. This changed during the Second World War when non-white servicemen – from the US and the Empire – came to Britain as crucial and welcomed support in the war. There was much less enthusiasm among working-class Britons when non-white immigrants were recruited to meet labour shortages notably in public transport and the new National Health Service. Symbolised by the arrival of the *Windrush* from the Caribbean in 1948, this set the frame for the political issues around migration that were to come to dominate culture, politics and sociology in subsequent years.

Most early projects on race relations in Britain took the form of community studies, seeking to understand the cultures of immigrants, and ultimately to build up a theory of race relations. Among these projects the work of Kenneth Little, Michael Banton and Sheila

Patterson was prominent.[10] Michael Banton became the first Director of the SSRC Race Relations Unit at the University of Bristol. He was followed later by John Rex at Warwick. Rex (1925–2011) came from South Africa and was a controversial figure. Having written the most important British work of social theory in the 1960s, *Key Problems of Sociological Theory* (1961), he went on to lead the landmark study of race relations in the inner Birmingham neighbourhood of Sparkbrook. Soon the field would branch out into a more critical approach identified especially with Stuart Hall (who came himself to work in Birmingham in 1964) and Paul Gilroy, who both emphasised the legacy of the slave trade and the two-way cultural interchanges which had developed through slavery and colonisation.[11] Before long gender also became an issue alongside race. We move from colonialism to postcolonialism.

The works that shaped the field in the early days now look somewhat anachronistic in their cultural assumptions: for example, Michael Banton's, *The Coloured Quarter. Negro Immigrants in an English City* (1955) and Sheila Patterson's *Dark Strangers* (1963), a community study of West Indians in Brixton. But John Rex and Robert Moore's *Race, Community Conflict* (1967) study of Sparkbrook in Birmingham became a landmark study: a new sort of community study focusing on ethnicity and the housing market. Published at a crucial time in British race relations, it was the first serious attempt to theorise the relationship between class and ethnicity, combining Chicago School approaches with Weberian theory. It focussed on housing because it was an area of competition. *Robert Moore* has written of the context for this book:

> By the mid-1960s, 'coloured immigration' was an issue central to political debate, with both the main parties wanting to show the electorate that they could be tougher than the other on immigration. Until it became a 'Celtic Tiger' Ireland was the main source of immigrants to the UK, but this seldom featured in the politics of immigration. A pivotal moment was the publication of Harold Wilson's White Paper *Immigration from the Commonwealth* in 1965. Then, as now – except for the most rabid racists – the debate centred around competition for resources, especially housing. The public were not altogether clear whether immigrants were the victims of housing shortages, or the cause of them. The Wilson White Paper closed the argument down; immigrants were the cause of the problems that city-dwellers faced. Labour joined a 'Dutch Auction' on immigration... Shortly thereafter we had the (Labour) 1968 Commonwealth Immigrants Act, the 1969 Immigration Appeals

Act which restricted access to appeals by persons refused entry to the UK, the 1971 Immigration Act (a Labour measure, enacted by the Conservatives), followed by almost continuous restrictive legislation on citizenship, immigration and asylum continuing into the twenty-first century...

When John Rex and I were working in Birmingham, people from India, Pakistan and the Caribbean were just seen as 'immigrants', a subordinated minority. The presence of these same (now older) immigrants, their descendants and newer arrivals, is now unremarkable. It is the all-white parts of Britain that seem strange. Minorities may be discriminated against but they accept subordination no longer. In the late 1960s minority populations mobilised against police harassment and violence. The case of the 'The Mangrove Nine' in 1970 resulted from resistance to police harassment and attempts to close down the Mangrove restaurant in Notting Hill. The persons charged were acquitted of all serious charges. Ten years later 'The Bradford Twelve' were similarly acquitted having argued 'self-defence' against charges. But two years earlier the Asian population of Southall had not fared so well when the police rioted, doing widespread damage to community property, inflicting injuries and causing the death of a school teacher. The year 1981 also saw resistance to heavy-handed policing and harassment in Brixton, Birmingham, Leeds and Liverpool. Although the period after the publication of the MacPherson Report saw substantial changes in policing, deaths in custody and police shootings continued to provoke responses, notably in 2011 when the shooting of Mark Duggan led to rioting across London which later spread to other English cities.[12]

Robert Moore discusses in his interview how the study was done:

I had read *Key Problems of Sociological Theory*, and I thought I would like to work with John Rex – if I could... It was the only post-war British book on sociological theory at that time... He was clearly Britain's leading writer on theory... So I wrote and said, 'Any chance of working with you?' And some time later I had a letter from him, saying, 'Can we meet some time?' So I met him at the Bamboo Coffee Bar under the railway bridge at Golders Green, and he said, 'I've got this money from the Survey of Race Relations in Britain to do a social survey of an inner part of Birmingham, if you want to come and work with me, how about it?' He started telling me all the things he wanted to do there, which was a kind of mixture of empirical data collecting, and participant observation. And then I, in all my brashness of youth, said, 'This is all very interesting, but how does this tie in with the theoretical positions that I've read in *Key Problems of Sociological Theory?*' I subsequently discovered that that challenge to him became the basis of one of the chapters of *Race, Community and Conflict*. (p 25)

John Rex was a notoriously difficult and irascible leading academic, and Robert is candid in his description of him as a co-researcher:

John is not the easiest person in the world to work with. I think it's felt that Sally Tomlinson and I were the two who were able to establish the best relationships with him. I think I only had one really flaming row with him, but that was after Sparkbrook. It was clearly an unequal relationship because he was a very distinguished sociologist and I was just a new researcher. But he had almost – I sensed a slight respect for me, because as he's said many times since, he said, 'You've got a nose for trouble.' And I'm one of these people who doesn't hesitate to poke my nose in where it's clearly going to be very unwelcome, and where I'm going to discover things that people would rather I didn't discover! So I was a fairly bold fieldworker, and I think he liked that, and I think he liked my kind of disciplined approach. (pp 27–28)

We looked at one another's chapters. We took sole responsibility for our chapters, but then we read one another's work. On the whole, John didn't take terribly kindly to any critical comments on what he'd written, but then he never did, and I knew that, so that I normally just made suggestions... No, but we sat in our own rooms, writing our own chapters, and then occasionally met and discussed what we'd been writing.

What about working out the design of the book, was that a joint thing?

It was a joint thing, but John was clearly the senior partner. But he listened to me, I appreciated that... To some extent, John and I had our own separate theoretical thoughts. He clearly had very strong views on race relations, partly rooted in his South African experience. I was more willing to be led by the data. I just found Sparkbrook so fascinating, and I'd only recently graduated, and so I don't think I brought any particular theoretical armoury to

182

it. It was that Sparkbrook, itself, set off, as I say, Durkheim and
the Chicago School and so on, and Whyte, in my mind. (p 43)

Another Pioneer who worked in race relations, was *Harry Goulbourne*,
a political scientist. Born in Jamaica in 1948, he grew up on the
mountain smallholdings of his extended family until 1958, when he
migrated to Britain to re-join his parents who had left six years before.
He wrote his PhD at Sussex on *Teachers, Education and Politics in Jamaica*
(1988). In the mid-1970s he began interviewing on the social history
of black people in Britain. He was interested in the co-operative saving
'partnerships' for housing which West Indians in Britain developed,
and also by their family gender roles. He came from a typical Jamaican
family in which the mother was in control of the family economy:

> She was a very very sharp leader of people... In my family, the
> person who ran the money entirely, was my mother. My mother,
> in terms of just human intelligence, was a superb person. In
> terms of arithmetic, in particular, you could throw any amount
> of numbers at her and ask her for the conclusion, and within a
> matter of minutes or seconds, you would have them. In buying
> and selling she used to say – she took her scales with her,
> because each of these sellers would have their scales, but that
> she could put them in her hands, throw them up, and tell the
> buyer what the weights are, and if they want to test it, they
> could test on the scale, and it would be exact! (pp 7–8)

Harry was also keen to explore the connections between Caribbean
and African culture, and so in 1975–80 he taught at the University of
Tanzania in Dar-es-Salaam, and then returned to Jamaica to teaching
at the University of the West Indies, Kingston, for five years. He came
back to Britain in 1985, this time to settle, to the Centre for Research
in Ethnic Relations at Warwick. From this point onwards he has played
an influential role in the wider development of British research on
migration, race relations and ethnicity. His own writing remained
primarily political, including *Ethnicity and Nationalism in Post-Imperial
Britain* (1991) and *Race Relations in Britain since 1945* (1998). In 1998
he became Professor of Sociology at London South Bank University
and Director of the Race and Ethnicity Research Centre. During this
later phase his focus shifted towards social issues in migration and its
impact on the Caribbean family as a transnational form. There is also
a striking parallel in his story with the active involvement of so many
women pioneers in the feminist movement. Harry explains how in

the 1970s he was not only researching about West Indians in Britain, but also working for them as an activist:

> During those two years, also, the big issue in Britain was, we were learning, for the first time, that the schools were pumping out a lot of black kids from ESN [educationally sub-normal] schools. and I got involved with John la Rose [of New Beacon Books] who had published, Bernard Coard, *How the West Indian Child is Made Educationally Subnormal in the British School System* [1971]. And so we took on that task of starting what is now quite popular, what was called the 'Alternative School System' of organising Summer Schools. I think one of the very first Summer Schools organised in London, was one I was involved with in '71 and '72, where we took these kids who were being sent to ESN schools, and we said, 'We're going to teach them the three R's, and some black history.' Which we did. (pp 70–71)

The negative treatment of black West Indian children in the British school system was only one of the issues with which he was engaged. A second big issue, which he took up along with his wife Selina, a lawyer, whose family come from Goa, was

> the question of black prisoners. Prisoners, black people in British prisons, because that started off, at the time, with young people, for youth, but in '72 the police brutality against middle-aged black men also started. So we founded, in Brixton, what was called the 'Joshua Francis Defence Committee', I was the Secretary for that, and one of the main organisers. And there's a number of black groups in London generally, who got together to organise around that. So those were two crucial areas which, in terms of activism, one became very involved in. (p 71)

Harry's work is also important in that he has always wanted to take a much wider approach than the earlier local community-based studies. He is interested by comparisons across the Atlantic between black African and West Indian cultures. He has also studied the cultures of other ethnic groups. In Britain he interviewed Asians from Guyana, Cypriot refugees, and Sikhs, exploring their attitudes to politics and culture of the Sikhs in Britain. He pursued this in part through participant observation, so attending Sikh festival 'gudwaras':

> I would not dress entirely appropriately, but it was required that you wear a sort of a scarlet headgear, which they'll give you, a kind of a scarf which you would put on the head. You would sit in the same way, you'd eat what they offer, etc., and just be around. So sometimes I would sit around all day, not necessarily talking to anyone other than informally. And what, what would I get from that? I would get a sense of exposure to what people felt was important to themselves. I'd get a sense of the cultural mores. (p 38)

Equally important, in his later work he looked at migrants as transnationals, rather than as simply moving from one culture to another – as in his co-edited (with Mary Chamberlain) *Caribbean Transnational Experiences* and *Caribbean Families in Britain and the Transatlantic Worlds* (both 2001) and his co-authored *Transnational Families: Ethnicity, Identities and Social Capital* (2010).

He also has strong views about studying race relations. He believes that anyone who is prepared to watch and listen with respect can be a successful researcher with another ethnic cultural group. He recalls an angry debate at a conference in 1979 on 'Oral History and Black History', at which a group of Asian participants were criticising a Jewish anthropologist for researching a Manchester Asian community and arguing that only Asians should interview Asians.

> Yes, that's right. It was a relativism that only Asians can write about Asians, in the way that some black Americans might say, 'Only blacks can write about blacks', and taking that kind of perspective. Which, in terms of the engagements that a number of us have had – or I have had – was an absurdity. And I still think it's an absurdity, that view.
>
> But in terms of methodology, you do hear this quite often, people saying that they have a particular advantage from being from the same group as they're looking at. And I often say, 'Well, okay, you might have an advantage. You also have a terrible disadvantage. It cuts both ways. Sometimes you have advantage in gaining access and openness, frankness, earnesty, precisely because you're from the outside. Other times, it might be the opposite, but it goes both ways'. And in terms of scholarship, we can't restrict it to the politics of empathy, to belongingness to the particular group. And that goes back to what I was saying about the comparative dimension, which does not allow for that.

> I've been in similar encounters, before and since. I recall a
> very progressive Southern African liberator – liberation fighter in
> the ANC – asking me how can I want to write a book on African
> politics, when I'm not an African? He, himself, at the time, was
> just about to write a book on the Feminist Movement! (p 97)

Focussing on his own research on the British Sikhs, he says:

> I've always taken the view that anybody can study anybody, that
> racism in Britain, if it's cast in that way, is as much a problem to
> be tackled by white academics as black academics… In terms
> of the insider/outsider debate to communities, in terms of
> research, it cuts both ways, it's a two-edged sword.
>
> When I was looking at the Sikhs, for example, the fact that
> I was an outsider gave me an edge with them, in the sense that
> I was powerless, whatever I did wasn't going to influence or
> affect them. Whereas I can imagine that a person coming from
> the Indian subcontinent, working amongst them, they would
> perhaps have closed the door, because that person, potentially,
> in terms of how they look at things, might have been able
> to influence them. So joining them as one of the first black
> academics, in Britain, to have gone that way, I saw nothing
> contradictory or weakening, and indeed, in terms of my links
> with communities, they saw it as a great strength. They saw it
> as a good thing that I was engaging in that way, and that I was
> a person, at Warwick, whom they could call upon, they could
> come and see, if they wished. They drew on that. (pp 132–134)

Thus, research on ethnicity has moved from local studies conducted
by white researchers towards a transnationalism in which the focus is
the impact of movement and can be taken up by researchers from any
background. Among our authors of this book, *Paul Thompson* has mainly
written from British material, but including many interviewees born
outside Britain. For him, as a suburban English child Scotland was the
first point of comparison. But he went on as a volunteer to interview
Moroccan migrants in Britain, and to become co-researcher and co-
author with Elaine Bauer of a book on transnational Caribbean families,
Jamaican Hands Across the Atlantic. And *Avtar Brah*, whose migrant Indian
family had moved to Uganda and then came as refugees to England,
where she fought for human rights alongside her Southall Black Sisters,
has woven her whole interdisciplinary intellectual focus successfully
around international movements and boundaries, as exemplified in

her *Cartographies of Diaspora*. Nevertheless she tells her life story as a continuing struggle against marginalisation in changing forms (Voices 6). In short, the issues remain raw.

Disability, ageing, sexuality

In short, ideas on class, ethnicity and gender started to crystallise in the mid- and late twentieth century into major fields of research linked to social divisions, inequalities, identities and cross-linking intersectionalities. We can also pick out other fields being shaped, if less conspicuously: disability, ageing, sexuality. *Mildred Blaxter* was an early researcher on disability. *Peter Townsend* linked his work on poverty with a major interest in researching age, looking not only at ageing in the community in *The Family Life of Old People* and institutions in *The Last Refuge*, but also conducting a major comparative study in *Old People in Three Industrial Societies*.

We will end with briefly considering one other 'division': how an interest in the study of sexuality was developing. Sexuality, of course, has been a central theme of Western literature and art for centuries, but from the 1890s onwards it becomes a blossoming theme in serious research explorations: in Havelock Ellis as an early champion of sexual diversity, in Freud and psychoanalysis, in anthropological observation such as by *Raymond Firth* or *Peter Loizos*, in the early survey work of Mass Observation.[13] But while gay practices were illegal and secretive, it was hard to feel good about, or even recognise, gay feeling.[14] Hence, the post-1945 decades are particularly interesting for two reasons. The first is how the changes in public opinion which led to the decriminalisation of homosexuality in the 1968 Sexual Offences Act opened up the research context. The second is the extent to which this new legal and cultural context change was experienced as personal bodily and emotional discovery by gay men of this generation, leading them into public activism. This is vividly expressed by *Ken Plummer* in his own Pioneers interview.

We can find these dualities again in the story of a neglected but important pioneer of sex research, and also a campaigner for civil liberties in diverse fields – on the treatment of prisoners, on drugs, on HIV – who we hoped to include among our interviewees: Michael Schofield (1919–2014). Trained in social psychology at Cambridge and business studies at Harvard before the Second World War, his career was mapped out to become part of his family department store business (Schofields of Leeds). But curious stirrings were happening within which led him to take a different path. He was discovering his homosexuality, much stigmatised and outlawed at the time. And so he wrote the book *Society and the Homosexual*, published bravely by Gollancz in 1952. Asked by *Ken Plummer* in 2008[15] why he had written this book he replied: 'I wanted to answer the question, "Why am I gay?" I reviewed the literature because I wanted to find out why? But the literature did not tell me'. The book was timely and well received; it was just before the Wolfenden Committee met to discuss changes in homosexual law. And Michael said that 'I got a lot of letters – letters for help. This was 1952'. But the book was not published under his own name. The publisher had advised him this would be safer; 'they insisted I use a pen name'. The author was now a 'Gordon Westwood'.

Michael had come out in his own consciousness. He had also decided to establish himself as a serious researcher under his real name. But on topics involving interviews with young people, funders would not have risked sponsoring a gay researcher. So – despite living with his lover – in public he succeeded in keeping his own orientation secret. Paradoxically, he had come out, but was still in hiding. With this strategy he won support for a series of important research projects which were published under his real name. In *Sociological Aspects of Homosexuality* (Longmans, 1965), he developed the view that it was not homosexuality in itself that was a difficulty. Rather it was the social hostility towards homosexuality that caused problems. He was starting to sense the wider formulation that was to be linked to the work of Howard S. Becker and others, highlighting how societal reactions could shape different social conducts, which came to be known as labelling theory and social constructionism.

Michael carried out two other later major studies. The first was *The Sexual Behaviour of Young People* (Longmans, 1965) – 'this was the big book. There was a lot of money behind it. And I could do it with good staff and training etc.' The same respondents were then later followed up in *The Sexual Behaviour of Young Adults* (Allen Lane, 1973). For a short while, these works became known not only for their findings but also their methods. *John Bynner* worked as a researcher on the first project, *Ken Plummer* on the second, finding in Michael a lifelong friend. John Bynner was less enthusiastic. And particularly interestingly, he pointed out how through only using a set of closed questions they deliberately avoided collecting any material on gay youth: yet one more twist in the zigzag between revelation and suppression along a legal and cultural borderline which was to continue to characterise research into sexual diversity.

VOICES 7

Reflections for the future

Here we bring together some of the ideas which our Pioneers drew from their own experience and felt important to pass on to future researchers.

Michael Young: an overview

Summing up his views at a time when he was in a perplexing restudy of his own early work, Michael Young was reflecting on effective research – by others as much as himself – which could help positive social change. He envisaged, at every stage in the research, space for creativity:

> *If you were to give advice to somebody else... are there any special tips now that you give them?*
>
> Yes, I would. Do all your formal interviewing yourself. Don't employ anyone else to do it, the most important thing of all. You'll get material ten times as valuable, even though the other interviewers are, in their way, expert, but they're expert, usually, in a different kind of interview. That's the first thing.
>
> The second thing is to follow your inner light... Find out what you're really interested in, what you really want to find out about, what you really want to say, even though you may change very much what you actually say later. But if you can touch some kind of deep cord in yourself, you'll probably have a good chance of doing something fairly decent.
>
> And third is to observe. Get around, meet people and talk to people, in wherever they are. Pubs are not so easy now, because life has become much more house-centred... It was much more an open-air life then, because people didn't have cars, and they walked. It was a pedestrian society, which, I think, in many ways, is a great advantage. It's a way of meeting people. You don't meet people in the same way if you have cars all the time...
>
> And last, ... but, last, for God's sake, learn to write! ... Unless you're humble about your probable incapacity to write well, you're not going to produce anything that's really going to make

an impact on other people. That means not just taking lessons in writing, which you can do, from someone who can do it... But it means, of course, because very few people can write it quite well in the first draft, is to take a very great deal of trouble about it, and show it to people and see if they do understand. Our rule became that... at least half of that time [on a project] must be given to the writing-up of the material we had, if it was going to be any good...

Analysis, I think it's difficult, can sometimes be very difficult, but it's the presentation of it all, and thinking out what the meaning of it is; and trying to remember the unusual small things that happen, that caught your attention, and giving them proper space in your writing, as a novelist would do. It's the small things about people, and the small things about the way they talk, and small things about their clothes, and what they put on their mantle-pieces, which are the most evocative of the style of life. (pp 13–14)

Peter Townsend: on sociology, anthropology and direct observation

Peter Townsend's life work was as a sociologist but there was a crucial lesson he drew from studying anthropology, the importance of direct observation:

The anthropological method was so important. That idea that you didn't do things in an aloof way, you didn't sort of send out teams of juniors to collect your data, and you sat at home in comfortable situations and looked through your... your microscope and wrote your reports, but you actually lived, you engaged with that society. There was a sense of you not being able to write anything decent about the societies you were trying to describe and understand, unless you at least spent part of the time there, and better, lived among them. And I think the idea that some anthropologists went and lived for several years, in very uncomfortable circumstances, sometimes in very dangerous conditions, and tried to understand the society as a whole, because they couldn't explain any detail within it, without understanding the whole. That was, that was a lesson that has lived with me all my life. (p 22)

Frank Bechhofer: on *The Affluent Worker* research design

One of its research team of four, Frank reflects on the prestigious *Affluent Worker* project, published in the early 1960s and a sociological research centrepiece for long afterwards. Its theme was a key public issue: whether rising living standards were undermining social class identity and political allegiance. Rather than taking a national survey, the project focussed on Luton with its concentration of well-paid skilled workers. If radical change was happening, it had to be here – but they found class feeling resilient. For Frank now that answer matters less than the way they got to it:

> The thing, of course, about *The Affluent Worker*, that, in my view, is its lasting legacy, but I would say that because the thing I'm interested in, one of the things I'm interested in, was its design. It was a very interesting research design, and I've used it ever since as an example. And I think it's about as good an example of that particular kind of design as any, and I wrote a book with Lindsay Patterson quite recently on research design, and we use it in there... The best thing about *The Affluent Worker*, its best legacy is the research design.
>
> Its worst legacy is 'embourgeoisement' as a word. But, never mind, we have to use it! This strange idea that the 'embourgeoisiement' of the working-class was taking place. I mean, it wasn't strange, lots of people espoused it in a big way. The idea that if you wanted to show this wasn't so, because you couldn't study the whole of Britain, not on the bucks available in those days, or, indeed, today, let's face it! What could you do? Okay, you try and find the locale which is most favourable to the thesis, and so if it's not happening there, it's not happening. Now, this was, I still think, in retrospect, a brilliant design...
>
> If you set the study up right, then it'll work. And if you don't set it up right, you've had it. And I've become very fascinated by that, and it's governed the way I've tried to do studies, and the way I've tried to get other people to do studies ever since. (pp 33–34)

Sandra Wallman: on the need to problematise the normal

Sandra Wallman has researched in both Africa and London: which makes for a different kind of starting point to define the research problem:

> If you're working in a society where people look different, they have a very different language, they have a very different livelihood, etc., you're constantly making an effort to normalise what they're doing. You're trying to say, 'Well, how is this like what I already know?' Whereas the other way round, working in Italy, for example, people look like you, you know the language much better, the language structure is the same, they apparently listen to the same music and eat similar food and so on, and it's very easy to assume you know how it is. And again, if you're working in London, on London too, it's very easy for you to assume you know how it is. So the effort, I think, is reversed... When it's an exotic culture, your effort is to normalise it, and when it's a familiar culture, your effort is to problematise it, you know what I mean? To assume nothing, which is very hard, but I think you have to do that, and I think that there again, you're trying to keep the insider/outsider balance going. (pp 27–28)

Paul Thompson: on choices in interpreting life stories

Paul Thompson recounts how, with over 400 oral history life story interviews as evidence for his book *The Edwardians* (1975), he interpreted and presented them through combining cross–analysis of the whole set with in–depth portraits:

> I found a conflict between the cross-analysis, and the whole stories. Once you knew a whole interview, somehow you wanted to have that whole person there, that you always feel... Yes, that was the first time I experienced it. And the way I solved it in the book was that I had a series of chapters which used the interviews as a whole, with short extracts. It might be a chapter on childhood and youth, or marriage, for instance, or there was one on politics, and so on. But then I also had two groups of portraits of people and their families. In the main group I juxtaposed different social [levels]. So it started with the daughter of a landed aristocrat, a really upper-class wealthy family, and it ended with the child of a poor, unemployed labourer. Right in the middle, a big block in

the middle, you see, about a quarter of the book roughly, and maybe more. And then two other [portraits] towards the end, which were both women, and one was a political woman who'd consciously tried to change society, and the other was an example of unconscious pressure for change, a poor woman who struggled to get a decent life. Actually, in the end, she failed. It's a very sad story, but it shows the pressure that's there all the time for ordinary people [to better themselves].

And that was an idea I got from the interviews, which I hadn't had before. Theories of social change were all about politics or megaforces like the economy, and there was nothing about this way in which ordinary people, all the time, are making decisions, trying to do better for themselves. Whether they marry, whether they have children, whether they move to somewhere else, whether they get a different job, all those kind of things. And that's an enormous part of the pressure for change. So that was symbolised at the end of the book. (pp 16–17)

Raymond T. Smith: is fieldwork different when you are with a child?

Many anthropologists, both men and women, took children with them for their fieldwork. Raymond T. Smith found it a great advantage when he went to Hopetown in British Guiana:

> We had a baby. My oldest son had just been born. I think he was, like, three months, when we went there. So it was a bit tricky, living in this old wooden house, right opposite a rum shop that played loud Indian music, during opening hours! Because it was a rice village. There were rats all over the place, they'd run around the house at night. Anyway, it was very useful having a child, because you immediately got incorporated into all kinds of domestic ritual, you'd go to weddings, and rituals, and everybody would want to hold the child. (p 18)

Colin Bell: on the merits of gossip in fieldwork

Colin Bell saw an unusual value in the suggestiveness of some of the gossipy asides in fieldwork – which were usually unrecorded:

> Hence, the really important insight, that you kind of gossip while you do fieldwork. You could chat on, you and I, and talk about

our children, and talk about colleagues we've had, and I think if we, if you weren't doing fieldwork, and you turned the tape off, it's just rolling reciprocity... I found I could gain enormous amounts by telling people things that I probably – I mean, I don't think it was ever either salacious or particularly damaging, or probably even terribly confidential. They just wonder, 'What does he really do?' 'Oh', I said, 'You know, he's just a Director of so and so'. 'Oh!' And I caught a frisson, a couple of times – you feel lack of authenticity in yourself, but also a realisation that they might not want to tell you that actually his job's not this, but his job's that. Or he's had a bad time at work and he's got sacked from that. Which is quite an important thing for me to know, but they won't tell you because you might tell somebody else. (pp 45–46)

Janet Finch: on handling gender issues in interviews

Janet Finch by contrast argues for a much more cautious approach, particularly when women are interviewing women:

[It's not] that men can't interview women. And I don't think I quite said that! ... The point is something rather deeper than that, about [how] in a society which is quite divided on gender lines, in terms of people's experiences and their assumptions about who you can trust and that kind of thing, that it is a different sort of dynamic when you get a woman interviewing a woman, than when you get a man interviewing a woman... I think it means that women in those situations need to be highly sensitised to what it is they're doing, and aware that they are trading on something which is about gender, and not just about their skills as an interviewer. And, therefore, prepared to have moral positions, if you like, on how far you push people in the interview situation, and how you use the material that you've got, afterwards... There's a danger of lulling the interviewee into some kind of false sense that this is a confidence between women... The danger is that the interviewee then forgets what you told them at the beginning, that you're going to do something with this, you know? ...

You must remember yourself, and you must keep reminding the interviewee that this is a research interview. It's not the beginning of a friendship, it's not somebody who you might meet on a train, and never have to see again, so you can tell them anything you like. It's not a potential counselling situation. It is a research interview, with its own rules and boundaries. (pp 60–62)

Harry Goulbourne: on dealing with antagonistic viewpoints

Especially when interviewing public personalities and politicians, as an interviewer your empathy may be threatened by encountering views you strongly dislike. Harry Goulbourne reflects on how he tries to react:

> I learnt, I developed a grunt, which meant, 'Yes, I can hear what you're saying, but don't think that I agree nor disagree with you', and I find that I still do that now! It's become a habit almost, because in talking to another human being, you can't sit there dumb and totally silent. (p 83)...
>
> In social science research, sometimes you have to grit your teeth and absent your personality, your own inner views, your own values, somewhat aside, and listen. Because you're not there to engage in exchange for understanding with the person you're interviewing. There is that, but really you want to get as close as possible to what the person thinks, feels – what they want to say... You're there as a listener. And I think, as a listener, you have to almost negate a degree of yourself as a person, as an individual, as a human being almost, so to speak, and just listen carefully. (pp 113–114)

George Brown: on research as sculpture

For George Brown, who has always sought systematic measurement in his research, there is also an important artistic dimension:

> I still like to go back to certain artistic elements in my nature, particularly. [It's like] carving a sculpture. I think it's because I wasn't very good at it, that I often didn't know [very well] what was going to emerge until I got fairly deeply into the product! And then there would be an interplay as I saw something emerging. I could interact with it, and something good might emerge. I find research very much like this, that

I don't know, very often, what's going to emerge, or I've got a very dim idea.

And the idea that you [must] have clear-cut hypotheses to test and so on, I don't think it's how most research works really, [or how] productive creative work [emerges]. And it is this sense that there's something there, like in the wood or stone, and by interplay, by looking at what's emerging, and feeding more in, it's this that I think I was trying to get at. (pp 183–184)

Pat Caplan on giving back to the community: website and film

At a later stage in her work on Mafia Island, Tanzania, in 2004 Pat Caplan used the new globalised technology to give something back to the people who had given so much to her:

It's a website for Mafia, it's their website, but I put it up, and it sits on the Goldsmiths' server, and it's quite extensive, because when I was there in 2004, for the first time there was an internet café in the district capital – well, internet café, that's too grand a term! – there were a couple of computers that sometimes worked and sometimes didn't. They were incredibly slow. But I could see this was the way things were beginning to move, and there were a few satellite dishes where they could get international football matches that the boys would gather to watch. In one place in Dar, somebody told me that that was how he got his broadband through a satellite thing, so I thought, 'Right, this is the time to do it'. So I put up this website, and lots and lots of links which need updating, actually, because some of the links don't work, and there's a lot more stuff available now. And so it was kind of giving back to Mafians...

The [BBC] producer, at the end, he said to me, 'I've got the rushes. I can give you a copy of the rushes, with all the Mafia stuff all linked up together'. Because it was actually chopped into bits in some series that were shown, so there were some quite long sequences and some very short sequences. So the people in the village desperately wanted to see this [1976 BBC] film, and I was incredibly worried because there were some interviews that I knew people had only agreed to, in the film, because they were confidential, so nobody else was there when we shot those interviews, and they didn't mind people in Europe hearing what they were saying, but they didn't want people in the village to hear what they were saying. Very fortunately, it's got a magnetic soundtrack, which means that the sound doesn't appear when it's played on the projectors I'd been able to get hold of on Mafia, which, as you can imagine, are pretty dicey anyway, with the generator and all the rest of it. But the last time I screened it, I screened a video on a television screen, and there were a thousand people watching a 14" television! ...

So I guess what I've been trying to do in these later years, is to engage with a different audience. Not just an anthropology audience, to try to give back more, but also to engage with a wider audience. (pp 73–74)

CHAPTER 8

Conclusion: what can we learn?

Our central task in this book has been to guide the reader into an awareness of an intriguing set of interviews with twentieth-century social researchers that are available for further reading, listening and scrutiny. Through the fragments of these voices we sense something of the excitement of earlier days of doing social research in Britain.

These interviews all throw light on a common problem: how empirical social research was conducted and given shape in mid-twentieth-century Britain. We have not aimed at a grand account of this history: we have referred to some more specific studies on this, and our own aims have always been much more modest. This is to put on record the fascinating stories of some earlier creative researchers working in intriguing new ways before they become forgotten. (Indeed, we have been a little surprised to find how already new generations have not heard of many of them.) We also wanted to capture something of the social and cultural contexts in which they worked and the dilemmas they faced. It is already – just a generation or two on – a very different world to the world of research we now live in. But we find all over these interviews the marks of the world we live in being gently shaped by some of these researchers. It is good to have them in the archive, on the record and full of future possibility.

On self-reflexivity

There are, of course, quite serious limits to our account: indeed, they illustrate some of the now well-documented problems of life story and oral history research. Our 58 interviewees cannot be taken as 'representative' of a wider scholarly pool. They are unique cases, and there are many other researchers who if alive and willing could easily have been included, and some who may have made even greater contributions and told very different stories. Nor can we be sure of the memories of our tellers; like almost all historical sources, whether created in the past or subsequently, what they say sometimes may be factually incorrect. Contemporaries shaped what they wanted recorded in documents, just as much as life story interviewees. Some facts which were once kept secret will be revealed in retrospect. Other facts will be reshaped – but this reshaping can be in itself a witness to changing consciousness. What our Pioneers told us was important to them. We doubt that anyone deliberately lied to us. But some of what they told us has gradually becomes an often-recounted narrative of their life. Over the same decades our wider understanding of interview and narrative has become increasingly sophisticated and we now no longer see memory as something simply within a particular person's brain, but also shaped through the context of each life, which is also social, collective, historical and shared. Sometimes it presents an exact moment. Sometimes it can be repetitive, even ritualistic telling. So while our fragments may not be '*the* truth', they can most surely tell us about the wider moments, issues and contexts in which research was done, of what could be said at the time, and of the language used.

Perhaps the central problem of life stories is the contrast between the *little stories* being told by our interviewees, and the *bigger stories* of overarching concerns. This book can be seen as a series of voices, some closely linked as colleagues, others marginal, even disconnected. In the data archive or library or internet you can read, or listen to, the full interviews, just as they are: as live fragmented voices speaking in the context of an interview. But we have also been trying here to understand better how research happens in practice and to bring together a wider account of how social research was starting to emerge, the puzzles it faced, the institutions it was building. History, and even more sociology, always speaks to a wider story than a single life can hope to achieve. In that sense this book demonstrates some of the very problems our researchers discuss.

The research process

As we have seen, our Pioneers lived and worked for at least part of their lives in a United Kingdom shaped by the sufferings of two major world wars, shadowed by a privileged colonialism and imperialism, transformed by an emerging welfare state socialism, liberated by the politics of 1968 and restricted by the rise of Thatcherism. It is true that changes in class, gender and ethnicity were in the air, but the privileges of hierarchy were most surely very deeply embedded. Most sociologists and anthropologists before the Second World War were white middle-class or upper-class 'gentlemen'. And racism and imperialism were prevalent too, even if hardly articulated as an issue. Most researchers (even on race) were conspicuously white males until the 1970s. Issues of disability, age, sexuality and more were largely hidden. Many of our Pioneers had little sense of the changes ahead – how could they know that they were standing at the brink of new fields of enquiry, methodology, technology, policy, ethics and theory? At the same time they were most surely part of its emergence.

So what might be concluded? What larger stories can be sensed? While our concern here is with voice and empirical detail, we can also start to see the emergence of a very grounded theory and account of the creative research practice. There is nothing sacred about the research method as these accounts clearly testify. Among the elements of a fuller account might be the following.

First, *research is a creative process*: it shows us a little of how creativity works. This is not an account of individual geniuses, talented as our researchers were. Rather, we can see here a process of historical opportunity, personal awakenings and social contingency. Our Pioneers could do their research because they were there at the right historical moment with the right interests and awareness and the chance encounters that brought them into this pathway of research rather than another. Typically, they did not create their own opportunities: but they had to see their chances and to seize them. And some among them, despite having to make up most of their own methodological rules, proved able to investigate, write and publish some of the most compelling social research books of any time.

Second, *research is both constructed and contingent*. Despite formal protocols and purposive planning, what happens is often unforeseen, less planned, with chance factors often playing key roles. Our voices tell us over and over again of the unpredictability of much of their research, and chance encounters that shaped it. Of course, plans are made. Today, elaborate research protocols have to be drawn up. For our Pioneers the plans were usually very simple, driven by intellectual curiosity rather than by political correctness, formal ethical rules and standard methodological procedures. But such rules and procedures are still challenged again and again by the unexpected. Research rarely turns out just like the plan, with chance factors such as bureaucratic bottlenecks or personal disasters or interpersonal rivalries and disputes upsetting the process. Ultimately, it is conducted between people in relationships with all the problems that this will bring as we live our lives in everyday work situations. Our Pioneers faced such challenges primarily through their own sensibilities rather than rules, but their dilemmas are very often shared in the social research process today.

Third, again as today, *research can be co-operative, or conflictual, or both*. Some of our Pioneers worked as colleagues, such as *John Goldthorpe, David Lockwood* and *Frank Bechhofer* on the *Affluent Worker* project. But research also grows from perpetual tensions across many lines and from many sources. These conflicts include the classic British debates between quantitative and qualitative social science raised sharply in Chapter 5. But we can also see the conflicts appearing across disciplines, across agencies, between researchers, across politics. And there are conflicts within research too: as the memories of *Margaret Stacey* and *Colin Bell* of the second Banbury study acutely show.

Fourth, *research itself is age cohort-based and generational and not necessarily cumulative.* Each generation has to face its own crises and develops its own research field. Schools, traditions, theories and people come and go. Through time the political, ethical and moral issues raise, fall, re-emerge and rise again. Most actors in the long run will get lost and forgotten. The issues typically recur in new forms. There are immense differences between the international world of today and how Raymond Firth and Stuart Hall, Mary Douglas and Avtar Brah lived through the final era of the British Empire. Progress, if it happens, does not follow neatly.

CHAPTER 9

Epilogue

In writing this book we have focussed above all on what we see as most interesting and valuable in the interviews. Yet, from the start it also seemed important to reflect on what is missing. Initially, that arose in terms of people. We noted significant researchers who we could not interview because they had died, or were unwell, or – rarely – did not want to record a life story in terms of our aims. We began with researchers who had direct experience of fieldwork research, but later added a group of purely quantitative researchers, and another group who came to Britain from elsewhere in the Empire. We were well aware that given funding and time many others could have been included – particularly, those working at the margins with other disciplines.

With our draft book sent to our publishers, we decided to look again at how far our Pioneers had responded to the key social changes in their working lifetimes, and the extent to which they had addressed through fieldwork research what now seem to be crucial issues for our future. One gap is immediately obvious. There is very little sign of interest in the environment and climate change.

Religious differences, now a major social flashpoint, were also largely sidelined by post-war researchers. However, we should note that anthropologists working abroad both before and after the Second World War did document and attempt to interpret local traditional religious rituals. Indeed, *Raymond Firth*, who as a young man was Superintendent of a Presbyterian Sunday School, later wrote two books on religion in Tikopia – *The Work of the Gods in Tikopia* (1940) and *Rank and Religion in Tikopia: A Study in Polynesian Paganism and Conversion to Christianity* (1970) – and later examples include the work of *Bruce Kapferer*, *Ruth Finnegan* or *Mary Douglas*. Among sociologists, however, *Colin Bell* was unusual in conducting a survey of religious attendance in Banbury. *Robert Moore* was a lifelong Methodist and made a point of regularly attending a variety of churches and chapels while researching his community studies.

In terms of personal belief at least six male Pioneers had intense but brief religious phases as late teenagers: *Ken Plummer* recalls setting up stalls for Methodists, *Harry Goulbourne* experienced an unhappy year trying out training as an evangelical preacher in Ulster, *Ray Pahl* took up 'muscular Christianity' with The Crusaders – he 'idolised' their leader, but equally his 'glamorous' French wife – and *Peter Townsend* described his two religious years as 'like a little rocket in the sky' (p 13). In addition, two lifelong couples met in Zionist youth groups. *David Hargreaves* persisted longest – in this phase – as an active High Church Anglican from his teenage years, 'smells and bells' – he went on to read Theology at Cambridge, but in retrospect interprets his religious conversion as a 'protection', an escape from accepting a gay identity (pp 12–13). Among women, *Pat Caplan* was an active teenage Methodist, and *Janet Finch* met her future husband, who became an Anglican clergyman, in a church youth group.

Typically, however, English sociologists, even if sent to Christian Sunday Schools, as adults became agnostics without friction, and did not see religion as relevant to current social issues. As *Raymond Smith* put it after reading a book on poor Jamaican women Pentecostals, 'I find the book very depressing, because so much energy is wasted on this religious stuff, that could go into real social protest. It saps the energy of the poor' (p 60).

What of social inequality? Yes, our Pioneers carried out much major work in terms of class, gender and ethnicity. But our sociologists researched on Britain, and while our anthropologists worked in many other countries, neither took to exploring inequality globally. Where the anthropologists went changed with colonial independence, depending on the political consequences. While we certainly hear some of our social activist Pioneers confronting danger, this was unusual because sustained research demands a stable and safe setting, and needs to be acceptable not only legally but also to local popular opinion. These constraints have had a particular impact on research on sexual diversity, with the changing laws of the 1960s redefining what could be safely published.

With climate change, it is remarkable that only one of our first 58 Pioneers took up the theme, and she was *Elizabeth Thomas-Hope*, social geographer, working at the end of her career in Jamaica after 2000. It is significant that *Howard Newby*, while not himself researching on climate change, did recognise the importance of the issue, and in 1990–95 as head of the ESRC sponsored a Global Environmental Change Programme. This was led by *Michael Redclift* who has now been interviewed for the project. But despite the ESRC programme none of our other Pioneer sociologists and anthropologists showed any sign of active interest. Was this because those in the mainstream remained unaware of its importance?

This seems unlikely. There is a long tradition of environmental writing in Britain, including Ruskin's prophetic denunciation of the change brought by industrial factory smoke, *Storm Cloud of the*

Nineteenth Century (1884), and in our Pioneers' generation the radical cultural humanism of Raymond Williams, such as in *The Country and the City* (1973). There was also popular environmental activism, including the successful campaigns by the Ramblers to win open access to the northern hillsides.

Moreover, in the US in 1962, Rachel Carson had published *Silent Spring*, demonstrating the environmental dangers of synthetic pesticides, and how human activity could de-stable nature. This aroused a powerful American popular response and inspired a grassroots environmental movement which – despite the fierce opposition of chemical companies – led to the national banning of DDT and the setting up of the US Environmental Protection Agency.

Perhaps the mainstreamers of the disciplines saw the environment as a scientific issue which was not a concern of their discipline. Or alternatively not a theme on which they could usefully do empirical research on in the UK. They showed no sign of wanting to emulate the enthusiastic younger NGO researchers, who saw themselves as aid workers rather than future academics, and from the 1980s were working – as with SOS Sahel and Panos – on how to deal with the climate changes which were already happening in Africa and Asia.

Rather than simply speculating, we decided on a symbolic step to demonstrate the need and potential for other life story researchers to explore the issues around social researchers and climate change: hence, we set about recording three new life story interviews with researchers who had focussed on this issue. So far, due to the COVID-19 lockdown, only the interview with *Michael Redclift* is complete. He has long sustained research interests in the relationships between human society, the environment, nature and climate change.

As he spoke of his life's work *Michael Redclift* vividly illustrated both his commitment and his sense of marginalisation in the British social research world. He was a prolific writer who felt ignored by the mainstream: 'most sociologists had cloth ears to the environment, to be quite frank!' (p 55). How and why did he experience that? Essentially, his account is of a journey down creative but ambiguous paths which never lead him to the centre grounds of conventional social research. This begins with his childhood. He was born in 1946 into the strong working-class culture of South Wales, at an ambiguous time of transition when the Welsh industrial heyday was well past. He was to become a grammar schoolboy and move out to university at Sussex, but Michael's childhood background remained highly significant to him. In his interview he speaks immediately and at length about how he found there an inspirational anchor for life.

This was through his close relationship with Arthur, his maternal grandfather: 'a very interesting man who developed my interest in nature and the environment'. Arthur had a rough start, 'beaten by a stepfather as a child'. From starting as a Devon blacksmith, 'like lots of other people he went, he came into the shipyards of South Wales, working as a blacksmith making ships'. Working in industry transformed his views. An autodidact, 'his background had been in Nonconformity. He used to "sky pilot for Jesus" as he called it. Then he discovered Marxism and gave that up!' He became a 'very militant' shop steward, suffering 'long periods of unemployment'.

'But his roots, his heart, were in the countryside. He had quite a lot of knowledge of nature and the countryside... He always had gardens, he used to collect horse manure to manure his garden, and he kept animals.' Looking back, Michael sees him like a beacon, with

> an interest in something other than the current Promethean urge to use and destroy nature. Today he could be seen as [having] quite an interest in sustainability... I dedicated *Sustainable Development* [in 1987] to my grandfather, 'Marxist and environmentalist', because he was very much a Marxist. But a very interesting one because he was interested in all kinds of green issues from an early stage. (pp 1–2, 5–7)

In Michael's own working life the paradox was that the elements which fed his insights also made his position more marginal: his beliefs in interdisciplinarity, in mixing rural and urban themes and methods, and in international comparisons. He saw the relevance of both modern scientific research and traditional practices in response to climate challenges such as hurricanes. Through his empirical research he became a Latin Americanist as well as a sociologist; and in Britain he was further isolated by the location of his workbase: Wye College, a research centre which was part of London University but 60 miles out of London in the Kent countryside – close to nature but isolating him from potential British colleagues. He found a more rewarding international network through a research committee of the International Sociological Association (ISA).

Michael sees British sociology, in contrast to the broader perspectives of other social science disciplines, as having been narrowly focussed on urban British issues and European-based theory. He recalls an occasion when he had been invited 'to write something about the environment in a mainstream sociology journal'. He sketched out a piece and sent it.

'And they said, "But there are none of the great masters here. There's no Marx, Weber or Durkheim, or anybody similar or anybody else." And my reply was, "That was because they didn't think an awful lot about the environment".' Michael was spurred to address this 'blind spot' (pp 46–47).

He discusses in his life story his series of major books through the 1980s and 1990s. First came *From Peasant to Proletarian* (with David Goodman, 1981) with a long time span, comparing the socio-economic impact of capitalism in Russia and in different Latin American countries; then three more books, still closely linked to case studies, with a stronger focus on the need to create new theoretical perspectives: *Development and the Environmental Crisis: Red and Green Alternatives* (1984), *Sustainable Development: Exploring the Contradictions* (1987) and then (jointly edited with Ted Benton) in 1994 *Social Theory and the Global Environment* – still the key theoretical work on the issue – calling for a much wider and more imaginative role for the social sciences in exploring environmental and climatic change, based on a radical re-think of existing inherited assumptions.

There was a moment, around midway, a turning point, when he was heard by the ESRC's head, *Howard Newby*, and as a result in 1990–95 became director of the ESRC's Global Environmental Change Programme. He recalls how from the start, 'sociology was a real challenge… I felt a bit evangelical at this stage. I felt I had to take it to sociology in particular'. Could he induce such a big shift? He remembers how a question at an early meeting demonstrated the gap in understanding:

'What about housing in Enfield? What's all this global climate change got to do with housing in Enfield?' It's a meeting of sociologists. And I thought about it, obviously it has an awful lot to do with the housing in Enfield. The way the houses are built, what they call 'part dependency' now, the links between housing stock and transport system, and where people work, what people spend, and then, how green is the housing estate going to be? How are the houses going to be heated? … So the more you think about it, housing in Enfield is very much a global environmental issue. (pp 50–51)

The programme was a turning point because it failed to change the perspectives of most British sociologists. Michael recognises this: 'There are people today, thirty years on, who are very committed to working on the environment, in sociology, but still not all that many. It's an uncomfortable position to be in' (pp 104–105).

But the early 1990s were a turning point in a wider and much more discomforting sense. They marked a growing international recognition of the inevitability of climate change, which has now culminated in the still more drastic stage of climate emergency. In short, a moment of change between generations, and at the same time in the material and social world context. Sustainability, which Michael had championed, was an optimistic middle path, still needed but only a partial solution. The answers have to come from a much younger generation of pioneers.

Michael today still challenges the times and still urges fresh thinking:

> People are inclined to say, from knowledge of climate change, 'What shall we do about it?' 'Should we feel guilty?' 'Are we capable of changing things?' 'Is it cultural?' All these issues. Obviously the existence of global climate change is bound up with all sorts of ways of living/existing, getting and spending, that we don't usually interrogate, we just take them as given. That's why the green agenda ultimately is so radical. It's much more radical than the Marxist agenda. Because you're actually saying, what if there wasn't positive growth, what if you have a stable state of economy? Everybody says how marvellous it is at Christmas when people are on the High Streets buying things. Well, I still slightly squirm when I hear that. Is it a good thing everybody's buying more stuff, to get rid of, or recycle? (pp 54–55)

Notes

Chapter 1

[1]   Paul Thompson and Louise Corti, 'Celebrating Classic Sociology', special issue, *International Journal of Social Research Methodology, Theory and Practice*, 7, 1 (2004); Chris Phillipson and Paul Thompson, 'Whither Community Studies? A special issue on researching community studies, past and present', *International Journal of Social Research Methodology, Theory and Practice*, 11, 2 (2008).

[2]   With some of whom interviews were agreed but could not be finished. See also 'Celebration of Julia Brannen's Contribution to Research Methods', *International Journal of Social Research Methodology*, 17, 2 (2019).

[3]   A great deal has been written on issues of memory, not only about factual accuracy and inaccuracy, but also on how mis-rememberings can offer important evidence of social attitudes. For a starting point, Paul Thompson, *The Voice of the Past*, 4th edn (Oxford University Press, 2017), Chapters 7 and 8: 'Evidence', and 'Memory and the Self'. A classic text on the recognition of 'false' memories as clues to changing consciousness is Alessandro Portelli, *The Death of Luigi Trastulli and Other Stories* (State University of New York, 1991). More recent and equally powerful is the new introduction by Svetlana Alexievich to her re-translated book on Russian women in the Second World War, *The Unwomanly Face of War* (Penguin Books, 2017), for which she was awarded the 2015 Nobel Prize in Literature.

[4]   There has been a growth of interest in the history of British sociology (see John Holmwood and John Scott, *The Palgrave Handbook of Sociology in Britain* (Palgrave, 2014)) and John Scott's briefer *British Sociology: A History* (Palgrave, 2020) but little recognition of the value of recorded interviews as a source. Also recent is Plamena Panayotova's edited collection, *The History of Sociology in Britain: New Research and Re-Evaluation* (Springer, 2019). Jennifer Platt was an early leader in this field, but when she did record interviews, as for her *The British Sociological Association: A Sociological History* (Sociology Press, 2003), she kept these interviews closed as confidential. A. H. Halsey's *History of Sociology in Britain* (Oxford University Press, 2004), refers to interviews but does not list them among his sources. It is striking that the most professional recent work on the history of British sociology, drawing on both archival sources and listed interviews, is by a journalist rather than a sociologist: Helen Pearson's *The Life Project* (Penguin Random House, 2016). Fortunately, as with anthropology there is also recent interview-based work coming up to the present: see Katherine Twamley et al (eds.), *Sociologists' Tales* (Policy Press, 2015) and Les Back's *Academic Diary* (Goldsmiths Press, 2016).

[5]   Bronislaw Malinowski, *Argonauts of the Western Pacific* (Routledge, 1922); Bronislaw Malinowski, *A Diary in the Strict Sense of the Term* (Routledge and Kegan Paul, 1967); Hortense Powdermaker, *Stranger and Friend: The Way of an Anthropologist* (Secker and Warburg, 1967).

[6]   http://alanmacfarlane.com/ancestors/audiovisual.html. Other published collections include Geert de Neve and Maya Unnithan-Kumar, 20 written personal accounts in *Critical Journeys: The Making of Anthropologists* (Ashgate, 2006).

Voices 1

[1] See also Michael Crick, *Sultan of Swing: The Life of David Butler* (Biteback Publishing, 2018).

Chapter 2

[1] In addition to our interview with *Hilary Rose*, the British Library holds a life story recording with Steven Rose as part of the Oral History of British Science. Similarly, they hold not only our interview with *Stuart Hall*, but also an interview with Catherine Hall from the Sisterhood and After oral history project (led by Margaretta Jolly and jointly based at the University of Sussex, British Library, and Women's Library at the LSE). These present different feelings, but the same core narratives.

[2] From this point onwards we have to take into account the fact that eight (out of 20) of the women Pioneers and 16 of the men (out of 40) had two or three marriages, and in interpreting their life stories we are using the information which we have for all of them.

[3] See also Richard Fardon, *Mary Douglas: An Intellectual Biography* (Routledge, 1999).

Chapter 3

[1] Ian Cobain, *The History Thieves: Secrets, Lies and the Shaping of a Modern Nation* (Portobello, 2016). See also Robert Gilea, *Empires of the Mind: The Colonial Past and the Politics of the Present* (Oxford University Press, 2019) and Julian Go, *Postcolonial Thought and Social Theory* (Oxford University Press, 2016.

[2] Stuart Hall with Bill Schwarz, *Familiar Stranger: A Life between Two Islands* (Allen Lane, 2017): 21.

[3] See Alan Walker (ed.), *The Peter Townsend Reader* (Policy Press, 2010).

[4] Others include Barbara Wootton, who became the first woman elected to be President of the BSA (1959–64), whose life has been well documented in Ann Oakley, *A Critical Woman: Barbara Wootton, Social Science and Public Policy in the Twentieth Century* (Bloomsbury, 2011). Olive Banks (1923–2006) studied sociology at the LSE and researched and taught at Leicester University on education, family planning and feminism. She wrote the influential *Faces of Feminism: A Study of Feminism as a Social Movement* (Martin Robertson, 1981). Her memoir was published in *Women's History Review*, 8, 3 (1999): 401–410.

Chapter 4

[1] Such academic micro-worlds can also be investigated. Here we have not followed that trail, but see Ken Plummer's *Imaginations: Fifty Years of Essex Sociology* (Wivenpress, 2014 and accessible from the University of Essex Library), which provides a case study of one sociology department at work in the time of our Pioneers.

[2] Jennifer Platt, *Social Research in Bethnal Green* (Macmillan, 1971).

[3] Helen Pearson, *The Life Project: The Extraordinary Story of our Ordinary Lives* (Allen Lane, 2016): 216.

Voices 4

[1] SPSS is a software package used for interactive statistical analysis. Developed in California by Norman Nie, Dale Bent and Hadlai Hull, it was first available in

1968 and thereafter in successive editions by SPSS Inc. It was acquired by IBM in 2009.

Chapter 6

1 Valuable broad histories of qualitative research can be found in the various volumes edited by Norman K. Denzin and Yvonne S. Lincoln, *The Sage Handbook of Qualitative Research* (Sage, 1994 etc). See especially Arthur J. Vidich and Stanford M. Lyman, 'Qualitative Methods: Their history in sociology and anthropology' (1994): 23–58, and Frederick Erickson, 'A History of Qualitative Inquiry in Social and Educational Research' (2011): 43–59.

2 A sense of the controversy in this formative period can be found in David Mills, *Difficult Folk: A Political History of Social Anthropology* (Berghahn Books, 2008) and Adam Kuper, *Anthropology and Anthropologists: The Modern British School* (Routledge, 1973).

3 A classic early text is Raymond Kent, *A History of British Empirical Sociology* (Gower, 1981). The major Mass Observation study was *The Pub and People* (Victor Gollanz, 1943). For a general analysis see Nick Hubble, *Mass Observation and Everyday Life: Culture, History, Theory* (Palgrave, 2006). Early sociology texts, which include Sidney and Beatrice Webb, *Methods of Social Study* (Longmans, Green, 1932), have been analysed by Geoff Payne in 'Research Methodology in Sociology', in John Holmwood (ed), *The Palgrave Handbook of Sociology in Britain* (Palgrave Macmillan, 2014): 413–436.

4 A key contemporary overview of this field is Colin Bell and Howard Newby: *Community Studies: An Introduction to the Local Community* (Allen and Unwin, 1971). Two important earlier reviews were Josephine Klein, *Samples from English Culture*, Vols 1–2 (Routledge, 1966) and Ronald Frankenberg in *Communities in Britain: Social Life in Town and Country* (Penguin, 1969). The most recent update is Graham Crow, *What Are Community Studies* (Bloomsbury Academic, 2018).

5 For a wide-ranging series of subsequent discussions of anthropological and sociological fieldwork, see especially Robert Burgess (ed), *Field Research: A Sourcebook and Manual* (Allen and Unwin, 1982) and *In the Field: An Introduction to Field Research* (Allen and Unwin, 1984). See also David Silverman, *Doing Qualitative Research: A Practical Handbook* (Sage, 2004) and more recently the articles in Paul Atkinson et al (eds), *Handbook of Ethnography* (Sage, 2001). This includes Sara Delamont, 'An Open Exploratory Spirit: The Cardiff School of Ethnography 1974–2017'. On life stories and oral history, see Paul Thompson, *The Voice of the Past*, 4th edn (Oxford University Press, 2017).

6 Paul Atkinson and David Silverman, 'Kundera's Immortality: The Interview Society and the Invention of Self', *Qualitative Inquiry* (2019) 3 (3): 304-25.

7 C. Wright Mills, *The Sociological Imagination* (Oxford University Press, 1959): 224.

Chapter 7

1 Geoff Payne's *Social Divisions* (BSA Publications, 2000, fourth edition 2020), now carves out a major research field. He discusses 'Three core social divisions' named as class, gender and ethnicity; and then turns to an array of other divisions like disability, age, sexuality, religion and nationality. But these divisions were never so clearly articulated in earlier days.

[2] For contemporary critical debates on meritocracy, see Jo Littler, *Against Meritocracy* (Routledge, 2017).

[3] See John Smyth, 'Education and the Working Class: A Conversation with the Work of Dennis Marsden and his Contribution to the Sociology of Education', *Journal of Education Administration and History*, 48, 4 (2016): 275–289.

[4] A much more detailed and valuable analysis of social class and methodology is made by Mike Savage in *Identities and Social Change in Britain since 1940: The Politics of Method* (Oxford University Press, 2010): 'A particular window on the social that was opened in the middle years of the twentieth century is now being closed, or at least stands as only one, by no means dominant, vantage point over the landscaped social': 24.

[5] As Geoff Payne writes: 'There can be few areas of British sociology that are so dominated by one study, as social mobility is dominated by David Glass's *Social Mobility in Britain* (Routledge and Kegan Paul, 1954).' See Payne's 'Social Mobility in Britain: The Old Evidence' in his *Mobility and Change in Modern Society* (Palgrave Macmillan, 1987).

[6] See Fiona Devine, *Affluent Workers Revisited: Privatism and the Working Class* (Edinburgh University Press, 1992).

[7] Savage: 97.

[8] For example, among our Pioneers, see Daniel Bertaux and Paul Thompson (eds), *Between Generations: Family Models, Myths and Memories* (Oxford University Press, 1993) and *Pathways to Social Class: A Qualitative Approach to Social Mobility* (Clarendon Press, 1997).

[9] For two rich accounts of feminism in North American sociology, see Myra Marx Ferre et al and Barbara Laslett, Ch 13 and 14 in Craig Calhoun, *Sociology in America: A History* (Chicago University Press, 2007): 438–501. Much less has been written on the impact of second-wave feminism on social research in Britain. For an early assessment, see Liz Stanley and Sue Wise, *Breaking Out: Feminist Consciousness and Feminist Research* (Routledge and Kegan Paul, 1983); and more recently Sara Delamont, *Feminist Sociology* (Sage, 2003). Ann Oakley's *Father and Daughter* (Policy Press, 2014) is about an earlier period; but see also her semi-autobiographical novel, *Taking It Like a Woman* (Jonathan Cape, 1984). Recorded memories are particularly valuable for this theme, and Margaretta Jolly's *Sisterhood and After: An Oral History of the Women's Liberation Movement in the UK: 1968–Present* (Oxford University Press, 2019) is an important new contribution.

[10] Kenneth Little, *Negroes in Britain: A Study of Race Relations in English Society* (Kegan Paul, 1948); Michael Banton, *The Coloured Quarter: Negro Immigrants in an English City* (Jonathan Cape, 1955) – see Howard Becker's review of *The Coloured Quarter* in *American Journal of Sociology*, 61 (1955–56): 497–498; Sheila Patterson, *Dark Strangers: A Sociological Study of the Absorption of a Recent West Indian Migrant Group in Brixton, South London* (Tavistock, 1963).

[11] Paul Gilroy, from the next generation, became one of the foremost theorists of race and racism with highly influential books such as *There Ain't No Black in the Union Jack* (Hutchinson, 1987) and *The Black Atlantic: Modernity and Double Consciousness* (Verso, 1993), marking a turning point in the study of diasporas.

[12] Robert Moore, '*Race, Community and Class* Revisited', in *Discover Society*, 6 (March 2014): 497–498.

[13] See Jeffrey Weeks, *Sex, Politics and Society: The Regulation of Sexuality Since 1800* (Routledge, 2017, 4th edn) and Liz Stanley, *Sex Surveyed, 1949 to 1994: From*

Mass Observation's 'Little Kinsey' to the National Survey and the Hite Reports (Taylor and Francis, 1995).

14   PT adds: Only two of our forty male and two of our twenty women Pioneers remembered living as one of a long-term gay couple. For all four these were seen as life-long relationships. Both of the women Pioneers had previously been in supportive married relationships with men: one of these husbands had died, while the other remained a very close friend living across the same square.

A further factor influencing these numbers was the lack of successful gay models among researchers or indeed writers more generally. There is a sharp contrast with the culture of artists and musicians, who since the times of Michelangelo and Leonardo have had models of great artists who were gay, and from the eighteenth century were further encouraged by the imagined links between bohemianism and creativity. Gay networks including leading painters were highly influential in the English art world of our Pioneers' generation. This was different from the apparently more 'respectable' world of social researchers, who preferred to stick to an almost Victorian middle-class reticence.

Our interviews were not intended to explore personal sexual behaviour, unless it was directly related to their research lives. Hence, with the exception of *Ken Plummer* himself they only give hints of their personal experiences of sexuality. Nevertheless, these hints are interesting in terms of gender differences in the shaping of memories. The most open memories come mainly from women Pioneers, some of whom were thrown into confusion and experimentation by second-wave feminism. These can be seen as stories of liberation. However, two women Pioneers accused older male colleagues of misogyny or serial sexual abuse. *Judith Okely* describes what would have been a not uncommon female experience in the academic world of the 1960s, when she worked as a part-time research assistant for an internationally famous social psychologist, who was a pioneer researcher on the cognitive aspects of prejudice and social identity. She was particularly keen to get this job. 'My interview consisted of me going to Wellington Square, to his room, and him touching me up all the way through the interview – running his hand up and down my arm, trying to grab my breast... And I couldn't protest because I wanted the job!' (p 52)

Judith also describes being once invited with her then partner to dinner with some 'very rich' academic Oxford friends. After the meal their host invited them to join a free love commune. 'He said, "We want a totally open commune type thing... so that we all sleep with somebody different every night... Would you like to join the commune?"' Judith declined (p 145).

Heterosexual men seem to have been the least willing to speak about their own sexual experiences. The most vivid item of evidence among our interviews was transmitted unintentionally. One eminent anthropologist sent our interviewer a google map, accidentally leaving on the reverse side of the page a detailed description by his lover of his slowly learnt sexual foreplay.

15   In 2008, Ken Plummer conducted an interview with Michael; but it was not a great success, as Michael's memory was fading. He keeps the interview in his archival papers. It is also particularly unfortunate that we did not interview Tony Coxon (d. 2012), both for his own personal life, and for his work on religion and in quantitative research, or Mary McIntosh (d. 2013) as a founder lesbian and gay activist and feminist sociologist.

Further reading

You can pursue the Pioneers broadly in four directions. The first is through the wider context in which they worked. The second – for which we also provide more detail in the endnotes – is to look at particular trails through disciplines and fields over a wider time span. The third is to look at other autobiographical work, including some recorded from younger generations. The fourth is to read some of the best of the Pioneers' own books. In each direction we have aimed to pick out books which are clear, readable and potentially stimulating.

The wider context

Eric Hobsbawm's *The Age of Extremes: The Short Twentieth Century 1914–1991* (Michael Joseph, 1994) combines broad vision with vivid detail to convey the global international context in which this generation of researchers worked.

George Steinmetz, *Sociology and Empire: The Imperial Entanglement of a Discipline* (Duke University Press, 2013) provides a broad understanding of British sociology's imperial connections. See also his *Rethinking Modernity: Postcolonialism and the Sociological Imagination* (Palgrave, 2007).

Ian Cobain, *The History Thieves: Secrets, Lies and the Shaping of a Modern Nation* (Portobello, 2016) shows how British governments have consistently but secretly manipulated official records to convey a positive view of colonial rule.

Randall Collin's *The Sociology of Philosophies: A Global Theory of Intellectual Change* (1998, Belknap) is a magisterial work – not for the fainthearted – which shows the ways in which generations shape human knowledge.

Stefan Collini's *Absent Minds: Intellectuals in Britain* (Oxford University Press, 2008) analyses the intellectual background in which this generation of Pioneers worked. See also his books on universities: *What Are Universities For?* (Penguin, 2012) and *Speaking of Universities* (Verso, 2017).

Particular trails

Gordon Marshall's *In Praise of Sociology* (Unwin Hyman, 1990) is a valuable review of the achievements of social research of the time of our Pioneers, which discusses the work of many of them.

Mike Savage's *Identities and Social Change in Britain since 1940: The Politics of Method* (Oxford University Press, 2010) draws on the Pioneers project to develop an original account of the development of class and identity research in Britain.

David Mills' *Difficult Folk: A Political History of Social Anthropology* (Berghahn Books, 2008) is an intriguing account of the conflicts around the making of British anthropology.

Sidney and Beatrice Webb's *Methods of Social Study* (Longmans, Green, 1932) is a classic early British example of a research methods text. It is so different from the blockbusters of today like Alan Bryman's *Social Research Methods* (5th edn, Oxford University Press, 2015).

A major early account of feminism was provided by Olive Banks in her *Faces of Feminism: A Study of Feminism as a Social Movement* (Martin Robertson, 1981).

Ronald Frankenberg reviews the entire field of community studies in *Communities in Britain: Social Life in Town and Country* (Penguin, 1969).

Paul Thompon's *The Voice of the Past: Oral History* (4th edn, Oxford University Press, 2017) is now a classic introduction to the history and methods of oral history and life stories.

Ken Plummer, *Documents of Life: An Invitation to a Critical Humanism* (Sage, 1983, 2nd edn 2001).

Other auto/biographical sources

Ann Oakley's *Father and Daughter: Patriarchy, Gender and Social Science* (Policy Press, 2014) provides a subtle study of family and research relationship. Her father was Richard Titmuss, founding professor of Social Administration at LSE.

Richard Hoggart's *Promises to Keep: Thoughts in Old Age* (Continuum, 2005) is a short autobiographical reflection by a man who could claim to be the founder of cultural studies in Britain.

Asa Briggs's *Michael Young: Social Entrepreneur* (Palgrave, 2001) on this astonishingly inventive Pioneer.

Stuart Hall's *Familiar Stranger: A Life between Two Islands* (with Bill Schwartz) (Allen Lane, 2017) draws a little from his Pioneers interview and provides a major account of an outsider turned insider.

Colin Bell's edited collection *Doing Sociological Research* (with Howard Newby) (Allen and Unwin, 1977) was the original early collection of researchers telling their research tales, and 'owning up'.

Helen Roberts (ed) *Doing Feminist Research* (Routledge and Kegan Paul, 1984) – more 'owning up'.

Bennett M. Berger's (ed) *Authors of their Own Lives: Intellectual Autobiographies by Twenty American Sociologists* (University of California Press, 1990) is a more developed set of biographical essays by US sociologists telling their life and research experiences.

Katherine Twamley, Mark Doidge and Andrea Scott's (eds) *Sociologists' Tales: Contemporary Narratives on Sociological Thought and Practice* (Policy Press, 2015) gives the very readable stories of some 30 sociologists working in Britain – of a current younger generation.

Twenty-five books from the Pioneers

All of our Pioneers were prolific writers and we cannot list all their works here. What follows is just a short list of a few of the major texts that have been featured and discussed in this book. Both the UK Data Service and the British Library can provide fuller details on the publications of our Pioneers (see pp vii–ix).

George W. Brown and Tirril Harris, *Social Origins of Depression: A Study of Psychiatric Disorder in Women* (Routledge, 1990).

Stanley Cohen, *Folk Devils and Moral Panics: The Creation of the Mods and Rockers* (Routledge, 1972).

Mary Douglas, *Purity and Danger: An Analysis of Concepts of Pollution and Taboo* (Routledge and Kegan Paul, 1966).

Ruth Finnegan, *The Hidden Musicians: Music Making in an English Town* (Cambridge University Press, 1989).

Raymond Firth, *We, the Tikopia: A Sociological Study of Kinship in Primitive Polynesia* (Allen and Unwin, 1936).

John H. Goldthorpe, David Lockwood, Frank Bechhofer and Jennifer Platt, *The Affluent Worker in the Class Structure* (Cambridge University Press, 1969).

Jack Goody, *The Development of the Family and Marriage in Europe* (Cambridge University Press, 1983).

Stuart Hall, Chas Critcher, Tony Jefferson, John Clarke and Brian Roberts, *Policing the Crisis: Mugging, the State and Law and Order* (Macmillan, 1978).

David Hargreaves, *Social Relations in a Secondary School* (Routledge, 1973).

Brian Jackson and Dennis Marsden, *Education and the Working Class* (Routledge and Kegan Paul, 1962).

Diana Leonard Barker and Sheila Allen (eds) *Sexual Divisions and Society* (Tavistock, 1976).

Claus Moser, *Survey Methods in Social Investigation* (Heinemann, 1958).

Ann Oakley, *Sex, Gender and Society* (Temple Smith, 1972).

Judith Okely, *The Traveller-Gypsies* (Cambridge University Press, 1983).

R. E. (Ray) Pahl, *Divisions of Labour* (Blackwell, 1984).

John Rex and Robert Moore, *Race, Community and Conflict: A Study of Sparkbrook* (Oxford University Press, 1967).

Margaret Stacey, *Tradition and Change: a Study of Banbury* (Oxford University Press, 1960).

Marilyn Strathern, *The Gender of the Gift: Problems with Women and Problems with Society in Melanesia* (University of California Press, 1988).

Paul Thompson (with Gill Gorell Barnes, Gwyn Daniel and Natasha Burchardt), *Growing Up in Stepfamilies* (Clarendon Press, 1998).

Peter Townsend, *The Family Life of Old People* (Routledge and Kegan Paul, 1957).

Peter Townsend, *The Last Refuge: A Survey of Residential Institutions and Homes for the Aged* (Routledge and Kegan Paul, 1962).

Peter Townsend, *Poverty in the United Kingdom: A Survey of Household Resources and Standards of Living* (Penguin Books and Allen Lane, 1979).

W. M. Williams, *The Sociology of an English Village: Gosforth* (Routledge and Kegan Paul, 1956).

Michael Young, *The Rise of the Meritocracy* (Penguin, 1958).

Michael Young and Peter Willmott, *Family and Kinship in East London* (Routledge and Kegan Paul, 1957).

Biographical summaries

Information includes birth date and place, and when to Britain; main discipline and pioneering focus; one or more key indicative works; main university research bases; other comment; year of recording and interviewer; British Library catalogue number/shelfmark when interview is held.

Sara Arber (b. 1949, London). Sociologist, focus on survey methods, gender and ageing, and on the sociology of sleep. Success in winning broader access to national statistics. *Doing Secondary Analysis* (with Angela Dale, Michael Procter) (Allen and Unwin, 1988). Surrey. Recorded 2017 by PT. British Library shelfmark: C 1416/58

Frank Bechhofer (1939–2018, b. Nuremberg; to Britain 1939). Sociologist: focus on class and identity, on affluent workers, lower middle classes, Scottish identity. *The Affluent Worker: Industrial Attitudes and Behaviour* (with John Goldthorpe et al) (Cambridge University Press, 1968); *The Petite Bourgeoisie* (with Brian Elliott) (Edinburgh University Press, 1981); *Principles of Research Design in the Social Sciences* (with L. Paterson) (Routledge, 2000). Cambridge, Edinburgh. Recorded 2001 by PT. British Library shelfmark: C 1416/07

Colin Bell (1942–2003, b. London). Sociologist, early work on middle-class families, community study enthusiast who led second Banbury study fieldwork and became key critic of the method. *Middle Class Families: Social and Geographical Mobility* (Routledge and Kegan Paul, 1968); *Community Studies: An Introduction to the Sociology of the Local Community* (with Howard Newby) (Allen and Unwin, 1971). Very much in the spirit of this book, Colin believed in 'owning up': *Doing Sociological Research* (with Newby) (Allen and Unwin, 1977) and *Social Researching: Politics, Process, Practice* (with Helen Roberts) (Routledge and Kegan Paul, 1984). Keele, Swansea, Edinburgh. Recorded 2002 by PT. British Library shelfmark: C 1416/34

Ted Benton (b. 1942 Leicester). Social philosopher who reworked Marxism in relation to ecology and green social theory; in parallel, local naturalist and environmental campaigner. *The Rise and Fall of Structural Marxism: Althusser and His Influence* (Macmillan, 1984); 'Marxism and Natural Limits', *New Left Review* 178, 1989; *Natural Relations: Ecology, Animal Rights and Social Justice* (Verso, 1993); *Social Theory and the*

Global Environment (eds . with Michael Redlclift) (Routledge, 1994); *The Bumblebees of Essex* (Lopinga, 2000); *Bumblebees* (HarperCollins, 2006); *Grasshoppers and Crickets* (HarperCollins, 2011); *A Naturalist's Guide to the Butterflies of Britain and Northern Europe* (John Beaufoy, 2017); *Philosophy of Social Science* (with Ian Craib) (Palgrave Macmillan, 2010); *Alfred Russel Wallace: Explorer, Evolutionist, Public Intellectual: A Thinker for Our Times?* (Siri Scientific, 2013). Leicester, Essex; Secretary, Colchester Trades Council, 1974–81; recording 2008 and 2020 in progress, by PT.

Daniel Bertaux (b. 1939, Paris). Leader of French school of life sociology and mixed method approach to social mobility. *Biography and Society* (Sage, 1981); *Pathways to Social Class* (with Paul Thompson) (Clarendon, 1997). CNRS, Paris. Recorded 2002 and 2011 by PT. British Library shelfmark: C 1416/04

Mildred Blaxter (1925–2010, b. Newcastle). Sociologist of health and disability. *The Meaning of Disability* (Heinemann, 1976); *Mothers and Daughters: A Study of Health Attitudes and Behaviour* (with Elizabeth Paterson) (Heinemann, 1982). Aberdeen, East Anglia. Recorded 2012 by PT. British Library shelfmark: C 1416/18

Avtar Brah (b. 1944, Punjab; childhood Uganda; came to Britain 1972). Interdisciplinary sociologist, focus on migration, borders, hybrid cultures. *Cartographies of Diaspora* (Routledge, 1996). Bristol, Open University, Birkbeck. BL Feminist/ethnic activist: founder Southall Black Sisters. Recorded 2018 by PT. British Library shelfmark: C 1416/49

George Brown (b. 1930, London). Sociologist/anthropologist and social psychologist: developing new methods with focus on the links between depression and women's life events and on expression of emotion. *Social Origins of Depression: A Study of Psychiatric Disorder in Women* (with Tirril Harris) (Routledge, 1990). London (Bedford College, University College). Recorded 2000 by PT. British Library shelfmark: C 1416/37

Sir David Butler (b. 1924, Oxford). Political scientist, early to use statistics as well as qualitative methods, pioneered media coverage in elections. *Political Change in Britain: Forces Shaping Electoral Choice* (with Donald Stokes) (Macmillan, 1969). Oxford. Radio/TV commentator especially at elections. Recorded 2014 by PT. British Library shelfmark: C 1416/44

John Bynner (b. 1938, London). Psychologist, educationist and statistician; early on youth culture, later on longitudinal studies, becoming director of both 1958 National Child Development Study and 1970 British Cohort Study. *The Young Smoker* (HMSO, 1969); *Changing Britain, Changing Lives: Three Generations at the End of the Century* (with Elsa Ferri and Michael Wadsworth) (Institute of Education, 2003). Bristol, Open, London (City, Institute of Education). Recorded 2015 by PT. British Library shelfmark: C 1416/45

Pat Caplan (b. 1942, Cheshire). Anthropologist: first on communities, land and kinship in Nepal and on Mafia Island, East Africa, next on women and gender in Madras, India, and later comparatively on food and other themes in Britain and elsewhere. Feminist activist. *Choice and Constraint in a Swahili Community* (Oxford University Press, 1975); *Class and Gender in India* (Tavistock, 1985). London (SOAS, Goldsmiths). Recorded 2009 by PT. British Library shelfmark: C 1416/19

Stanley Cohen (1942–2013, b. Johannesburg, came to Britain 1963). Sociologist, best known for his new perspectives on deviance, examining its media exaggeration in 'moral panics'; also focussed on human rights issues, including the impact of imprisonment, and how and why we deal with others in suffering. *Folk Devils and Moral Panics: The Creation of the Mods and Rockers* (Macgibbon and Kee, 1972); *Psychological Survival: The Experience of Long-term Imprisonment* (with Laurie Taylor) (Penguin, 1972); *States of Denial: Knowing about Atrocities and Suffering* (Polity, 2001). Witswatersrand, LSE, Durham, Essex, Jerusalem. Recorded 2001 by PT. British Library shelfmark: C 1416/31

Sir David Cox (b. 1924, Birmingham). Pioneer of statistical social science. *Principles of Statistical Inference* (Cambridge University Press, 2006). Leeds, London (Birkbeck and Imperial). Recorded 2010 by Anne Murcott. British Library shelfmark: C 1416/35

Sir Ivor Crewe (b. 1945, Manchester). Political scientist, focus on elections and voting behaviour. *Decade of Dealignment: The Conservative Victory of 1979 and Electoral Trends in the 1970s* (with Bo Sarlvik) (Cambridge University Press, 1983). Headed Data Archive. Oxford, Essex. Recorded 2008 by PT. British Library shelfmark: C 1416/46

Leonore Davidoff (1932–2014, b. New York, came to Britain 1953). Sociologist and social historian, founding editor of *Gender and History. Family Fortunes: Men and Women of the English Middle Class 1780–1850* (with Catherine Hall) (Hutchinson, 1987). LSE, Essex. Recorded 2003 by PT. British Library shelfmark: C 1416/14

John Davis (1938–2017, b. London) Anthropologist, focus on Mediterranean family and honour systems. *Land and Family in Pisticci* (Athlone, 1973); *People of the Mediterranean: An Essay in Comparative Social Anthropology* (Routledge and Kegan Paul, 1977). Oxford, Kent. Recorded 2010 by PT. British Library shelfmark: C 1416/13

Meghnad Desai, Lord Desai (b. 1940; to US 1961, London 1965, Life Peer 1991). Economist, journalist and Labour activist. Focus includes Marxist theory, Indian films and agrarian societies. *Marxian Economic Theory* (Blackwell, 1979); *Power and Agrarian Relations* (LSE, 1984). Bombay, Pennsylvania, LSE. Recorded 2017 by PT. British Library shelfmark: C 1416/57

Mary Douglas (1921–2007, b. San Remo, Italy, to Britain 1929). Anthropologist, first worked in Congo, then became influential theorist. Not a feminist. *Purity and Danger: An Analysis of Concepts of Pollution and Taboo* (Routledge and Kegan Paul, 1966); *The World of Goods* (Allen Lane, 1979). Oxford, London (University College), New York (Russell Sage Foundation), North-Western, Princeton. Recorded 2003–04 by PT. British Library shelfmark: C 1416/16

Dame Karen Dunnell (b. 1946 Los Angeles, came to rural Britain 1949). Sociologist, focus health and family; broadened scope of national surveys to include marriage and sexuality. *Family Formation* (HMSO, 1979). Bedford College, Institute of Community Studies, OPCS; Director, ONS. Recorded 2017 by PT. British Library shelfmark: C 1416/55

Glen Elder (b. 1934, Ohio). Sociologist, pioneered 'life course' method in longitudinal studies. *Children of the Great Depression* (Chicago University Press, 1974). Penn State, Berkeley, North Carolina. Recorded 2001 by PT. British Library shelfmark: C 1416/08

Dame Janet Finch (b. 1946, Liverpool). Sociologist, focus on gender, family and inheritance. *Married to the Job: Wives' Incorporation in Men's Work* (Allen and Unwin, 1983); *Family Obligations and Social Change*

(Polity, 1989). Bradford, Lancaster, Keele. Recorded 2001 by PT. British Library shelfmark: C 1416/12

Ruth Finnegan (b. 1933, Londonderry). Anthropologist, focussed internationally but especially in Africa on myths and storytelling and myths as literature; later work in Britain on the social culture of music. *Oral Literature in Africa* (Clarendon, 1970); *The Hidden Musicians: Music-making in an English Town* (Cambridge University Press, 1989). Oxford, Open. Recorded 2010 by PT. British Library shelfmark: C 1416/29

Sir Raymond Firth (1901–2002, b. New Zealand, came to Britain 1924). Anthropologist, a link with earlier generations, as Malinowski's pupil and heir. Lifelong interest in Polynesian cultures, classic study of the remote Pacific island of Tikopia; later research on Malay fishermen, and kinship in London. *We the Tikopia* (Allen and Unwin, 1936); *Malay Fishermen* (Routledge and Kegan Paul, 1946); *Families and their Relatives* (Routledge and Kegan Paul, 1969). His book *Human Types* (Nelso, 1938) was an influential early textbook; and he played a key role in the Colonial Social Research Council. Auckland, LSE. Recorded 2000 by PT. British Library shelfmark: C 1416/25

Ronald Frankenberg (1929–2015, b. London). Anthropologist/sociologist, with broad interests, influential especially as editor of *Sociological Review*. His research was earlier on communities, later on health. *Village on the Border* (Cohen and West, 1957); *Communities in Britain* (Penguin, 1966). Manchester, Keele. Recorded 2010–11 by Ray Pahl and PT. British Library shelfmark: C 1416/28

Duncan Gallie (b. 1946, Guildford, England). Sociologist, focus on industrial organisation and trade unions, link with French sociology. Led Social and Economic Change Initiative. *In Search of the New Working Class: Automation and Social Integration within the Capitalist Enterprise* (Cambridge 1983). Oxford, Essex. Recorded 2018 by PT. British Library shelfmark: C 1416/50

Jonathan Gershuny (b. 1949, London). Sociologist, focus on innovation and the switch to a service economy, and in methods, time-use diaries. *After Industrial Society? The Emerging Self-Service Economy* (Macmillan, 1978); *Social Innovation and the Division of Labour* (Oxford, 1983). Glasgow, Sussex, Essex, Oxford. Recorded 2016–17 by Blanche Girouard. British Library shelfmark: C 1416/54

Harvey Goldstein (b. 1939, London). Sociologist, focus on child health, education and on survey analysis. *Multilevel Statistical Models in Educational and Social Research* (Griffin, 1987). Manchester, London (Institute of Child Health), Bristol. Recorded 2017 by Blanche Girouard. British Library shelfmark: C 1416/52

John Goldthorpe (b. 1935, nr Barnsley, Yorkshire). Sociologist of male class and social mobility. Led mixed-method *Affluent Worker* project, but later passionately quantitative; with novel use of odds ratios. *The Affluent Worker in the Class Structure* (with David Lockwood, Frank Bechhofer and Jennifer Platt) (Cambridge University Press, 1969); *The Constant Flux: A Study of Class Mobility* (with Robert Erikson) (Cambridge University Press, 1992). LSE, Cambridge, Oxford. Recorded 2013 by Anne Murcott. British Library shelfmark: C 1416/38

Sir Jack Goody (1919–2015, b. London) Anthropologist, interdisciplinary and multi-theme, mediaeval to modern – marriage and family, death and inheritance, food and flowers, orality and writing. WW2 fought in North Africa, prisoner-of-war and escapee in Italy. *Myth of the Bagre* (Clarendon, 1972); *The Domestication of the Savage Mind* (Cambridge University Press, 1977); *The Development of the Family and Marriage in Europe* (Cambridge University Press, 1983); *The Culture of Flowers* (Cambridge: Cambridge University Press, 1993). Recorded 2008 by PT. British Library shelfmark: C 1416/11

Harry Goulbourne (b. 1948, Jamaica; to Britain, 1958). Political scientist, focus on ethnic relations and transnationalism. *Ethnicity and Nationalism in Post-Imperial Britain* (Cambridge University Press, 1991); *Caribbean Transnational Experience* (Pluto, 2002). Sussex, Dar es Salaam, Kingston Jamaica, Warwick, London (South Bank). Recorded 2004 by PT. British Library shelfmark: C 1416/09

Sir Peter Hall (1932–2014, b. London). Social geographer, prophetic urbanist and town planner. *The Industries of London* (Hutchinson, 1962); *London 2000* (Faber and Faber, 1963); *World Cities* (Weidenfeld and Nicolson, 1966). Cambridge, London (Birkbeck), Reading. Recorded 2011 by Blanche Girouard. British Library shelfmark: C 1416/21

Stuart Hall (1932–2014, b. Jamaica, came to Britain 1951). Social, political, literary and media analyst, fusing these approaches as founder of cultural studies. Activist in student New Left in 1950s, first editor of *New Left Review*, led the new Centre for Contemporary Cultural Studies in Birmingham 1964–79. Innovative teaching methods. Jointly from the Centre, *Resistance Through Rituals: Youth Sub-cultures in Post-war Britain* (jointly) (1976); *Policing the Crisis: Mugging, the State and Law and Order* (jointly) (Macmillan, 1978); *The Hard Road to Renewal: Thatcherism and the Crisis of the Left* (Verso, 1988). Oxford, Birmingham, Open. Recorded 2017 by PT. British Library shelfmark: C 1416/42

David Hargreaves (b. 1939, Bolton). Educational sociologist, combining in-depth research on class culture in schools with influential role as Chief Inspector of Inner London schools, and later teaching doctors to teach. *Social Relations in a Secondary School* (Routledge and Kegan Paul, 1967). Manchester, Cambridge. Recorded 2010 by PT. British Library shelfmark: C 1416/03

Tirril Harris (b. 1940, Oxford). Social psychologist, long-term co-worker with George Brown on mental illness among women. Jointly with Brown: *Social Origins of Depression: A Study of Psychiatric Disorder in Women* (Routledge, 1990), and *Life Events and Illness* (Guilford, 1989). London (Institute of Psychoanalysis, Bedford College, St Thomas' Hospital). Recorded 2000 by PT. British Library shelfmark: C 1416/32

Sonia Jackson (1934, London). Psychologist and educationist. With Brian Jackson ran Advisory Centre for Education and edited its magazine, *Where*. Initial research on day care for preschool children but main focus thereafter on the education of children and young people in out-of-home care. *Childminder: A Study in Action Research* (with Brian Jackson) (Routledge and Kegan Paul, 1979); *People Under Three: Young Children in Day Care* (with Elinor Goldschmied) (Routledge 1994, 3rd edn, 2015 with Ruth Forbes); *Improving Access to Further and Higher Education for Young People in Public Care: European Policy and Practice* (with Claire Cameron) (Jessica Kingsley, 2014); *Educating Children and Young People in Care: Learning Placements and Caring Schools* (with Claire Cameron and Graham Connelly) (Jessica Kinglsey, 2015). Huddersfield, Bristol, Swansea, UCL Institute of Education. Recorded 2019–20 by Rebecca Abrams. Processing for British Library shelfmark: C 1416

Bruce Kapferer (b. 1940, Sydney, Australia; scholarship to Britain 1963). Anthropologist, his work on Zambian factories part of shift to an urban colonial anthropology; also early use of social network theory. *Strategy and Transaction in an African Factory* (Manchester University Press, 1972). Sydney, Rhodes Livingstone Institute, Manchester,

Adelaide. Recorded 2010–11 by Elaine Bauer. British Library shelfmark: C 1416/02

Diana Leonard (1941–2010; to Britain 1947). Anthropologist and sociologist; focus on gender and family. *Sex and Generation: A Study of Courtship and Weddings* (Longman, 1980). With Sheila Allen organised and published 1974 crucial Aberdeen BSA conference: *Dependence and Exploitation in Work and Marriage* and *Sexual Divisions and Society* (Tavistock, 1976). Swansea, London (Institute of Education). Recorded 2010 by PT and also recollections of her by Miriam David. British Library shelfmark: C 1416/06

Richard Lipsey (b. 1938, Victoria, Canada; to Britain 1953). Economist, famous for his classic book *An Introduction to Positive Economics* (Weidenfeld and Nicolson, 1963) in which he argues for economics as a socially and practically useful discipline which needs to be tested by facts. Since its first publication in 1963 it has sold more than 5 million copies and in over 13 editions. LSE, Essex, Yale, Toronto, Simon Fraser. Recorded 2010 by PT. British Library shelfmark: C 1416/47

David Lockwood (1929–2014, b. Holmfirth, Yorkshire). Sociologist, focussing on working-class culture and images of society. *The Blackcoated Worker* (Allen and Unwin, 1958); *The Affluent Worker in the Class Structure* (with John Goldthorpe, Frank Bechhofer and Jennifer Platt) (Cambridge University Press, 1969). LSE, Cambridge, Essex. Recorded 2001–02 by PT. British Library shelfmark: C 1416/05

Peter Loizos (1937–2012, b. London). Anthropologist: of Mediterranean kinship, and of forced migration of a Cypriot Greek community, to which his father's family belonged. *The Greek Gift: Politics in a Cypriot Village* (Blackwell, 1975); *The Heart Grown Bitter: A Chronicle of Cypriot War Refugees* (Cambridge University Press, 1981). LSE. Recorded 2011 by PT. British Library shelfmark: C 1416/22

Dennis Marsden (1933–2009, b. Huddersfield, Yorkshire). Sociologist who focussed on working-class culture and education, the unemployed, and women alone and in couples. *Education and the Working Class* (with Brian Jackson) (Routledge and Kegan Paul, 1962); *Mothers Alone: Poverty and the Fatherless Family* (Penguin, 1969). London

(Institute of Community Studies), Essex. Recorded 2002 by PT. British Library shelfmark: C 1416/36

Maxine Molyneux (b. 1948 Pakistan, came to Britain 1965). Sociologist, focus on women and gender, in Middle East, and then in Latin America. *The Ethiopian Revolution,* (with Fred Halliday) (Verso, 1982); *Women's Movements in International Perspective* (Palgrave Macmillan, 2000). Essex, Birkbeck, Institute of Latin American Studies. Recorded 2017 by PT. British Library shelfmark: C 1416/56

Robert Moore (b. 1936, London). Sociologist, early researcher with John Rex on race, later on religion in northern communities. *Race, Community and Conflict: A Study of Sparkbrook* (with John Rex) (Oxford University Press, 1967); *Pitmen, Preachers and Politics: The Effects of Methodism in a Durham Mining Community* (Cambridge University Press, 1974); *The Social Impact of Oil: The Case of Peterhead* (Routledge and Kegan Paul, 1982). Hull, Birmingham, Durham, Aberdeen, Liverpool. Recorded 2011–12 by PT. British Library shelfmark: C 1416/27

Claus Moser, Lord Moser (1922–2015, b. London). Social statistician, first Director of Central Statistical Office in 1967. *Survey Methods in Social Investigation* (Heinemann, 1958). Resisted political interference. Recorded 2019 by PT as British Library shelfmark: C 1416/33, a supplement to his full interview by Jennifer Wingate C408/029

Sir Howard Newby (b. 1947, Derby). Sociologist, focus on rural societies, and with Colin Bell on methods. *The Deferential Worker* (Allen Lane, 1977); *Green and Pleasant Land* (Penguin, 1980); with Colin Bell *Community Studies* (Allen and Unwin, 1971) and *Doing Sociological Research* (Allen and Unwin, 1977). Essex, Southampton, Liverpool. Recorded 2009 by Ray Pahl. British Library shelfmark: C 1416/10

Ann Oakley (b. 1944, London). Sociologist, early feminist, focus on women and gender, housework and motherhood; later, evidence-based health research. *Sex, Gender and Society* (Temple Smith, 1972); *The Sociology of Housework* (Martin Robertson, 1974); *Becoming a Mother* (Penguin, 1981); with Juliet Mitchell co-edited *The Rights and Wrongs of Women* (Penguin, 1976). London (Bedford College, Thomas Coram, Institute of Education). Also novelist, including semi-autobiographical *Taking it Like a Woman* (Cape, 1984), and televised, *The Men's Room* (Virago, 1988). Most recently, in parallel with our aims in this book,

Women, Peace and Welfare: A Suppressed History of Social Reform, 1880—1920 (2019) and as auto/biographer, daughter of Richard Titmuss, *Father and Daughter* (Policy Press, 2014). Recorded 2010–11 by Liz Spencer and PT. British Library shelfmark: C 1416/01

Judith Okely (b. 1941, Malta, to Britain c. 1945). Anthropologist, beginning as ethnologist and defender of gypsies, later autobiographical and gender-focussed, including on own schooling. *The Traveller-Gypsies* (Cambridge University Press, 1983); *Own or Other Culture* (Routledge, 1996). Oxford, Essex, Hull. Recorded 2011 by PT. British Library shelfmark: C 1416/39

Ray Pahl (1935–2011, b. London). Sociologist: innovative projects on communities, families and work. First his thesis, 'Urbs in rure', on commuter villages outside London, then on managers with an early gender dimension, later on formal and informal work in Sheppey, Kent, and last on friendship networks. *Managers and Their Wives* (with Jan Pahl) (Penguin, 1972); *Divisions of Labour* (Blackwell, 1984); *Rethinking Friendship* (with Liz Spencer) (Princeton University Press, 2006. Cambridge, LSE, Kent. Recorded 1998 and 2004 by Michele Abendstern and PT. British Library shelfmark: C 1416/24

Ken Plummer (b. 1946, London). Sociologist, founder-editor *Sexualities*, and also broad concern with past and present research methodologies. Major substantive area of research is sexualities. *Sexual Stigma* (Routledge and Kegan Paul, 1975); *Telling Sexual Stories* (Routledge, 1995); and on methods, *Documents of Life* (Allen and Unwin, 1983, 2nd edition 2001) and *Narrative Power* (2019). Middlesex, LSE, Essex, Santa Barbara. Recorded 2015 by PT. British Library shelfmark: C 1416/48

Michael Redclift (b. 1946, South Wales). Leading environmental sociologist, early recognising conflict between sustainable development and climate change. Carried out empirical research in very diverse localities, especially Latin American, for example in *From Peasant to Proletarian: Capitalist Development and Agrarian Transitions* (with David Goodman) (Basil Blackwell, 1981); and also a leader in theoretical development, especially in *Development and the Environmental Crisis: Red and Green Alternatives* (Methuen, 1984); *Sustainable Development: Exploring the Contradictions* (Macmillan, 1987); and *Social Theory and the Global Environment* (eds with Ted Benton) (Routledge,

1994). Wye College, Kent (London). Recorded 2019–2020 by PT. To be archived British Library shelfmark: C 1416

Hilary Rose (b. 1935, London, childhood in Framlingham, England). Sociologist, social policy activist, focus on marginal poor, squatters and benefits claimants; with Steven Rose, sociology of science. *Science and Society* (Penguin, 1970). LSE, Bradford. Recorded 2016–18 by PT. British Library shelfmark: C 1416/53

Raymond T. Smith (1925–2015, b. Oldham, Lancashire). Anthropologist, leading interpreter of family and kinship in the Caribbean. *The Negro Family in British Guiana* (Routledge and Kegan Paul, 1956); *Kinship and Class in the West Indies* (Cambridge University Press, 1988); *The Matrifocal Family* (Routledge, 1996); Cambridge, Kingston Jamaica, Chicago. Recorded 2001 by PT. British Library shelfmark: C 1416/26

Margaret Stacey (1922–2004, b. London). Sociologist, led Banbury community studies; feminist, 'role model' for younger academic women. WW2 factory work and adult education. *Tradition and Change: A Study of Banbury* (Oxford University Press, 1960); *Women, Power and Politics* (with Marion Price) (Tavistock, 1981). LSE, Swansea, Warwick. Recorded 2003 by PT. British Library shelfmark: C 1416/15

Dame Marilyn Strathern (b. 1941, North Wales). Anthropologist, worked on gender and kinship in Papua New Guinea and in Elmdon, Essex, the latter theorised through secondary materials. *Women in Between: Female Roles in a Male World* (Seminar Press, 1972); *Kinship at the Core: An Anthropology of Elmdon, Essex* (Cambridge University Press, 1981). Cambridge. Recorded 2011 by Elaine Bauer as a supplement to interview by Alan Macfarlane for Leading Thinkers, Cambridge. British Library shelfmark: C 1416/40

Elizabeth Thomas-Hope (b. 1943, Jamaica). Social geographer, focus on migration, gender, environment. *Explanation in Caribbean Migration* (Macmillan, 1992). Oxford, Liverpool, Kingston Jamaica. Recorded 2018 by PT. British Library shelfmark: C 1416/51

Paul Thompson (b. 1935, Surrey). Social historian/sociologist, pioneered usage of life stories and oral history, in themes from class and gender to transnational families and stepfamilies – and social researchers. *The Voice of the Past* (Oxford University Press, 1978; 4th edn 2017); *The Edwardians: The Remaking of British Society* (Weidenfeld and Nicolson, 1975); *Growing Up in Stepfamilies* (with Gill Gorell Barnes, Gwyn Daniel and Natasha Burchardt) (Oxford University Press, 1997); *Jamaican Hands Across the Atlantic* (with Elaine Bauer) (Ian Randle, 2006). Founded National Life Stories at British Library. Oxford, Essex. Recorded 1996 by Karen Worcman and 2007 by Julie Boekhoff. British Library shelfmark: C 1416/20 and 41

Peter Townsend (1928–2009, b. London). Sociologist, innovative researcher on poverty, ageing, health and disability, leading public campaigning for social justice for the underprivileged. His first two classics were both based on surveys and rich qualitative fieldwork carried out personally: *The Family Life of Old People* (1957); and *The Last Refuge* (1962), a study of old people's homes. He went on to build a strong research team for his third classic, *Poverty in the UK* (2009). His later work was more innovative in terms of using computer-based analysis and measures of need. Cambridge, London (Institute of Community Studies, LSE), Essex. Founded Child Poverty Action Group and Disability Alliance. Recorded 1997–98 by PT. British Library shelfmark: C 1416/23

Sandra Wallman (b. 1934, London but much of childhood in Canada and South Africa). Anthropologist: early work in Africa on hunger and foreign aid, later on multi-ethnic neighbourhoods in London. *Take Out Hunger* (Athlone, 1969); *Eight London Households* (1984, Tavistock). LSE, Bristol, London (University College). Recorded 2010 by Elaine Bauer. British Library shelfmark: C 1416/30

W. M. Williams (1926–?, b. South Wales). Anthropologist/sociologist, whose two English community studies, both rural, were important because while the first emphasised tradition and continuity, the second showed how change was a continuous part of the social structure. WW2 Welsh Guards. *The Sociology of an English Village: Gosforth* (Routledge and Kegan Paul, 1956); *West Country Village, Ashworthy: Family, Kinship and Land* (Routledge and Kegan Paul, 1963). Aberystwyth, Keele, Swansea. Recorded 2003 by PT. Of the audio, only the extracts survive. British Library shelfmark: C 1416/43

Lord Michael Young (1915–2002, b. Manchester, childhood in Melbourne Australia until 1923). Anthropologist/sociologist and unique social entrepreneur. Worked at PEP, drafted the Labour Party's 1945 manifesto, set up the Institute of Community Studies in Bethnal Green. *The Rise of the Meritocracy* (1958), and with Peter Willmott *Family and Kinship in East London* (1957) and *The Symmetrical Family* (1973). Among numerous initiatives founded the Consumers' Association, the magazine *Which*, envisaged and became first chairman of the SSRC, also envisaged the Data Archive and the Open University. Recorded 1990 and 2001 by PT. British Library shelfmark: C 408/12 and C 1416/17

Index

childhood and family life 22
influence of Becker on 75
on marginality 10
political values and activities 52
writing and literary skills 158
colleges of advanced technology
(CATs) 80
colonial context of research 46–48, 180
see also British Empire
Colonial Office 73
Colonial Social Science Research
Council 3, 46, 79, 82
coming out 13
Commonwealth Immigrants Act
1968 180
community studies 90–94, 137
and race relations 179–180
and social class 165–166
computer technology 118
and quantitative data analysis 94–96,
105–108
research methods 126–127
confidentiality issues, in
fieldwork 155–156
Congo, Douglas' research in 4, 31,
150–152
consciousness raising groups 63, 70, 173
see also feminism
Cowley study 114, 115, 116
Cox, David 27
biographical summary 221
Coxon, Tony 2
Crewe, Ivor 82, 86–87
biographical summary 221
university administration 53
CSO (Central Statistical Office) 84–85
cultural studies 81, 138
and Stuart Hall 64–68
culture, and social class 165–166
Cyprus 4, 12–13, 156–157

D

danger in research, Afghanistan 4, 161
Dartington School 41–42, 82
Davidoff, Leonore (Lee) 3, 174
biographical summary 222
feminism 63
gender-based obstacles 171
parenthood 31
Davis, John 4
biographical summary 222
de Beauvoir, Simone 77
Deflem, Mathieu 6
Delphy, Christine 175, 178
depression in women
Brown's research 11–12, 122–124,
152–153

post-natal 11–12, 14, 61, 175
Desai, Meghnad 32
1968 student protests 58
biographical summary 222
childhood and family life 22
fieldwork experiences 9–10
deviancy 75
Dickens, Charles 136
digital technologies, and fieldwork 139
see also computer technology
disability 88, 187
Disability Alliance 55, 165
disciplines, shifts and transformations
in 80–82
Donnison, David 164
Douglas, James 43, 94
Douglas, Mary 4, 202
biographical summary 222
Congo research 4, 31, 150–152
on dirt 14
education 25, 40–41
feminism 59
fieldwork 140, 150–152
parenthood 31
partnership and marriage 43
religion 203
Du Bois, W. E. B. 137
Duggan, Mark 181
Duncan, Otis Dudley 95, 169
Dunnell, Karen 97
biographical summary 222
research methods 126–127
Durant, Will 40

E

East Anglia University 79
Eaton, Peter 40
Economic and Social Research
Council *see* ESRC (Economic
and Social Research Council)
Economic Planning Councils 56
economics, nature of 9–10
education
and gender 26–27
influences of on Pioneers 26–27
and social class 165–166
treatment of black West Indian
children in British schools 184
educationally sub-normal (ESN)
schools 184
Elder, Glen 3
biographical summary 222
research methods 121–122, 124
elections 16
Eliot, George 136
Ellis, Havelock 187
'embourgeoisement' thesis 167, 191

gender relationship
  experiences 28–29
  as a role model 174–175
  wartime experiences 27, 49–50
Stanley, Liz 2
Statistical Package for the Social
  Sciences (SPSS) 95, 106–107
Stoller, Robert 170
Strachan, Walter 25
Strathern, Marilyn 6
  biographical summary 229
  parenthood 31
  partnership and marriage 28
Strauss, Anselm 137
structural functionalism 76
student protests, 1968 55, 57–59
suicide 11
Surrey University 88–89
survey research methods 115–117,
  118–119, 120–121, 141, 167–168
Sussex University 79
sustainability 208

T

Tanzania 4, 196–197
tape recorders 148–150
Taylor, Marcia 86–87
Thatcher, Margaret 85, 86
Thatcherism 68, 93, 138
Theosophical Society 39
Thomas, W. I. 136–137
Thomas-Hope, Elizabeth 95, 105–106
  biographical summary 229
  childhood and family life 22
  climate change 204
  partnership and marriage 30
  research methods 125
Thompson, Paul 3, 186
  biographical summary 229–230
  education 25
  fieldwork 140
  reflections for the future 192–193
Tikopia, Firth's research in 46,
  129–132, 135, 153–154, 203
Titmuss, Richard 2, 5, 55, 61, 88, 164
Tomlinson, Sally 182
Townsend, Peter 1, 84, 86, 88, 96, 97
  anthropology 80–81
  biographical summary 230
  childhood and family life 21
  community studies 90
  education 26
  fieldwork 137, 149–150
  National Service 28
  old people's homes research 19–20,
    55, 84, 90, 164, 165, 187
  partnership and marriage 29

political values and activities 52
post-war reconstruction period, as
  research context 53–56
poverty studies 53–56, 164–165
reflections for the future 190
religion 204
research methods 118–121
and the spirit of 1968 57
wartime experiences 50–51
transnationalism 186
  and Brah 69–72
triangulation 120, 125
Tropp, Asher 89, 167

U

UCL 99
Uganda 69
UK Centre for Longitudinal Studies 99
UK Data Archive 1–2, 82
UK Data Service 1, 82
Unit of Analysis problem 107
universities
  administration roles of Pioneers 53
  audit culture 159
  ethic committees 154
  expansion of 79–81
University of Essex 55, 57, 79
University of Tanzania 183
University of the West Indies 183
University of Wales at
  Aberystwyth 132
US (United States) 3, 6
  American sociology 113, 122, 128
  and the culture of flowers 18–19
  development of fieldwork 137–138
  ethnography 136–137
User Support Bureau 98

W

Wallman, Sandra
  biographical summary 230
  parenthood 31
  reflections for the future 192
Walton, Cecil 26
war 27, 48–51, 72–75
Warwick University 79, 180
  Centre for Research in Ethnic
    Relations 183
Webb, Beatrice 59
welfare state 83
  rise of 53–57
Whitehead, Annie 173
Whyte, William Foote 76
Williams, Raymond 2, 205
Williams, W. M. 91
  biographical summary 230
  fieldwork 137

Index

Gosforth research 132–133, 135,
  137, 165
research methods 117, 125
wartime experiences 27, 75
Willis, Paul 2, 138
Willmott, Peter 1, 84, 137, 165
Wilson, Harold 56, 84, 97, 180
Windrush 65, 179
  see also migrants and migration
Wolfenden Committee 188
women
  consciousness raising groups 63,
    70, 173
  depression in
    Brown's research 11–12, 122–124,
      152–153
    post-natal 11–12, 14, 61, 175
  gender research 169–179
  influences of education on
    Pioneers 26–27
  new agendas in research 170,
    175–179
  obstacles experienced by
    Pioneers 170–172
  role models, Pioneers as 170,
    174–175
  support and solidarity networks 170,
    172–174
  see also gender
Women's Caucus, BSA 63, 172
Women's Liberation Movement 63, 70

and ethnicity 71–72
Women's Research and Resources
  Centre 63, 173–174
women's studies 81
Wootton, Barbara 210n4
working class 21–22, 163–164,
  165, 166
Wright Mills, C. 158, 159
writing, importance of in social
  research 157–158, 189–190
Wye College 206

Y

York University 79
Yorkshire
  and Goldthorpe 33–34
  and Marsden 34–35
Young, Jock 80
Young, Michael 1, 55, 82, 85, 165
  biographical summary 230–231
  career overview and the PEP 82–84
  education 25, 41–42
  fieldwork 137, 141–142
  reflections for the future 189–190
  research methods 128, 148
  writing and literary skills 158

Z

Zambia (Southern Rhodesia) 4
Znaniecki, Florian 136–137